TRANSACTION BURGON SOCIETY

Volume 20   2020
Published October 2021

TRANSACTIONS OF THE
BURGON SOCIETY

Volume 20 (for 2020)
Published October 2021
newprairiepress.org/burgonsociety

Published by The Burgon Society
© 2021 The Contributors
burgon.org.uk

ISBN 978-1-8380679-1-5
Printed in England

Back issues of the *Transactions*, together with books about academic dress published by the Society and others, are available at **www.burgon.org.uk/shop**.

Opinions expressed in this journal are those of the contributors and are not necessarily those of the Burgon Society. Neither the Editors nor the Burgon Society can vouch for the accuracy of material in the journal or accept legal responsibility or liability for any errors or omissions that may be made.

The Burgon Society

Officers

(as at 1 August 2021)

President

Professor Graham Zellick, CBE, QC, MA, PhD (Cantab), Hon LLD (Birmingham & American International University), LHD (New York), DLit (QMUL), AcSS, Hon FRAM, Hon FSALS, FBS

Executive Committee (Trustees)

Chairman Andrew J. P. North, MChem (Oxon), PhD (Cantab), FBS

Secretary Alice Hynes, BA (Exeter), MA (London), FCIS, MAPM, MInstLM, FAUA, FRSA, FBS

Treasurer Ian Johnson, BA (CNAA), FRSA, FBS

Ordinary Members

Jonathan C. Cooper, BSc (St Andrews), PhD (Central Lancs), FRGS, FBS *(Dean of Studies and Communications Officer)*

Professor William Gibson, MA (Wales), PhD (Middlesex), DLitt (Wales), FSA, FRHistS, FRSA, FBS

Thomas Goodman, BSc (Birmingham), FRSA, MBCS, FBS

Nicholas Jackson, BA (York), MSc, PhD (Warwick), FBS

Sandra Wearden, MA, PhD (Lancaster), FBS

Professor Stephen L. Wolgast, BA (Kansas State), MS (Columbia), FBS *(Publications Editor)*

Non-Executive Officers

Curator Chris Williams, MA (Cantab), MA (Colchester Inst.)

Marshal John C. Horton, BSc (Manchester), PhD (Cantab), MInstP, FBS

Social Media Officer Paul Coxon, MPhys, PhD (Newcastle), MRSC, MInstP

Burgon Society Events in 2020

Most events planned for 2020 were cancelled on account of the novel coronavirus pandemic.

10 October   Congregation

The AGM and admission of new Fellows were deemed to have taken place on 10 October.

> The Trustees' Annual Report and Financial Statements for 2019 had been circulated in advance and Fellows and Members had been invited to send in questions and comments. Responses from the Executive Committee were included in the Minutes circulated on 11 October.

> Admission to the Fellowship of the Burgon Society
> Jack Lindsay (by submission — Academic Dress of Australia)
> Brian Newman (by submission — The Evolution of Undergraduate Academic Dress at the University of Cambridge and its Constituent Colleges)
> Scott Pilkington (by submission — History and Development of University Doctoral Academical Dress in Aotearoa (New Zealand))
> Martin Hardcastle (by submission — Cap and Gown? Use of Headgear at Graduation in UK Universities in the 21st Century)
> David Parker (by submission — University of Leeds Academic Dress)

17 October   Virtual Speaker Event
Talk given online by Zoom

> Martin Hardcastle — *Cap and Gown? Use of Headgear at Graduation in UK Universities in the 21st Century*

Fellows & Members

(as at 1 August 2021)

Fellows

Mr Robert Armagost

Professor Sir John Baker
Dr Richard Baker
Mr David J. P. Baldwin
Sqn Ldr Alan Birt
Mr Christopher Bottley
Dr David T. Boven
The Revd Dr John Lester Brennan
Mr Michael Brewer
Dr Giles Brightwell
Mr Ronald Brookes

Mr Stephen Callander
Mr Arthur B. Casey
The Rt Revd and Rt Hon. Lord Chartres
Professor Peter Chiu
Professor Bruce Christianson
Mr Peter Clarke
Dr Jonathan C. Cooper
The Revd Dr Noel S. B. Cox
The Revd Kenneth Ian Crawford

The Revd Dr Graham Deans
Dr Neil Kay Dickson
Mrs Kathryn Douglas
Dr Donald L. Drakeman
The Revd Matthew Duckett
Mr Peter Durant

The Revd Edmund J. Eggleston
Dr Michael W. Everett

Mr Paul Fielder
Mr Colin A. M. Fleming
Ms Kerstin Fröberg

Professor William Thomas Gibson
Dr Nicholas Gledhill
The Revd Philip Goff
Mr Thomas Anthony Goodman
Professor John N. Grant
Dr Nicholas Groves
Dr Valentina S. Grub

Professor Martin Hardcastle
The Revd Dr John James Harding
Mrs Nicola Hardy
Mr Seamus Addison Hargrave
Dr Thorsten Hauler
Lieutenant Nicholas A. Hoffmann
Dr John Charles Horton
Miss Alice Ruth Hynes

Dr Francis Jackson
Dr Nicholas James Jackson
The Revd Canon Dr Stephen James
Mr Ian A Johnson

Dr Michael Kearsley
The Revd Fr Oliver James Keenan
Dr Alex Kerr
The Rt Revd Graeme Knowles
Mr Charles Ka Shing Ko
The Very Revd Harry E. Krauss

Dr John Lancaster
Mr Martin Lewis
Mr Jack Lindsay
Mr Philip Lowe
Dr John Lundy

Professor Yves Mausen
Mr Timothy Nicholas Milner

Mr Brian Morley Newman
Professor Leonard E. Newton
Dr Andrew James Peter North
Dr Susan North

Mr David Parker
Mr Scott Pilkington
Dr Steven E. Plank
Dr Michael Powell

Mr David Christopher Quy

Dr Byron W. Rangiwai
Professor Aileen Ribeiro
Dr Leslie M. M. Robarts

Dr Alan J. Ross

Dr Matthew Cheung Salisbury
Miss Elizabeth Scott
Dr Mary Shaw
Mr Nick Shipp
Professor Klaus Solberg Søilen
Professor Kenneth L. Suit, Jr

Mr Jason T. Testar
Dr James P. S. Thomson
Mr Charles Rupert Tsua

Mr John Venables

Dr Sandra Wearden
Professor Stephen L. Wolgast

Mr Alexander K. Yen

Professor Graham Zellick

Deceased Fellows

Dr John Birch, *died 2012*
Mr Leonard Brown, *died 2007*
Mr Clifford Dunkley, *died 2019*
Professor Bruno Neveu, *died 2004*
The Revd Dr Steven A. Peay, *died 2020*
Dr Robin Rees, *died 2021*
Dr George Wenham Shaw, *died 2006*
The Revd Canon Ambrose Southward, *died 2019*

Members *Indicates fellow-elect*

Dr Malcolm Aickin
The Revd Fr Kevin J. Alban, *died 2021*
Dr Christian Anderson
Mr James Douglas Anderson

Jayne Ball Designs
Ms Emily Barber
Mr Paul Barber
Mr Terence N. Barcock
Dr John J. Barnes
The Revd Dr Anthony M. Barratt
Mr David C. M. Barton
Dr Melissa Beauregard
Dr Andrew-John Bethke*
Mr John Bishop
The Revd Dr Christian D. Boyd
Mr Thomas W. Brian
The Very Revd Dr Godfrey Brown
Mr Graeme Bruce
Mr Paul Butcher
Mr Ian James Burton

Mr Jimmy Campbell
Dr Peter Campbell
Dr Jack Carlson
Mr Leslie Carrick-Smith

Cécile Biôt
Mr Emilio Chiquito
Churchill Gowns
Mr Peter Mark Close
The Revd Jonathan Collis
Mr Jeremy Colman
Mr William G. Condé
Mr Martin Cooke
The Revd Philip Corbett
The Revd Ivor Cornish
Mrs Janette Corporal
Ms Eilis Courtney
Cosprop Ltd
Dr Paul Robert Coxon
Mr Shane Creppel
The Revd Dr James Curry

Professor James H. Davenport
Mr Andrew Mark Davidson
Dr Josu de la Fuente
The Revd Dr Michael Diamond
Mr Andrew Jan Dobrzanski
Mr James Anthony Drabble
Dr Michael A. K. Duggan
Dr Jason Dunn

Mr Matthew James Edwards
Ede & Ravenscroft Ltd
Dr Paul Ellison

The Revd Dr David Roderick Evans
The Revd Dr Keith James Eyeons

Mr Duanran Feng
Dr Gordon Fletcher
Mr Ron Fletcher
Dr Anthony William Fox
Professor Peter French
Mr David Salsbery Fry
Mr Theodore Frydensberg
Dr Heinz Fuchs

Dr Ian Baird Galbraith
Mr Thomas M. Garrett
Mr Edmund Hugh Gazeley
Mr Roberto Gherseni
Mr Joseph Goldsmith
Dr Peter John Gorton
Dr Christopher Goulding
Gowning Street Pty Ltd
Graduate Gowning Company
Graduation Attire
Dr Walter G. Green
The Revd Canon Mark N. Gretason
Mr Leslie Grout

Mr Christopher J. Ha
Mr Morgan Hale

Mr Patrick Martin Harrigan
Mr Patrick Hampshire
Mr Robin Arthur Hanford
Mr Paul Anthony Hayward
Dr Nicholas G. Heavens*
The Revd Gregory Henderson
Cllr Karl Hobley
Dr Andrew J. C. Hogg
Mr Peter Edward Holden
Mr Ian Martin Howard
Mr Jake Humbles
Mr Garry Paul Humphreys
Dr Robyn Humphries
Mr Paul Stephen Hunt
Mr Paul Hutchings

Dr Steven Jackson
Mr Anthony Johnson
Dr Colin Graeme Johnson
The Revd Anthony J. L. Jones

Professor Stephen F. Keevil
Mr Malcolm David Kemp
The Revd B. David Kennedy
Mr Thomas Francis King
Mr Stephen John
    Klimczuk-Massion
His Honour Judge Graham
    Roy Knowles
Dr Nikolas Krawchenko
Mr Petter Kringberg

The Revd Dr William Roy
    Large
Mr Blake Lawrenson
The Revd Fr Edward Lewis
Dr Simon Lindley
Professor Benedikt Loewe
Mr Bryan George Lowe, *died
    2021*

Dr Ian B. Maclennan
Dr Leonard Madden
Mr Mitchell Josef Marinac
Mr Philip Marshall
Marston Robing Ltd
Mr Jack Mason
Mr Christopher Maynard
Mr Matthew McCallum
Canon Brian McKay
Ms Liz McMahan
Professor Thomas McSweeney

Mr Dennis Shane Miller
The Revd Christopher James
    Mogridge
Mr Joel James Luke Moore
Dr Simon James Morris*
The Right Revd David Moshier
Mr Roger Moult
The Revd Graeme Watson
    McKinnon Muckart
Dr Keith Munday

Mr Behroz Sasan Nanevasadeh
The Revd Robin Nash
Dr Roderick Forsyth Neilson
Mr H. G. Gordon Nevill
The Revd Dr Peter Newing
Dr Stuart Newton
Dr Andrew Nicoll
Mr Mitchell A. Nicholls*
Mr Jeremy Nigel Fortescue
    Norman
William Northam & Co. Ltd

Mr Mark Ockenden
Dr Gustavo Adolfo Ornelas-
    Almaraz
OSBO China
Dr David M. O'Shea

Cdr Thomas Packer
M. Perkins & Son Ltd
Dr Andrew Plant
Dr David John Chandler Price
Mr Chad Proudfoot

Dr Anthony Razzi
The Revd Anthony
    Reader-Moore
Dr Richard P. Reece
Reed Graduation Services Pty
    Ltd
Mr Steven Marc Rhodes
Dr Jakob K. Rinderknecht
Mr Alan S. Robertson
Mr Timothy Charles Roll-
    Pickering
The Revd Sion Rhys-Evans

The Rt Revd Dr Ronald
    Saunders
Dr Tim Schmalz
Chev. Angelo A. Sedacca

The Revd Norman William
    Shaw
Shepherd & Woodward Group
Mr Kevin William Stone
Mr Ian Stuart Henry
    Sudlow-McKay

The Very Revd Michael E.
    Tavinor
Mr Olivier Louis Tedde
Mr Samuel G Teague
Mr Stewart Lee Thompson
Mr Benjamin Francis Titmus
Mr Julian A. Torres-H-Bonilla
Mr Brian Turvey

Mr Richard Maria van der
    Beek

Mr Lee Walker
Dr Anthony Michael Dermot
    Gerard Walsh
Mr Fergus James Patrick
    Walsh
Mr Patrick Walsh
Dr Geoffrey D.
    Wandesforde-Smith
The Revd Dr Robin Ward
Mr Philip Edward Waters
The Revd Dr Derek Herbert
    Webster
Mr Luke Webster
Dr Michael Wells
Mr Richard Whitaker
Mr Ivo Wiesendanger
Mr Sandro Wiggerich
Mr Dominic Wilks
Mr Anthony George
    Willenbruch
Mr Chris Williams
Dr Robert B. Williams
Dr Patrick Wills
Miss Lizelle Wiltshire
J. Wippell & Co. Ltd
Professor Marcin Wiszowaty
Dr Roger Wood
Dr David Andrew Woolf

The Revd Ian Ira Yemm

In Memoriam
Robin L. D. Rees, BSc, MPhil (Lond), PhD (Sheff), MAstatus (Oxf), MInstP, CPhys, ACertCM, FBS

25 September 1946–7 June 2021

I forget exactly how and when I came into contact with Robin: it was long before the internet and emails, but sometime around 1990. It may have been when I wrote to ask for back numbers of *Hoodata*, or it may have been via Robin Richardson of Wippell: in those days when we all worked independently, the robemakers were quite good at putting us in touch with each other.

Born at Clevedon in Somerset, Robin attended Westminster School, and read physics at Bedford College, London (of which he was a Governor for ten years), and followed his BSc with an MPhil. He worked with computers for many years for the University of Oxford. When it became clear that Oxford would allow him to work part-time, he undertook a PhD at Sheffield, researching the often fraught relationship between clergy and church musicians; it went behind the C of E's official 1992 report 'In Tune with Heaven'. A book based on his research was published by Gracewing in 1993 as *Weary and Ill at Ease: a survey of clergy and organists*. He was granted the status of MA by Oxford, something he much enjoyed, and I recall that he had the hood made up in the Edinburgh shape, as an attested historical variant.

His achievements in terms of academic dress were several. Possibly the major one was persuading the Institute of Physics in 1977 to introduce a set of robes, and then to design them. The scheme used violet, combined with Oxford MA shot crimson. The colours (violet and red) are the extremes of the spectrum; that the length is one metre—the SI standard; and the shot red signifies the phenomenon of interference. Alas, the robes, while not actually decommissioned, are not now promoted.

His next project was the design of the original hood for the award of Archbishop's Certificate in Church Music (ACertCM). He held the award himself, and had an active career as a church musician—always ensuring that members of his choir were suitably behooded! Holders initially wore a medal on a ribbon, but cost and other considerations made a hood more practical. Robin used a hood in a modified simple shape, somewhat like a reduced Burgon shape; bearing in mind the 1882 restrictions on theological hoods, and the level at which the Certificate was examined, he came up with a black hood lined with black Italian cloth, bordered inside the cowl for 0.5" with royal blue, and bound on all edges with terra-cotta cord—blue and terra-cotta being the colours of the Guild of Church Musicians which administer the award. He was much annoyed when the hood was changed to full shape without being consulted; I don't know what he thought of its current form.

His final piece of input was the addition of a 1" strip of claret ribbon to the gowns of MPhils of the University of London so as to mark its status as being something more de-

Dr David Woolf

Dr Nicholas Groves

Institute of Physics, Members' and Fellows' hood.

Archbishop's Certificate in Church Music, original hood.

manding than a taught master's degree. One has to wonder what Dr Franklyn might have said.

He took on the editorship of *Hoodata* when Alan Birt relinquished it. It ran to four editions under his care, and then ceased in December 1981.

He also worked with Hugh Smith on the never-to-be-completed second edition of his great work, and indeed introduced me to him (via surface mail). He was also an active contributor to the old Yahoo! AD group. He was thus an obvious person to ask along to the initial meetings that became the Burgon Society, and he was on Council for several years.

He had been unwell for some time, and spent the last year in and out of hospital undergoing various procedures. He died peacefully on 7 June 2021.

Helen, his widow, wrote to me that 'Academic dress was one of Robin's passions, and he enjoyed your gatherings. It was enormous fun to go to Encaenia with him, as he could identify all the UK robes and hoods for me.' Let that stand for his memorial.

—*Nick Groves*

Editor's Note

What have we learned in the last year? Masks work, isolation makes one glum, and gowns aren't going away anytime soon.

The first two are no surprise. Science works despite the sceptics, and time with friends nourishes the soul.

I would have been hesitant, on the other hand, to predict that academic gowns would remain popular, despite the social science research published in the *Transactions* showing their popularity. Perhaps I was a bit of a sceptic too.

The ceremonial use of academic dress is thriving even though the pandemic is whipsawing many other social patterns. We've learned to change how we shop, how we travel, and of course how we dress.

University uniforms, however, haven't changed, and as a symbol of success in an centuries-old rite of passage their very uniformity is a point in their favour. Even though robes appear (to some) anachronistic and awkward in the twenty-first century, as elements of a tradition they give us comfort in uncertain times. Students may not be able to study in the library, but when they pose for photos in their gowns they carry forward the outward representation of their accomplishment.

Losing the library as a place to study for exams certainly frustrated students, but they weren't the only ones left without a critical resource. Researchers also found themselves unable to browse the stacks or delve into archives, which slowed their scholarly work or put it on hold entirely. Many of our authors look into historical university records, and while a vast cache of old books is available online, archival material is rarely uploaded. You can't open a cardboard box over the internet or pick up the ephemera and turn it over, seeking a hidden clue.

Yet even with the limitations of lockdowns, we are pleased to present another abundant collection of research and ideas. A handful of the articles in Volume 20 did not fit into Volume 19, and I thank those authors for their patience in bringing their discoveries to light. The result is the set of eleven articles that follow and our special issue on the formation of the Burgon Society, a history inspired in part by the Society's twentieth anniversary last year.

The editors and reviewers, who joined me in reading and re-reading more than 100,000 published words, hope this year's *Transactions* helps make up for closed libraries and all these months apart.

—*Stephen Wolgast*

Transactions of the Burgon Society, 20 (2020), pag 9–14

Examining Official Dress in Universities
in Aotearoa New Zealand

Officers' robes change over time, but finding reasons for their evolution from university sources proves difficult, *Scott Pilkington writes*

While collecting data on doctoral academic dress in New Zealand universities which formed the basis of my Burgon Society Fellowship submission, I also became aware of how the academic dress of university officials changed over time. The biggest question, of course, was why change the dress—surely once robes have been purchased for the Chancellor and Vice-Chancellor (excepting drastic changes in size), that is that? The 'what' was apparent—after all, it is listed in the university calendars. The 'how' and 'why' less so. The need to visit the various university archives and explore minutes and memoranda to determine the reason and mechanism for change became clear.

Primary Source

Wherein a Fellow's expertise and the outside world meet

Unfortunately, this is not as easy as it first seemed. When the universities were emailed, the replies varied from 'we don't know what you're talking about' to 'sorry, don't think we ever wrote any of that down, and if we did, it's already thrown out' to 'there might be something in the former registrar's papers but there are 1000 boxes'. Covid-19 restrictions and lockdowns further complicated efforts.

A further, proper, and detailed analysis and comment on the history of change in the dress of officials in New Zealand universities will be undertaken and submitted to this journal for consideration once I have visited the archives of the extant eight universities and the national government archives for the former University of New Zealand. This article, then, is a brief look at of some of the items found in the University of Auckland Administrative Archive. A magnitude of thanks goes to the University Archivist Dr Libby Nichol for her *mahi* (work) helping me wade through these items and signing off that the items in these records could be shared with the public.

Founded in 1883 as the Auckland College of the University of New Zealand, the University of Auckland first specified the dress of officials in the 1963 University Calendar.[1] At the time, all graduands and graduates of the university wore trenchers (as graduates of the University of New Zealand had done from 1884), but from 1973 doctors from University of Auckland (the constituent colleges became separate universities in 1963) wore Tudor-style bonnets. However, this change was not applied to the official party who still wear trenchers.[2] The dress for university officials at this university have not changed (other

1 University of Auckland, *The University of Auckland Calendar 1963* (Auckland: The University of Auckland, 1963), pp. 41-42, 504.

2 Noel Cox, 'Academical Dress in New Zealand,' *Burgon Society Annual 2001*, pp. 15–24, at <newprairiepress.org/burgonsociety> https://doi.org/10.4148/2475-7799.1003; University of Auckland, *The University of Auckland Calendar 1961* (Auckland: The University of Auckland, 1961), p. 36; University of Auckland, *The University of Auckland Calendar 1973* (Auckland: The University of

than the occasional requirement for different sizes) since then, although new officials have since been added: Kaumatua and Kuia (Māori elders) in 2000 and for graduation officials (marshals) in 2007, summarised below in Table 1.[3]

Table 1: Prescribed academic dress for university officials at University of Auckland

Position	Description	Year set
Chancellor	The robe for the Chancellor of the University is a blue damask gown with facings of gold lace, bearing on each shoulder the coat of arms of the University. The cap is a black velvet trencher with gold lace and tassel.	1963
Pro-Chancellor	The robe for the Pro-Chancellor is a black silk gown with facings of blue silk and gold lace, bearing on each shoulder the coat of arms. The cap is a black velvet trencher with gold tassel.	1963
Vice-Chancellor	The robe for the Vice-Chancellor is a blue silk gown with facings of silver lace, bearing on each shoulder the coat of arms. The cap is a black velvet trencher with silver lace and tassel.	1963
Registrar	The robe for the Registrar is a gown of black silk with facings of blue silk, bearing on each shoulder the coat of arms. The cap is a black velvet trencher with black silk tassel.	1963
Kuia and Kaumatua	The robe for the Kaumatua and the Kuia is the Fellow's gown of the colour University blue to be worn with a black scarf lined with the colour University blue bearing on each lapel the coat of arms. The cap is a black velvet trencher with a black silk tassel.	2000
Officials	The academic dress for Graduation Officials shall be the costume appropriate to their degree. In addition, the gown shall bear on each shoulder the coat of arms of the University, and the trencher shall have a blue tassel. Graduation Officials who are not graduates shall wear an undergraduate gown bearing the coat of arms of the University on each shoulder.	2007

As the Auckland University College became the fully fledged University of Auckland in the early 1960s, a great flurry of activity took place as it set to distinguish itself from the other former University of New Zealand colleges, now also independent universities. 1961 saw the meeting of a Heraldry Committee, formed of the Pro-Chancellor and Chair (Sir Douglass Robb, MD), the Chancellor (William Hollis Cocker), Vice-Chancellor (Kenneth Maidment), and Professor Paul Beadle (sculptor and Dean of Elam School of Fine Arts who joined the university that year), who were entrusted by the university Council to carry

---

Auckland, 1972), pp. 50-52, 828; University of New Zealand, *The New Zealand University Calendar 1884* (Wellington: The University of New Zealand, 1884), p. 55.

3   University of Auckland, *The University of Auckland Calendar 2000* (Auckland: The University of Auckland, 2000); University of Auckland, *The University of Auckland Calendar 2007* (Auckland: The University of Auckland, 2007). Prior to these changes, these staff wore their own academic dress if they were entitled to them, or a plain black bachelor's gown and no cap, making them difficult to find when in a crowd of graduands!

out recommendations for ceremonial robes and a coat of arms. Professor Beadle submitted coloured sketches for robes for the university officials, taking into consideration feedback received from the Committee.[4] The resolution is provided below.

> It was resolved —
> That the sketches of the four robes be approved, and that a badge of the university's coat-of-arms be worn on the right shoulder of all four, and that the blue to be used be as near as possible to heraldic blue.
> That the sketches be now forwarded to Messrs Ede & Ravenscroft with a request for an estimate of time and cost, all robes to be made for 6ft figure and in as lightweight material as possible.
> That the firm be also requested to send samples of materials when it is supplying its quotation.
> That the respective head sizes be forwarded in respect of the mortarboards.

Later that same month—in what must be a world record for university speed on an issue—the University Registrar, James Andrew Stanley Kirkness JP, exchanged with London (UK) robemakers Ede and Ravenscroft Ltd. The university had previously bought academic dress for graduating students in December 1955 from AG Almond Ltd of Cambridge (UK).[5] Ede & Ravenscroft provided a list of prices and recommended design changes following their receipt of Beadle's coloured sketches.[6] Their recommendations included adding lace to the back of the chancellor's gown, placing the university crest on both shoulders (Beadle had suggested only the right shoulder), and tapering the width of the lace on the sleeves and cap. Records do not survive in the university archives of Beadle's sketches, but a written description is provided by Ede & Ravenscroft, along with their suggested changes are available in Table 2.

The Registrar and the Heraldry Committee agreed, and the dress was accordingly made.

Shortly after this in 1963–64 Professor Hugh Smith wrote from Rhodes University (specifically mentioning official dress) to update his files on academic dress around the world.[7] This was followed in 1965 with letters exchanged between the Assistant Registrar, Victoria University of Wellington (VUW, another former University of New Zealand college) on behalf of the Deputy Vice Chancellor and Kirkness at University of Auckland, as VUW began the process of designing their own dress for university officials (which has never been specified in the university calendar).[8]

---

4   Report of Meeting of Heraldry Committee 6.6.1961 (adopted by Council 19 June 1961), 6 June 1961, University of Auckland Archives, Admin Collection (henceforth Auckland Archives)—Heraldry, 304, 1960–1961.

5   Registrar University Auckland, and A.G. Almond (Ltd) Cambridge, multiple telegrams, 17–18 December 1955, Kirkness Files, Auckland Archives—Academic Dress, 299, Academic Dress 1954–1955.

6   Ede and Ravenscroft Ltd to University of Auckland Registrar, Letter, 26 June 1961, Heraldry Folder, Kirkness Files, Auckland Archives—Academic Dress, 304, 1960–1961.

7   Professor Hugh Smith and University of Auckland Registrar, multiple letters, 29 May 1963, 24 Jan 1964, 10 April 1964, Kirkness Files, Auckland Archives, 310, 184, 195, 1962-1963, 1964-1965, 1966-1967. This information went into Hugh Smith and Kevin Sheard, *Academic Dress and Insignia of the World*, 3 vols (Cape Town: A. A. Balkema 1970).

8   D. G. Edwards (Assistant Registrar Victoria University of Wellington) to Kirkness, letter, 14 April 1965, Kirkness Files, Auckland Archives—Academic Dress, 184, 1964–1965.

Table 2: Written descriptions of dress recommended by University of Auckland (following the design of Professor Beadle) and the suggested modifications by Ede & Ravenscroft, 1961
Modern prices in Pounds sterling and New Zealand Dollars in square brackets.

Robes as illustrations

Chancellor's Robe, of blue damask with 2½" gold oakleaf lace, and 2½" lace on the sleeve slits and one badge ... ... 123 guineas [£2348/$4607].

Pro-Chancellor's Robe, as above, but with black damask and blue silk facings ... ... 127 guineas [£2425/$4757].

OR as above, but using black corded silk and blue facings ... ... 119 guineas [£2272/$4458].

Vice-Chancellor's Robe, of black corded silk, with 2" silver oakleaf lace and blue facings and one badge ... ... 97 guineas [£1852/$3634].

Registrar's Robe, of black corded silk with 2½" blue facings and one badge 57 guineas [£1088/$2135].

Suggested modifications

Chancellor's Robe, of blue damask with 2½" gold oakleaf lace, and 1¾" gold lace on the sleeve slits and one extra badge ... ... 116 guineas [£2215/$4345].
Extra for lace on the back slit ... ... 18 guineas [£344/$674].

Pro-Chancellor's Robe, as above, but of black damask and blue silk facings. 120 guineas [£2291/$4495].

OR as above, but using blue corded silk and therefore no extra for blue facings ... ... 110 guineas [£2100/$4121].

Vice-Chancellor's Robe, of black corded silk, with 2" silver lace and ¼" lace on the sleeve cuts and one extra badge ... ... 97 guineas [£1852/$3634].

Hats as illustrations

Chancellor's Hat – Black velvet mortar board with gold bullion tassel. 7½ guineas [£143/$281]

Pro-Chancellor's Hat – Black velvet mortar board with silver bullion tassel. 7½ guineas [£143/$281]

Vice-Chancellor's Hat – Black velvet mortar board with silver bullion tassel. 7½ guineas [£143/$281]

Registrar's Hat – Black velvet mortar board with black silk tassel ... ... 6 guineas [£115/$225].

Suggested modification

Chancellor's Hat – Black velvet mortar board, with gold lace on the skull and gold bullion tassel 9 guineas [£172/$337]

In 1974 the university encountered a problem which occurs when all the university officials change office, and the replacement appointments did not have 'a fixed head size', requiring the university to order new trenchers for them all.[9] Of note, D. W. Pullar, the new University Registrar, has also scribbled Smith & Caughey (a local large department store whose tailors formerly also made gowns for graduating students) and a phone number on the bottom of the letter. It is unclear who eventually prepared the new trenchers, although the reader does hope the Pro-Chancellor did get to wear his before his term was up!

22 July 1974

Messrs Ede & Ravenscroft Ltd,
Robe Makers & Tailors
93 & 94 Chancery Lane,
London, W.C.2,
ENGLAND.

Dear Sirs,

University of Auckland – Ceremonial Robes

It would be appreciated if you would supply four new mortar boards—we have had a change in office for all four officials and unfortunately we did not make one of the terms of appointment 'a fixed head size'. The robes were supplied by your firm in 1961.

The requirements are:

Chancellor:	One black velvet mortar board with gold lace on skull and gold bullion tassel. Size: 7 3/8ths.
Vice-Chancellor:	One black velvet mortar board with silver lace on skull and silver bullion tassel. Size: 7".
Pro-Chancellor:	One black velvet mortar board with gold bullion tassel. Size: 7¼.
Registrar:	One black velvet mortar board with black silk tassel. Size: 7 1/8th.

I hope you are able to fill the order without undue delay. Under our new arrangements the Pro-Chancellor holds office for one year only—it would be a great pity if during his term of office he never had a hat to fit.

Yours faithfully,
D.W. Pullar
REGISTRAR

This short article serves to illustrate the origin of the dress of university officials at the University of Auckland in the early 1960s. There are eight more universities to examine (which may or may not have information about academic dress in their archives), and once they have been visited, explored, and examined, a follow-up article will be presented examining the history and changes in New Zealand universities.

---

9   Pullar to Ede & Ravenscroft, letter, 22 Jul 1974, Pullar Files, Auckland Archives, 380, 1972–1979.

Transactions of the Burgon Society, 20 (2020), pages 14–50

'Different Forms of Gowns for All Sorts of Scholars in their Several Ranks': Academic Undress at Oxford in 1635

By Alex Kerr

This is a study of a one-page manuscript in the Oxford University Archives with the title 'Different Forms of Gowns for All Sorts of Scholars in their Several Ranks'. It is dated 'June 1635'. No previous writers, with one exception, seem to have known this remarkable document, but it is of unquestionable significance for the history of academic dress. It was clearly written in connection with the Laudian Code of statutes, which was drafted in 1634 and finally adopted in 1636. The Code included regulations on university dress and its use at Oxford that would remain in force for 134 years, despite disruptions in actual practice during the Civil War and Commonwealth. 'Different Forms' gives a concise specification for Oxford gowns at a time when other written records providing such detail are lacking and pictorial evidence is sparse. It would be over thirty years before anything comparable would be produced in text or image, by which time, in the Restoration, some particulars of the dress had changed. Vice-Chancellor John Fell would issue his *Orders to Tailors* in 1666; George Edwards and David Loggan would publish their superb engravings of Oxford dress in 1674 and 1675 respectively.

This article places 'Different Forms' in the context of the Laudian Code and provides a transcription. It then explains the various ranks and the requirements for the gowns and their facings and ornament. A section is devoted to four problematic terms for articles of dress. A commentary discusses significant points in the document, comparing the dress with Oxford gowns in the period leading up to 1635 and in the later seventeenth century. A table summarizing the provisions in 'Different Forms', the text of a second manuscript (at Magdalen College) and a glossary of materials to be used for trimming the gowns are given in appendices. Because details of black gowns in paintings of the time are difficult to make out, photographs of monuments and engravings are used to illustrate features of the dress. Unless otherwise stated, images are from the author's collection.

The Laudian Code and 'Different Forms'

William Laud was elected chancellor of the University in 1630. He was well acquainted with the workings of Oxford: he had studied at St John's College, where subsequently he was a fellow, a University proctor in 1603 and the College's president from 1611 to 1621. He left Oxford to take up a succession of senior church appointments, rising to be bishop of London and then archbishop of Canterbury. For over a century there had been moves to review and codify the University's mass of statutes, but a thoroughgoing overhaul had not been achieved. As chancellor Laud saw it as a priority to bring the project to fruition and he set to work at once. He appointed like-minded men in the University as special dele-

I am very grateful to Professor Bruce Christianson for his many valuable comments and suggestions on earlier drafts of this article and to Dr Susan North for her advice on various seventeenth-century garments and materials.

Photos reproduced courtesy of the Bodleian Library, University of Oxford

Figs 1 (above) and 1A. 'Different Forms of Gowns for All Sorts of Scholars in their Several Ranks'. Manuscript in the Archives of the University of Oxford. Above, a detail of the title and date.

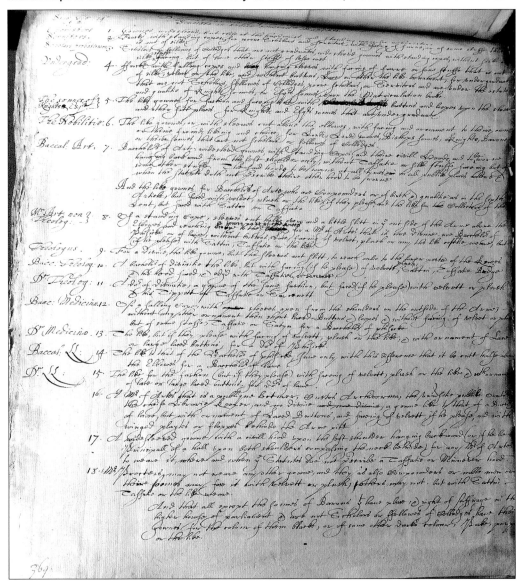

gates to work on a new Code with the intention of imposing order on chaos. They were to compile and consolidate the existing statutory materials rather than create new ones. The aim, however, was to realize Laud's conservative and high-church vision of a rigorously disciplined academic institution. Under his chancellorship more power was given to senior officers than in the past and less to the body of resident MAs. In the end Laud took over the task of reviewing and establishing the text of the Code personally. By 1634 a draft was ready and circulated to the Hebdomadal Board, set up in 1631 and comprising the heads of houses with the vice-chancellor, who met every Monday to transact University business.[1]

One of the statutes in the Code, Title XIV, was concerned specifically with university dress and its use. It laid down certain regulations and the sanctions that were to be imposed for non-compliance. It did not go into much detail about the dress itself. Undergraduates who were on the foundation of a college were to go out in gowns with wide or loose sleeves (*laxe manicatis*) and square caps; those who were non-foundationers were to go in gowns reaching the ankles (*talaribus*) and round caps.[2] Laud required the Hebdomadal Board to make inquiry concerning the academic dress suitable to each degree and faculty. It was to have a pattern of each article made up, and deposited in a press (cupboard) or chest provided for the purpose.[3] 'Different Forms' is proof, however, that a University functionary had already made a start on a record of one aspect of correct dress, the undress gowns, twelve months before Laud's Code was finally promulgated by the University's Convocation in June 1636.

Some paragraphs from 'Different Forms' were printed in *Notes and Queries* in 1879 in a contribution by W. H. Turner of Oxford. This appeared at the end of a discussion over several months about whether MAs would have worn the old full-dress gown with wide sleeves, now used by the proctors, when the allied sovereigns visited Oxford in 1814. Turner believed that the paragraphs he quoted supported the conclusion that they would not. He did not comment further on them but noted that the document was preserved among the papers of Gerard Langbaine.[4]

'Different Forms' is bound with miscellaneous manuscript and printed documents in one of twenty-one large-format volumes donated to the University Archives by Lang-

---

1   See Anthony Milton, 'Laud, William (1573–1645)', in *ODNB*; Charles Edward Mallet, *A History of the University of Oxford*, 3 vols (London: Methuen, 1924–27), Vol. II (1924), pp. 303–19; Kenneth Fincham, 'Oxford and the Early Stuart Polity', in *History of the University of Oxford*, Vol. IV, *Seventeenth-Century Oxford*, edited by Nicholas Tyacke (Oxford: Clarendon Press, 1997), pp. 179–210 (pp. 199–204); L. W. B. Brockliss, *The University of Oxford: A History* (Oxford: Oxford University Press, 2016), pp. 144–50.

2   Latin text in John Griffiths (ed.), *Statutes of the University of Oxford Codified in the Year 1636* (Oxford: Oxford University Press, 1888), p. 144; English translation by G. R. M. Ward, *Oxford University Statutes*, 2 vols (London: Pickering, 1845–51), Vol. I, pp. 152–53.

3   Griffiths, p. 145; Ward, Vol. I, p. 154. Mallet's statement (Vol. II, p. 333 n. 3) that these were drawings or engravings is not borne out by the Laudian text, which speaks of patterns in some cheap material, each one with a label attached (*titulo affixo*).

4   *Notes and Queries*, 5th ser., 12 (1879), 27 Sept. 1879, pp. 250–51. Turner was an Oxfordshire antiquary engaged on work for the Bodleian Library from 1870 until his death in 1880 <archives .bodleian.ox.ac.uk/repositories/2/resources/732> [all online material cited in this article retrieved 9 May 2021]. Langbaine the elder was keeper of the Archives of the University from 1644 and provost of Queen's College from 1646 (A. J. Hegarty, 'Langbaine, Gerard (1608/9–1658)', in *ODNB*). Thanks are due to Dr Paul Coxon, who came across the item in *N&Q* and drew it to my and others' attention.

baine, to which more were added by the antiquary Anthony Wood and by purchase after Langbaine's death. The contents are papers and publications collected by Langbaine while keeper of the Archives. The volume that includes our document, MS Langb. 3, comprises 530 folios, of which this item is fol. 369. 'Different Forms' is identified in the Archives' shelf list as WPγ/26/1/369. To judge by the handwriting it might tentatively be attributed to John French, University registrar from 1629 to 1651.[5]

The document itself does not identify who the intended readers were or why it had been written. A clue is obviously in the heading '*Stat: Tit: 14º. §. 2.*' just below the title. This refers to the section in the draft Laudian Code entitled '*De reprimendis et puniendis novos et insolitos habitus invehentibus*', issued in 1634 for the consultation with the Hebdomadal Board.[6] As it happens, §2 was retained unchanged in the finished statute of 1636; its heading has been translated as 'Concerning the repression and punishment of persons who introduce new and unwonted dresses'.[7] This section requires the vice-chancellor and heads of houses to prevent or punish any scholars or other persons, including cutters and tailors, who introduce new and unusual fashions of dress. Perhaps 'Different Forms', written in English rather than Latin, was intended to provide a schedule of correct gowns for the robemakers in the city, as well as those responsible within the University for seeing it implemented. If so, it serves a similar purpose to Fell's *Orders* of 1666, although that document deals only with dress for junior members (undergraduates and BAs).[8] This manuscript of 'Different Forms' looks like a working draft: there are several words and phrases crossed out and others inserted, corrections or amendments, one by another hand. It is a set of notes, awkward in expression and not written up in fluent prose. Of course, we can only assume that it gives accurate descriptions of gowns current in 1635 and that the patterns in Laud's press or chest would match them.

At a late stage in the research for this article another copy of 'Different Forms' came to my notice, preserved in the Archives of Magdalen College. It is now bound as item 81 in a volume of 104 documents, mostly letters, MS 367. The format is the same as the University Archives copy and the text differs from it in only a few details. It looks as though the text could have been copied either from the University Archives manuscript before the alterations were made or from a common source. It is undated. Its position in MS 367, which has documents generally in date order, would put it between 1639 and 1648. However,

5   I am indebted to Simon Bailey, keeper of the Archives of Oxford University (now retired), for comparing the manuscript with other contemporary documents and giving his opinion as to the possible writer.

6   *Corpus statutorum universitatis Oxon., siue; Pandectes constitutionum academicarum: e libris publicis et regestis universitatis consarcinatus* (Oxford: Oxford University Press, 1634), annotated copy in Oxford, Bodleian Library, Caps. 10.9 (1), unnumbered pages.

7   Griffiths, pp. 143–44; Ward, Vol. I, p. 152. Two changes were made elsewhere in the text of the draft Title XIV before the Code was approved in 1636 (indicated by handwritten marginal notes in the Bodleian copy of the 1634 *Corpus statutorum*). In §3, to the regulation that required graduates to wear square caps was added that the lawyers and medical men were to wear round ones. Christ Church was added to the places where graduates must wear their habits and hoods when attending solemn sermons (Griffiths, p. 144; Ward, Vol. I, p. 153). Of course, these amendments are immaterial for 'Different Forms' as they do not concern gowns.

8   Reprinted in L. H. Dudley Buxton and Strickland Gibson, *Oxford University Ceremonies* (Oxford: Clarendon Press, 1935), pp. 30–31.

since the other documents in the volume are mainly to do with College business, it may not have been filed with them originally, in which case it could be earlier than 1639.[9]

'Different Forms' gives specifications for undress gowns worn by undergraduates and graduates. However, it does include the wide-sleeved gowns for MAs that later commentators have generally taken to be 'full dress'. It does not include the coloured robes or the convocation habits worn by doctors: perhaps these robes and habits were not seen as the same class of dress as gowns. The black wide-sleeved MA gown, while a more formal alternative to the gown with hanging sleeves, appears not to have been regarded, here at any rate, as a festal garment as the DD, DCL and DM scarlet or the DMus white damask full-dress robes were.[10]

The text

Figures 1 and 1A are photographs of the manuscript, Oxford, University Archives, WPγ/26/1/369. Below is a semi-diplomatic transcription of the text. ˆ ˆ = text inserted above the line; <–> = text crossed out; [ ] = letters supplied by editor to resolve abbreviations or numerals to signal notes. For a summary table of the provisions in 'Different Forms' see Appendix A. For a transcription of the Magdalen College copy see Appendix B.

Different formes of Gownes for all sorts of
Scholars in theire severall Ranckes.

June 1635

Stat: Tit: 14º. §. 2.

Choristers
    1. Gownes wide sleev'd, but close at the hand wrist, and standing capes, for choristers.

Servitors.
    2. Frocks with standing capes, for poore Scholars and servitors, with facing of furre, or of some stuffe that is not of silke.

Scholars probationers:
    3. Scholars or fellowes of Colledges that are not graduates, wide-sleev'd gownes with standing capes, without silke or silke ˆstuffeˆ facing, but of some other stuffe of lesse cost.

Vndergrad[uates]:
    4. ffrocks with falling capes and <long>[1] hanging sleeves with facing of furre or some stuffe that is not of silke, velvet or the like, and without buttons, Lace or other the like ornament, for undergraduates that are not Scholars, ffellowes of Colledges,

---

9   I am grateful to Dr Charlotte Berry, archivist of Magdalen College, for kindly sending me photographs of the manuscript and for her comments about its possible date.

10 Writers on academic dress adopt a variety of terms for the different styles of sleeve. Here the terms *wide sleeves* and *hanging sleeves* are used as they are the most common in seventeenth-century usage and in modern reference works on dress history such as Valerie Cumming, C. W. Cunnington and P. E. Cunnington, *The Dictionary of Fashion History*, 2nd edn (London: Bloomsbury Academic, 2017).

poore scholars, or Servitors and are vnder the estate and qualitie of Knights sonnes, or Esq[ui]res sonnes, vpon the Matriculation booke.

The sonnes of Knights & Esq[ui]res.

5. The like gownes for fashion and faceing but with *<several words inked over and indecipherable>* buttons and loopes vpon the sleev[es] and other fitt places. for Knights and Esq[ui]res sonnes that are vndergraduates.

The Nobilitie:

6. The like gownes, or with sleeves cut above the elbowes, with facing and ornament to theire owne or theire freinds likeing and choice, for Lords, Lords sonnes, Bishops sonnes, Knights, Baronets or theire sonnes, that are not scholars or fellowes of Colledges.

Baccal: Art,

7. Bacchelors of Arts, wideslev'd gownes, with standing Capes, and theire civill Hoode, and to ˆbeˆ worne hanging backward from the left shoulder only, without Taffatie or silke stuffe faceing but of some other stuffe. The said hoode to be worne at all tymes and in all publike places where & when the statute doth not prescribe theire other hood to be worne[2]

And the like gownes for Bacchelors of Arte who are Compounders or of birth & qualitie as in the sixth Article, but faced with velvet, plush or the like, if they please, and the like for <the> Collectors of the Lent, but faced with Sattin or Taffatie.

Mr Art. non Theolog:

8. Of a standing Cape, sleeves cut halfe over, and a little slitt in [th]e out side of the Arme[3] above the Elbowes and reaching onlye to the ˆlower part of the kneesˆ <skirts>,[4] for a M[aste]r of Artes that is noe divine, noe Bacchelor of Phisicke or of lawe, without buttons, Lace, facing of velvet, plush or any the like costlie weare, but (if he please) with Sattin, Taffatie or the like.

Theologus.

9. For a divine, the like gowne, but the sleeves not slitt, to reach onlie to the lower parte of the knees.[5]

Bacc: Theolog:

10. A bachelor of divinitie the like, but with facing (if he please) of velvett, ˆplush,ˆ Sattin, Taffatie Budge & his hood faced & edg'd with Taffatie, or Sarcenett.[6]

Dr. Theolog:

11. A d[oct]or of divinitie, a gowne of the same fashion, but faced (if he please) with velvett or plush & his Tippett of Taffatie or Sarcenett

Bacc: Medicinæ.

    12. Of a falling Cape, with \<open\> sleeves open from the shoulders on the outside of the Armes without any other ornament than short laced Buttons & loopes & without facing of velvet or plush but of some stuffe, Taffatie or Satyn for a Bacchelor of phisicke

Dr Medicinæ.

    13. The like, but if they please with facing of velvett, plush or the like, & with ornament of Lace or large laced buttons, for a d[oct]or of Phisick.

Baccal: LL:

    14. The like to that of the Bachelor of phisicke, save only with this difference that it be cut halfe above the Elbowes for a Bacchelor of Lawe.

Dr. LL:

    15. The like for the fashon (but if they please) with faceing of velvett, plush or the like & w[i]th ornament of lace or large laced buttons, for d[oct]ors of lawe.

    16. A M[aste]r of Artes that is a publique lecturer, Custos Archivorum, the Universitie publike Orator, the cheife Librarie Keeper, and no divine \<and noe divine\>, a gown like to that of a Bacch[elor] of lawe, but with ornament of Laced Buttons, and faceing of velvett, if he please, and with winged playtes or flappes behinde the Arme pitt.

    17. A wide sleeved gowne with a civill hood upon the left shoulder hanging backward (or if he be a Principall of a hall upon both shoulders compassing the neck behinde) for any M[aste]r of Artes to weare it, where and when [th]e Statutes doe not prescribe a Taffatie or Minnever hood.

    18. M[aste]r Procters may not weare any other gowne, and they as also Compounders or noble men or theire sonnes may face it with Velvett or plush, others may not, but with Sattin, Taffatie or the like weare.[7]

        And that all except the sonnes of Barons [tha]t have place & right of suffrage in the higher house of parliament & are not Scholars or ffellowes of Colledges have their gownes for the color of them blacke, or of some other darke colour, Puke, purple or the like.

Notes

[1] long *crossed out, but stands in the Magdalen College copy (M).*

[2] *Entire sentence lacking in M.*

[3] and a little slitt in [th]e out side of the Arme *lacking in M.*

[4] down *has been overwritten as* onlye; lower part of the knees *inserted above the line;* skirts *crossed out; the original reading* (down to the skirts) *stands in M.*

[5] *M reads* but the sleeves to reach only to the knees.

[6] or Sarcenett *written by a different hand; lacking in M.*

[7] *Articles 17 and 18 lacking in M.*

20

Scholars in their several ranks

Most of the ranks in the list are those we are accustomed to in later periods, if not always down to the present day.[11]

1. Choristers formed a lowly class of non-graduate foundationers who sang in their college chapel choir.

2. Servitors, some also called poor scholars, worked their way through university by waiting on fellows in hall and acting as servants for wealthier students.[12] Laud also includes *batellarii* in his list, a rank a little above servitors, who paid some fees and made up the rest by undertaking tasks in college like servitors.

3. Scholars were undergraduate students on the foundation of a college. At some colleges no undergraduates were fellows; at some all scholars were fellows; at some undergraduate fellows were drawn from among the scholars—during the period before they became fellows, with a voice in college business, these were sometimes called probationers or scholar probationers. Scholar status survives today and attracts a token sum in recognition of academic achievement and a right to wear a distinctive gown.[13]

4. Those here called undergraduates were generally known as commoners. They were fee-paying students usually of modest or medium social status. The term commoner is still in use for any undergraduate not entitled to wear the scholar's gown.

5. Those here identified as sons of knights and esquires would later generally be termed gentlemen-commoners. They paid higher fees and enjoyed enhanced privileges.

6. Those here identified as the nobility include two classes that are differentiated from one another in Laud's Code. Sons of lords in the upper house of Parliament might wear brightly coloured gowns, while those without that status, as well as bishops' sons and baronets and their sons, were restricted to black or at any rate subdued colours—see the final, unnumbered, indented paragraph of 'Different Forms'.[14] Noblemen paid higher fees than gentlemen-commoners and enjoyed considerable privileges.[15]

The ranks above except those in 3 and 4 became obsolete during the nineteenth century and their distinctive dress fell out of use.

7. The BA was the first degree for all students, with one exception.[16] Although undergraduate courses in a widening range of disciplines were developed, this remained the case

11 For a fuller explanation and discussion of the different ranks of junior members see Brockliss, pp. 225–34. Although chiefly about a later period, see also William Gibson, 'The Regulation of Undergraduate Academic Dress at Oxford and Cambridge, 1660–1832', *Burgon Society Annual 2004*, pp. 26–41 (pp. 27–34), at <newprairiepress.org> https://doi.org/10.4148/2475-7799.1027.

12 At most colleges poor scholars were non-foundationers. Queen's College had a class of foundationers called 'poor boys' or 'poor children'.

13 Some colleges also have choral and organ scholars. At some the holder of the lesser award of an exhibition is counted as a foundationer and may wear the scholar's gown.

14 W. N. Hargreaves-Mawdsley, *A History of Academical Dress in Europe until the End of the Eighteenth Century* (Oxford: Clarendon Press, 1963), p. 93. The privileges of Scottish and Irish peers' sons were augmented by an addendum to Title VI in 1738/9 (Griffiths, p. 308; Ward, Vol. I, p. 313). Thereafter, Title XIV explicitly exempted them from the rule on black or dark gowns.

15 Knights, already included in article 5, are repeated here between bishops' sons and baronets and their sons, out of their proper place in the order of precedence, which is puzzling. If, however, we disregard the comma between the words 'Knights' and 'Baronets' as an error, we can take 'Knights Baronets' as a phrase meaning simply 'baronets', an emendation supported by the Magdalen College copy, which reads 'Knight Baronetts' (see *OED*, s.v. 'Knight').

16 Brockliss, pp. 234–35, 276.

until the BEd was introduced in 1969.[17] The only exception in the 1630s was the Student of Civil Law (a status abolished in 1873), who bypassed the BA and MA and studied for the BCL.[18] Compounders (petty or grand) were graduands who on a scale according to their social rank and wealth were required to pay graduation fees several times higher than the regular fees. Grand compounders wore a scarlet habit over their gown and walked in procession next to the vice-chancellor. Although this status ceased in 1855, it had in reality been in abeyance for four decades.[19] Collectors were representatives of the BAs, at this time appointed by the proctors rather than elected, who made the arrangements and collected the fees for Lenten disputations, the final exercises for new BAs (determination). Determination was phased out in the early nineteenth century, the last collectors being appointed in 1822.[20]

8 and 9. To complete the Arts course BAs continued as student-teachers until they were admitted to the degree of MA (inception). At this period the BA usually took four years and the MA a further three.[21] Requirements for the MA were reduced little by little until from 1859 BAs could apply for admission to the degree some seven years after matriculation without further academic study or residence and this remains the case today.[22] The distinction made here between MAs who were clergymen ('divines') and those who were not hardly figures in the Laudian Code and not at all so far as academic dress is concerned.

10–15. The bachelors' degrees that were awarded in the superior faculties of Theology, Medicine and Civil Law were all higher degrees requiring advanced study. The BD and BCL remained so, while the BM came to be awarded with the BCh as the medical joint degree; medical students are now awarded the BA (in Medical Sciences) after their three years of study on the pre-clinical course before proceeding to the second half of their degree programme. The corresponding doctorates were what we would now call higher doctorates, awarded after a considerable period of further study. The DD and DCL still are, but the DM is now normally awarded on the basis of a thesis as for the Doctor of Philosophy degree.

---

17 Andrew James Peter North, 'The Development of the Academic Dress of the University of Oxford, 1920–2012', *TBS*, 13 (2013), pp. 101–41 (pp. 126–27), https://doi.org/10.4148/2475-7799.1111. The BFA, BTh and a number of first-degree masters' awards followed (ibid., pp. 129–30, 131–32). For the range of courses currently provided and degrees awarded visit <www.ox.ac.uk>.

18 Provision in the Code's Title IX sect. 6 §2 (Griffiths, p. 115; Ward, Vol. I, p. 115). See also Hargreaves-Mawdsley, pp. 91–92; W. Gibson, 'Regulation', p. 27 n. 8; Alan J. Ross, '*Togas gradui et facultati competentes*: The Creation of New Doctoral Robes at Oxford, 1895–1920', *TBS*, 10 (2010), pp. 47–70 (p. 59), https://doi.org/10.4148/2475-7799.1084.

19 See Mallet, Vol. II, p. 130; Hargreaves-Mawdsley, pp. 102–03; W. Gibson, 'Regulation', p. 39; G. V. Cox, *Recollections of Oxford* (London: Macmillan, 1870), p. 251.

20 Mallet, Vol. II, pp. 128–29, 324; Cox, pp. 51, 102, 152 n. 1, 241–42, 257.

21 The Code's Title VI sect. 1 §1 made an exception of the sons of peers and eldest sons of baronets and knights, who could take their BA degree after three years (Griffiths, p. 45; Ward, Vol. I, pp. 31–32). Later in the seventeenth century, and until the nineteenth, these ranks of undergraduates were routinely created honorary MA after only two years from matriculation (Anthony Wood, *The Life and Times of Anthony Wood, Antiquary of Oxford, 1632-1695, Described by Himself*, edited by Andrew Clark, 5 vols (Oxford: Clarendon Press, 1891–1900), Vol. I, p. 414; L. S. Sutherland, 'The Curriculum', in *History of the University of Oxford*, Vol. V, *The Eighteenth Century*, edited by L. S. Sutherland and L. G. Mitchell (Oxford: Clarendon Press, 1986), pp. 469–91 (p. 478); Buxton and Gibson, pp. 87–88).

22 Brockliss, pp. 235, 237; Cox, p. 443; Buxton and Gibson, p. 6 n. 2.

16. A public lecturer was at this time a teacher engaged to give lectures in the University, as opposed to a holder of only a college post. Some held endowed lectureships, the number of which had increased steadily since the mid-sixteenth century and included readerships and professorial chairs. Others were appointed every second year by the four colleges supplying the proctors for the current and the following year.[23] The keeper of the Archives, the public orator and the chief library keeper (with the title Bodley's Librarian) are all posts that still exist.

17. The academic halls were residential communities for non-collegiate members of the University. Mostly small and unendowed, they were licensed by the vice-chancellor and presided over by a principal. From about a hundred in the late Middle Ages the number dwindled and by the 1630s only seven remained.[24] The last, St Edmund Hall, became a full college in 1957.

18. The two proctors, regarded as representatives of the MAs, were (and are) senior officers responsible for enforcing discipline and sanctions, supervising examinations and performing a range of other administrative functions. From 1628 they were elected by pairs of colleges in rotation rather than by the whole body of resident MAs, as they had been previously.[25]

Different forms of gowns

The range of basic gown patterns laid down in the 1635 document is essentially what had become commonplace in the late sixteenth century and has remained down to the present day, although there have been far-reaching changes in the detail. The gowns can be characterized primarily by the sleeves (or lack of them) and the collar.

So far as sleeves are concerned there are two basic styles:

Wide sleeves. The chorister, scholar, BA and MA are to have this wide-sleeved style—in the MA's case as an alternative to the gown with hanging sleeves, although the proctors are required always to wear the wide-sleeved gown.[26] The chorister's gown has the sleeves drawn in at the cuff ('close at the hand wrist') to form what would later be called pudding sleeves.

Hanging sleeves. These have various types of opening:

At the elbow
- with a horizontal slit ('sleeves cut above the elbowes', 'sleeves cut halfe over', 'cut halfe above the Elbowes'). The MA, BD and DD are to have this style. It is also one of two styles assigned to the nobleman undergraduate. The description refers to the fact that the tube forming the sleeve has a slit on the front of the upper arm with the back of the sleeve left intact (see Fig. 2).[27] The sleeves are to reach no further than just below the knee.

23 Mallett, Vol. II, pp. 321–23.

24 See Brockliss, pp. 56–57, 144, 754 (Map 4).

25 Brockliss, pp. 146–47.

26 A fine example of the wide-sleeved MA gown is in a 1636 portrait possibly of Richard Lovelace at Worcester College <artuk.org/discover/artworks/portrait-of-a-young-gentleman-224077>.

27 For an example in an oil painting, see the portrait of Christopher Potter, DD, in Queen's College, painted in about 1636 <commons.wikimedia.org/wiki/File:Christopher_Potter.jpg>. The status and degrees of members of the University have been verified in Joseph Foster, *Alumni Oxonienses, 1500–1714*, 4 vols (Oxford: Parker, 1891–92).

Photograph by Nicholas Groves

Fig. 2. Henry Caesar, DD, d. 1636, monument in Ely Cathedral, with a horizontal opening at the elbow and the sleeve reaching to the knee, ending with an open cuff.

Fig. 3. Sir William Paddy, DM, d. 1634, monument in St John's College, with large buttons for ornament and sleeves open up to the shoulder.

Fig. 4. Jerome Keyt, BCL, d. 1631, monumental brass in St Mary Magdalene Church, Woodstock, Oxon., with small buttons linked by lace, an inverted T with the vertical slit buttoned up and possibly also an opening (hand-slit) halfway down the lower part of the sleeve.

Fig. 5. Hugh Barker, DCL, d. 1632, monument in New College, with large buttons and lace for ornament and inverted-T sleeves, the vertical slits open only halfway up the upper arm. Two loops at the end of strips of lace on each arm show that the buttons just above the elbow could be done up if the wearer wished.

Fig. 6. John Pendarves, commoner of Exeter College, d. 1617, aged seventeen, brass in St Michael's Church. There are no known images of undergraduates closer to 1635. Notice the shoulder-level openings with wings, the sleeves hanging behind the arms, the fur-covered facings and flap collar.

Fig. 7. John Walrond, gentleman-commoner of Christ Church, d. 1602, aged eighteen, on his brass in the Cathedral, in a gown with a prominent wing round the shoulder-level armhole and a sleeve behind the arm, open at the foot, decorated with seven strips of lace. Walrond's gown matches the prescription for a gentleman-commoner's gown to appear in 'Different Forms' except that the trimming on the hanging sleeve seems to be simple lace rather than 'buttons and loopes'.

- with an inverted-T slit. MAs who are not clergymen are to have in addition a small, presumably vertical cut ('a little slitt in the out side of the Arme'), so making the opening an inverted T.[28]
- with a horizontal slit and a vertical slit up to the shoulder. The BM and DM are to have this style ('open from the shoulders on the outside of the Armes'). It seems that the BCL and DCL in contrast are to have a horizontal or perhaps an inverted-T opening; pictorial evidence shows that in practice their vertical slit reaches halfway to the shoulder (see Figs 3, 4 and 5). The distinction between the medical and legal faculties could be achieved by using similar gowns but unbuttoning or buttoning the upper sleeve.[29] The MA holding one of certain posts, if not a clergyman, wears an enhanced version of the BCL gown.

At the shoulder, with an armhole behind which the entire sleeve hangs free. The servitor, commoner and gentleman-commoner (to use familiar later terminology) are to have this style, the gowns referred to as 'frocks'. The 'frock' is evidently a subtype of the gown as gentlemen-commoners are to have 'like gownes for fashion and faceing' which follows immediately after the commoners' 'ffrocks' (see discussion below). Commoners and gentlemen-commoners have this style of opening to their 'hanging sleeves' (see Figs 6 and 7) and so do noblemen unless they opt for the style with a horizontal slit at the elbow. There is no mention of sleeves for the servitor; perhaps his gown did not have them at this time.

There are two styles of collar:

A stiffened yoke, probably now always without the original upstanding collar. The chorister, servitor, scholar, BA, MA, BD and DD have this style ('standing capes').

A flap collar. The commoner, gentleman-commoner, nobleman, BM, DM, BCL, DCL and certain post-holder MAs who wear a version of the BCL gown have this style ('falling capes').[30]

---

28 The Magdalen College copy does not mention 'a little slitt in the out side of the Arme'. However, it requires the divine to have sleeves that 'reach only to the knees' while the non-divine's are to reach 'down to the skirts' (an echo of Psalms 133. 2?); that could be anywhere between the waist and the hem (Cumming, Cunnington and Cunnington, p. 244), but here possibly a little below the knees. The wording for the non-divine in the University Archives copy before it was emended was 'down to the skirts'.

29 The question of upper sleeves being held shut or left open is explored by Bruce Christianson and Joan Kendall, 'A Portrait of an Oxford Nobleman, *circa* 1705', *TBS*, 15 (2015), pp. 30–40 (pp. 36–39), https://doi.org/10.4148/2475-7799.1132. They note (with illustrations) that Peter Turner, Doctor of Medicine of both Cambridge and Oxford, d. 1614, on his monument in St Olave's Church, Hart Street, London, has his sleeve open almost to the shoulder, unlike Thomas Bodley, d. 1615, in Merton College, MA and office holder, who has his upper sleeve almost closed, the opening in the form of a modest inverted T.

30 In his *Orders of Apparell* of 1585 the chancellor of Cambridge University, Lord Burghley, required graduates' gowns there 'to be made with a standing coller [...] and not falling' (quoted in Charles Henry Cooper, *Annals of Cambridge*, 5 vols (Cambridge: Warwick, 1842–53), Vol. II (1843), p. 410). No doubt 'standing capes' in 'Different Forms' is what in Canon 74 of 1604 is termed 'standing collars' (John Henry Blunt, *The Book of Church Law*, revised by Walter G. F. Phillimore and G. Edwardes Jones (London: Longmans, 1913), p. 405). In our document foundationer undergraduates and graduates in the clerical faculties of Arts and Theology are to have a 'standing cape' (a stiffened yoke). Non-foundationer undergraduates, graduates in the lay faculties of Medicine and Civil Law,

The last, unnumbered paragraph of 'Different Forms' indicates a certain leeway in the question of colour, permitting 'blacke, or some other darke colour, Puke [blackish brown or blue], purple or the like'.[31] Sons of peers in the House of Lords, however, could choose any colour they pleased. The fabric from which the body of the gowns should be made is not specified. At this period, it would most likely be prunello, a strong silk or woollen fabric commonly used for academic, clerical and legal gowns. Presumably, robemakers were free to make them up in material to suit the customer's status and budget.

Facings and ornament

Quite elaborate directions are set out for what trimming was required or allowed on the gowns. (For a glossary of materials prescribed in 'Different Forms' for facings and ornament see Appendix C.)

Facings

No particular facings are specified for choristers: presumably they would be of the same material as the body of the gown. Servitors, commoners and gentlemen-commoners could have fur facings. This would no doubt be inexpensive fur such as budge. An alternative for servitors is some stuff other than silk and for commoners and gentlemen-commoners some stuff other than silk or velvet. Was it assumed that servitors would not aspire to velvet? Similarly, scholars are to have facings of a fabric cheaper than one containing silk. Undergraduate noblemen may have facings of any material they choose—or, as the text puts it, 'to theire owne or theire freinds likeing and choice'. Perhaps friends here means family or sponsors, a usage at this time.

BAs have to face their gowns in a material not containing silk, while the collectors are required to have their gowns faced with satin or taffeta. BAs who are compounders or noblemen can use velvet or plush. The MA, BD, BM and BCL can, if they choose, face their gowns with satin or taffeta. The BD has the additional options of velvet, plush or budge. Doctors can, if they choose, face their gowns with velvet or plush or the like.

Certain post-holder MAs can have velvet facings on their BCL-style gowns. The proctors and MAs who are compounders or noblemen can have velvet or plush. Other MAs, as already mentioned, are restricted to satin or taffeta.

Ornament

Gentlemen-commoners are to have buttons linked by lace (of the kind later called braid) between them with loops or buttonholes. This ornament is to be laid on the sleeves, that is sleeves hanging behind the arms, and 'other fitt places'. This probably means the sides and possibly the lower back of the skirt, but that is not stated. Noblemen undergraduates can have ornament of their choice.

Laced ornament is prescribed for graduates in lay faculties, but it is not explicitly stated whether this is required or optional. The BM and BCL have what is called 'short

---

and certain post-holder MAs are to have 'a falling cape' (a flap collar). Servitors appear to be an anomaly in this regard, being non-foundationers but having a yoke—if 'Different Forms' is correct.

31 Puke was an imported woollen fabric used for gowns, etc., in the sixteenth century. The word is used here for the very dark colour in which it was dyed (Cumming, Cunnington and Cunnington, pp. 337, 357; *OED*, s.v. 'Puke'). At Cambridge in 1585 Burghley similarly prescribed that gowns must be 'blacke, puke, London Browne, or other sad color' (Cooper, Vol. II, p. 410).

Fig. 9. Sir Henry Savile, MA, d. 1622, monument in Merton College, with two wings round the armholes at the shoulder and sleeves hanging behind the arms. Savile was Warden of Merton, among other appointments and offices.

Fig. 8. Sir Eubule Thelwall, MA, d. 1630, monument in Jesus College, with small buttons linked with lace and a horizontal sleeve opening. Thelwall was Principal of Jesus and may have been depicted in this BCL-style gown because of his office.

laced Buttons & loopes'. The DM and DCL have what is called 'Lace or large laced buttons', no doubt a more sumptuous lace and/or buttons larger in size.[32] Certain post-holder MAs have the BCL-style gown, with the same ornament. Charles Rupert Tsua has provided a concise description of the ornament on seventeenth-century academic gowns:

> Typically, a strip of braid around 8" long has a button installed at the middle with tufts installed at both ends and sometimes above and below the buttons. Where there is an opening in the form of a vertical slit on the sleeve, the braid is divided in two: the button is installed at the opening side of one braid strip, and the other braid strip on the side facing the button is formed into a buttonhole or loop so it could be functionally buttoned to close the opening slit.[33]

We are fortunate in having contemporary pictorial evidence of what the ornament on the graduate gowns looked like in the 1630s (Figs 3, 4, 5 and 8). At that time the buttons were conspicuous, with tufts, if present, very modest in size.

---

32 The Magdalen College copy has the lay bachelors' sleeves 'with buttons & loopes without lace or tuffes' and the lay doctors' 'with ornament of lace and laced buttons'.

33 'A Study of the History and Use of Lace on Academical Gowns in the United Kingdom and Ireland', *TBS*, 12 (2012), pp. 103–27 (p. 116), https://doi.org/10.4148/2475-7799.1103.

Difficult terms

Frock

The term *frock* is here restricted to a gown with an opening at the shoulder to release the arm. In the early modern period the word *frock* generally meant a loose outer garment with sleeves.[34] Joseph Strutt, however, comments on frocks in the wardrobe of Henry VIII: 'It does not appear that this garment had any sleeves'.[35]

In his will of 1544 John Holden, rector of Gamlingay, Cambs., bequeathed his 'clothe frock lined with sattin of cypress' to Jone Grene.[36] The word is used in 1570 for one of the styles of gown worn by Puritan ministers, those who are said to eschew 'Popish ragges', and it is referred to as a 'lay fashion'.[37] An inventory of the property of John English, fellow of St John's College, Oxford, compiled in 1613, includes this article: 'A frocke gowne'.[38] These references do not help with defining what the frock was like, but are an indication that clergymen and academics owned garments in the sixteenth and early seventeenth centuries which they called by that name.

The term *frock* is found in university documents in the sixteenth century, although the distinction between that and other kinds of gown is not explained. For example, Oxford Decrees and Orders issued in 1576 impose fines for graduates who attend St Mary's Church, Convocation or Congregation 'without having on [...] a Gowne or frock' or various academic exercises without 'theyr Gowne or frock'.[39] By 1635 it seems the frock as a gown without sleeves or with sleeves open at the shoulder and hanging behind the arms was confined to undergraduates, although only twelve years before that Sir Henry Savile, who was an MA and office holder, is shown in one on his monument in Merton College (Fig. 9).

Civil hood

'Different Forms' prescribes the wide-sleeved gown for the BA with in addition a civil hood:

> to be worne hanging backward from the left shoulder only, without Taffatie or silke stuffe faceing but of some other stuffe. The said hoode to be worne at all tymes and in all publike places where & when the statute doth not prescribe theire other hood to be worne.

When wearing the wide-sleeved gown rather than one with hanging sleeves the MA similarly is to wear:

> a civill hood upon the left shoulder hanging backward (or if he be a Principall of a hall upon both shoulders compassing the neck behinde) for any Master of Artes to weare it, where and when the Statutes doe not prescribe a Taffatie or Minnever hood.

---

34 Cumming, Cunnington and Cunnington, p. 116.

35 *A Complete View of the Dress and Habits of the People of England*, revised by J. R. Planché, 2 vols (London: Bohn, 1842), Vol. II, p. 246.

36 Quoted in J. R. Planché, *History of British Costume*, new edn (London: Cox, 1847), p. 313.

37 Thomas Harding, *Confutation of a Booke Intituled An Apologie of the Church of England* (Antwerp: Laet, 1570; repr. Ilkley: Scolar Press, 1976), p. 397; quoted by Janet Mayo, *A History of Ecclesiastical Dress* (London: Batsford, 1984), p. 73.

38 W. C. Costin, 'The Inventory of John English, B.C.L., Fellow of St John's College', *Oxoniensia*, 11–12 (1946–47), pp. 102–31 (p. 105).

39 Strickland Gibson (ed.), *Statuta antiqua Universitatis Oxoniensis* (Oxford: Clarendon Press, 1931), p. 403.

The BA's 'other hood' would be black, lined or part-lined with cheap fur, usually budge, while the MA's would be black, lined with silk or more expensive fur such as miniver, according to the occasion and the season, and possibly turned out, or even inside out, to display the lining.[40]

Although *civil hood* appears in passages from earlier texts quoted by some modern writers on dress history, none of them has identified exactly what this article is and I have not discovered any pictorial evidence to help.[41] Some do discuss the Latin term *epomis*, which, as we shall see, is most probably the same thing at this period. The phrase *civil hood* is found in a variety of late-sixteenth- and early-seventeenth-century written material, in most cases referring explicitly to an item of academic dress. Consequently, we may assume that the writer of 'Different Forms' was using an established term that readers would know.

An eyewitness account by a Cambridge man of the visit of James I and his consort, Queen Anne, to Oxford in 1605 includes the following observation:

> The young Masters of Arts & the Batchelors of arts wore gowns & hoods so much alike as not to be distinguished, viz., black wide sleeved gowns, faced to the foot with taffeta and about the arm to turn up to the elbow, and black civil hoods on the left shoulder.[42]

Regulations drawn up when the king visited Cambridge in 1615, recorded by the Registrary, James Tabor, ordered that

> Regents and Non Regents come to S' Marie's Church in the tyme of Disputacions with hoods and capps; viz., Regents with white hoods, and Non Regents with civill [*but quite possibly* sable—*the handwriting is unclear*] hoods.[43]

Two inventories include a civil hood: one, of Paul Kisby or Gisby, bursar of All Souls College, compiled in 1594, has an item 'a schollers gowne & civill hoode';[44] the other, of John English from 1613, whose frock gown was mentioned in the previous subsection of this article, also included 'An old suite and an hatte, an old cloake an old paire of drawers & a civill hoode' and also 'A batchelors hoode'.[45]

Letters written in 1611 by a college tutor to the father of two brothers who were students at Brasenose College, Oxford, and whose finances he managed (as was then the custom) ask for money to buy cloth for gown and civil hood. Evidently the brothers required

---

40 Hargreaves-Mawdsley, pp. 89, 81.

41 Hargreaves-Mawdsley must be mistaken when he writes (p. 83) that the civil hood mentioned in the inventory of Edward Cooper, BD, of 1640 'was an ordinary lay cape to put round the shoulders in cold weather and had nothing to do with an academical hood'.

42 From 'The Preparation at Oxford, in August 1605 against the Coming of King James', London, British Library, MS Harl. 7044, fols 201–16; transcription in John Nichols, *The Progresses, Processions and Magnificent Festivities of King James I*, 4 vols (London: Nichols, 1828), Vol. I, p. 557; also quoted in F. W. Fairholt, *Costume in England*, 4th edn, edited by H. A. Dillon, 2 vols (London: George Bell, 1909), Vol. I, pp. 288–89. The account is probably by Philip Stringer, who is known to have written the account of Elizabeth I's progresses, from which this, in the same hand, follows on.

43 Transcribed by William Cole, preserved in the Cole MSS, Vol. XLII, London, British Library, MSS Adds 5843, p. 286; printed in Nichols, Vol. III, p. 43; Cooper, Vol. III (1845), p. 68; also quoted in Fairholt, *loc. cit.*

44 Transcription by Ronald Caseby, Bodleian Library, Oxford <kisby.one-name.net/old-site /note/gisby-inventory.html>. 'Schollers' here no doubt means belonging to an academic or just an educated man and not a foundationer undergraduate.

45 Costin, p. 105.

the civil hood once they had graduated and more especially when the older one was apply-ing for a fellowship at All Souls.[46] An earlier letter, written in December 1610, contains a similar request when the younger brother needed a hood—not a civil hood in this case.[47]

Records at Wells Cathedral include a note that at hearings about vicars choral the attorneys wore a civil hood to award seisin.[48] Also at Wells it is recorded that in February 1633/4:

> Mr. Martin Simon appeared to answer certain articles. [...] To the eighth article he an-swered 'that he did not weare a civill hood untill he was a Mr. of artes of fower yeares standing, and since that he hath worne one, which he beleeveth he may doe by the priv-ilidges of the university of Cambridge, wheare he tooke his degree.' He was willing to discontinue it if the dean and canons 'doe dislike therewith,' etc.[49]

Presumably Simon had been accused of wearing something he was not entitled to or which was inappropriate in the context in which he wore it. His assertion does confirm, however, that the civil hood at this period was worn at Cambridge (as well as at Oxford). The significance of his waiting four years before donning it is unclear: if the criterion had been moving from regent to non-regent status that would have occurred two years after his inception. Simon, a vicar choral and priest, 'appears not to have been amenable to any kind of discipline, if one may judge from the frequent references to him in the Chapter Acts.'[50]

A work in the style of Edmund Spenser entitled *Thule; or Vertue's Historie* published in 1598 by Francis Rous the Elder includes lines on Philedonus, a seducer, donning re-spectable, professional, possibly scholarly garb in order to deceive his victim:

> Yet faire he seemeth at the sudden sight,
> Yet foule he is at last when men him weete;
> Under a pleasing hew and civill hood,
> He carries poyson'd baytes and venom'd food.[51]

A dramatic allegorical interlude, *Time's Complaint*, performed at St John's College, Oxford, on 1 January 1607/8 as part of the Christmas revels, mentions the civil hood: 'After these six of the privie Counsell in Schollars gownes and civill hoods, everie one attended on by a Footman [...].' and 'After these the [Christmas] Prince himselfe in a scholler's gowne and civill hood, with a coronett of laurell about his hat, attended by fower footmen [...].'[52]

---

46 Quoted in Lady Newton, *The House of Lyme: From its Foundation to the End of the Eigh-teenth Century* (London: Heinemann, 1917), pp. 93, 94.

47 Newton, p. 92.

48 Historical Manuscripts Commission, 'Acts and accounts: 1630–41', in *Calendar of the Man-uscripts of the Dean and Chapter of Wells*, Vol. II (London, 1914), pp. 392–425. See British History Online <www.british-history.ac.uk/wells-mss/vol2/pp392-425>.

49 Historical Manuscripts Commission, *Report on the Manuscripts of Wells Cathedral: A Calendar of Abstracts*, ed. by James Arthur Bennett (London, 1885), p. 255 <archive.org/details/reportonmanuscr00cathgoog/page/n270/mode/2up?q=civill+hood>.

50 Wyn K. Ford, 'The Life and Works of John Okeover (or Oker)', *Proceedings of the Royal Musical Association*, 84 (1957–58), pp. 71–80 (p. 74).

51 Spenser Society Publications, 23 (Manchester: Spenser Society, 1878), p. 15.

52 *The Christmas Prince*, edited by F. S. Boas and W. W. Greg, Malone Society Reprints (Ox-ford: Oxford University Press, 1922), pp. 105–06.

Wikimedia

Fig. 10. Physician and surgeon (left) and members of the Grocers' Company (right) in two styles of mourning hoods in Sir Philip Sidney's funeral procession, 1586/7. The former have their liripipe wrapped round the neck with an open fold at the back; the latter's liripipe goes straight over the shoulder and ends in a little bag. Details from the Lant Roll, engravings by Derick Theodore De Brij after drawings by Thomas Lant.

The identifiable item of dress from the period that seems to come closest to the civil hood is the mourning hood worn at great funerals by various officials and civil dignitaries, as in Philip Sidney's funeral procession in 1587. Some figures wear a full hood with a cape and the cowl pulled up over the head, a sign of mourning, and some wear a mourning hood on the left shoulder (see Fig. 10).[53] The black mourning hood was invariably worn on the left shoulder. It was adopted by barristers on the death of Charles II in 1685 and they have retained it ever since.[54] This is in contrast to the judges and serjeants, who wore their casting-hood on the right shoulder. The Judges' Rules of 1635 suggest that the scarlet casting-hood worn on the right was a sign of temporal dignity and the black mourning hood on the left a sign of spiritual status.[55] A similar article formed part of the dress of certain livery companies in the early seventeenth century and was not especially for mourning. The Leathersellers' officers wore it in livery colours on the right shoulder—no doubt following convention.[56] Perhaps Oxford BAs and MAs were to wear their civil hood on the left shoulder because they were graduates in the Arts faculty, which was deemed to be clerical, like

---

53 Articles of dress in this form are variously named elsewhere as a *capuchon*, *chaperon*, *chausse*, and latterly *epitoge*. For a brief description and the origins see Nicholas Groves (ed.), *Shaw's Academical Dress of Great Britain and Ireland*, 3rd edn (London: Burgon Society, 2011), pp. 16–17.

54 J. H. Baker, 'History of Gowns Worn at the English Bar', *Costume*, 9 (1975), pp. 15–21 (pp. 18–20).

55 Baker, 'Gowns at the Bar', pp. 19, 21 n. 44.

56 See image of officers of the Company in the 1604 Charter given by James I <leathersellers .co.uk/wp-content/uploads/2016/11/Leathersellers-Book.pdf>, p. 6.

Theology and unlike Civil Law and Medicine, which were lay faculties.

In the 1635 document an MA who is the principal of a hall is required to wear a civil hood in the way certain clergymen on several sixteenth-century brasses wear their hood, i.e. with it fixed on the left shoulder, the hanging part brought round the back of the neck and draped over the right shoulder. Note that with this item unlike the mourning hood the liripipe part seems to be short and pinned on the shoulder rather than hanging at length at the front (Fig. 11).[57] The civil hood described in 'Different Forms' is explicitly said to hang backwards from the shoulder; there is no reference to anything hanging at the front.

Part of Title XIV §3 in the draft of the Laudian Code of 1634 and the finished version of 1636 reads:

Fig. 11. Richard Bethell, d. 1518, from his brass in St Peter's Church, Shorwell, Isle of Wight, shown in a gown with a scarf or hood worn in the style of a Cambridge squared hood. Engraving by Charles Tomkins, published by George Kearsley, c. 1794.

> Lectores etiam et Professores publici, in Lectionibus suis ordinariis, Togis Gradui vel Facultati suæ competentibus, Epomide et Pileo induti, ad Scholas accedant, et eodem Habitu induti legant, ac iterum a Scholis recedant. In solennibus autem Lectionibus in Vesperiis, Pileis, Capis, et Caputiis, Gradui et Facultati suæ competentibus induti ad Scholas accedant, legant, ac iterum recedant.[58]

> The public readers and professors, too, at their ordinary lectures shall go to the schools dressed in gowns suitable to their degree or faculty, and in the scarf and cap, and lecture, and return again from the schools in the same habit. But during the solemn lectures at Vesperies, they shall go to the schools, and lecture, and withdraw in caps, capes, and hoods, conformable to their degree and faculty.[59]

Ward translates *epomide* here as 'in the scarf', but it must be what Laud's contemporaries were calling the civil hood in English. However, Laud requires the *epomis* to be worn for giving 'ordinary' lectures whatever the wearer's degree or faculty. 'Different Forms' pre-

---

57   N. F. Robinson took the 'scarf' on the brass of John Yslyngton, priest at Cley-next-the-Sea, Norfolk, to be some kind of veil for the chalice and paten that the figure is holding ('The Pileus Quadratus', *Transactions of the St Paul's Ecclesiological Society*, 5.1 (1901), pp. 1–16 (pp. 4–5)). This seems unlikely as the figures on the brasses of Richard Bethell, vicar at Shorwell, Isle of Wight, and at least seven others listed by Herbert Druitt wear it in the same way without holding a chalice (*A Manual of Costume as Illustrated by Monumental Brasses* (London: Alexander Moring, 1906), pp. 106–07). J. H. Baker has shown it to be a hood worn squared in the manner of the Cambridge proctors and describes and illustrates examples of lawyers wearing it in this way but fixed on the right and brought round to lie on the left shoulder ('A Comparison of Academical and Legal Costume on Memorial Brasses', in *Commemoration in Medieval Cambridge*, ed. by John S. Lee and Christian Steer (Woodbridge: Boydell, 2018), pp. 90–105 (pp. 102–05)).

58   Printed in *Corpus statutorum*. This passage from the 1636 finished text is printed in Griffiths, p. 144.

59   Ward, Vol. I, p. 153.

scribes the civil hood only for Arts graduates when in the gown with wide sleeves; there is no mention of it for graduates in Theology, Civil Law or Medicine, who wear a gown with hanging sleeves.

The same section in the Laudian Code also has:

> Statutum est, quod Præfecti Collegiorum et Aularum in Conventu suo Hebdomadali, diligenti inquisitione habita, de Toga, Capa (seu clausa, seu aperta), Caputio, Epomide, Pileo, cuique Gradui et Facultati (præsertim Medicis ac Iuristis) competentibus, determinabunt.[60]

> [I]t is enacted that the heads of colleges and halls shall determine at their weekly meeting, after making diligent inquiry concerning the gown, cape (whether close or open), hood, scarf, and cap suitable to each degree and faculty, particularly to those of the physicians and jurists.[61]

As this list includes both *Caputio* and *Epomide* they are clearly different articles. Again Ward, in 1845, translates *epomide* as 'scarf'.[62]

The next reform of the statute on academic dress after Laud was conducted in 1770. The new statute Title XIV refers to what in modern Oxford usage is called a *tippet*, as shown in plates of the nobleman and the baronet in the engravings commissioned from Charles Grignion to illustrate it.[63] By this date it is a pyramidal fold of cloth fixed behind the shoulder to the lower left-hand corner of the yoke. This tippet figures in the engravings of the proctor, the pro-proctor and the collector as well, but their dress is not described in Title XIV—they are to wear what was already in use.[64] The tippet in this sense of *epomis* has now been dropped from the dress worn by other graduates.

> Baronum filii in superiore Parliamenti Domo suffragii Jus habentium, nec non Baronum ex gente Scoticâ et Hibernicâ, Togâ talari deauratâ, sive Togâ nigrâ laxè manicatâ sericâ cum Epomide, et Pileo quadrato cum Apice deaurato, induti incedant. Baronetti autem Togâ talari nigrâ, deauratâ, sive Togâ laxè manicatâ sericâ cum Epomide, et Pileo quadrato cum Apice deaurato.[65]

---

60 Griffiths, p. 145.

61 Ward, Vol. I, p. 154.

62 E. C. Clark took the *epomis* to be the same as the *exomis* and read John Caius' statutes of 1557/8 to require undergraduates in his college to wear it when graduates wear the *caputium* (hood) ('English Academical Costume (Mediæval)', *Archaeological Journal*, 50 (1893), pp. 73–104, 137–49, 183–209 (p. 90)). Hargreaves-Mawdsley (p. 132) read Caius' statute to require all members of the college to wear an *exomis*, but is vague as to what it was. Caius' statute 27, *De vestitu*, is printed in *Documents Relating to the University and Colleges of Cambridge*, 3 vols (1852), Vol. II, pp. 258–60.

63 See Alex Kerr, 'Layer upon Layer: The Evolution of Cassock, Gown, Habit and Hood as Academic Dress', *TBS*, 5 (2005), pp. 42–58 (p. 55), https://doi.org/10.4148/2475-7799.1038. A set of Grignion's engravings is held in the Bodleian, MS Top. Oxon. c. 16 (20–45).

64 *Parecbolae; Sive excerpta e corpore statutorum Universitatis Oxoniensis* (Oxford: Clarendon Press, 1771), p. 165; Ward, Vol. II, p. 9. See Hargreaves-Mawdsley, Plate 11A.

65 *Parecbolae*, p. 167. The Latin text of the academic dress statutes of 1636 and 1770 is given in Christopher Wordsworth, *Social Life at the English Universities in the Eighteenth Century* (Cambridge: Deighton, Bell & Co., 1874), pp. 481–85.

When the statute on academic dress was being revised in 1770, a draft dated 1 July still had BAs (but not MAs) in an *epomis*, retained from the Laudian Code, even though they had not worn such a thing for at least a hundred years. Perhaps it was intended to insist on the statutory *epomis* to distinguish them from undergraduate scholars, whose gown was otherwise rather similar. This was omitted in a later draft, dated 10 July, despite a suggestion in the interim that both BAs and MAs should be able to wear one if they chose (proposed *Amendments* issued 1 July). In the final draft, with text ex-

Here Ward, in 1851, translates *epomide* as 'tippet', different from his translation of the word in the 1636 statute.[66]

> The sons of barons who have the right of voting in the upper house of parliament, and also of barons of the Scotch and Irish peerage, are to go dressed in the gown of gold brocade reaching the ankles, or in the black loose-sleeved silk gown with the tippet, and the square cap with gold tuft. Baronets in the black gown of gold brocade reaching to the ankles, or in the loose-sleeved silk gown with the tippet, and the square cap with gold tuft.[67]

This usage must be distinguished from the DD's 'Tippett' in 'Different Forms': it is highly implausible that the two are the same thing.

It appears likely that the civil hood was a kind of chausse or epitoge something like the mourning hood worn at great funerals such as Philip Sidney's in 1587. Or perhaps more like the article with a back part that could be drawn round the back of the neck by principals of halls and fixed on the other shoulder rather as the full hood at Cambridge can be worn 'squared'[68] and as Richard Bethell has on his brass of 1518 (Fig. 11). It seems that the civil hood as such had disappeared by the 1670s. In their Oxford academic dress engravings George Edwards has the proctor in the tippet (in the modern sense)[69] and David Loggan has the collector (Fig. 12) and the proctor in one—and the proctor has a tippet even when wearing the ermine hood.[70] Did this tippet evolve from the civil hood and shift from hanging backwards to hanging sideways over the shoulder by 1674?[71] Or is it a completely different item from the civil hood? Is it the remnant of the cape of a hood like the back of an

---

tensively rearranged, promulgated and approved on 13 July, the distinction between scholars and BAs was marked by the latter being allowed a gown, probably reflecting actual contemporary practice, with significantly longer sleeves than the former. At the same time the requirement for noblemen and baronets in undress to have an *epomis* was inserted: no prior discussion of this has been found or evidence that they had worn it in the past—or indeed that they had not; none of the known pamphlets published in the debate about the new statute touches on the topic. For a brief account see V. H. H. Green, 'The University and Social Life', in *History of the University of Oxford*, Vol. v, *The Eighteenth Century*, pp. 309–58 (pp. 324–27). Copies of the printed drafts are collected in Bodl., Don. b.12.

66 The term *tippet* does not appear in the drafts or discussions in 1770, but is used in the modern sense in William Combe's text for *History of the University of Oxford*, 2 vols (London: Ackermann, 1814), Vol. II, p. 17 (reprinted in Nicholas Jackson (ed.), *Ackermann's Costumes of the Universities of Oxford and Cambridge* (London: Burgon Society, 2016), p. 15).

67 Ward, Vol. II, p. 10.

68 J. H. Baker, 'The Dress of the Cambridge Proctors', *Costume*, 18 (1984), pp. 86–97 (pp. 92–95). Hargreaves-Mawdsley states (p. 81) that the Laudian Code had new MAs wearing the old 'shoulder piece' as a kind of cape (*mantellum*) when incepting and he cites Ward's translation of Title VII §4. In fact, the word *mantellum* does not appear anywhere in the Code and what Ward translates here as 'in their capes' is, as elsewhere, for the Latin '*in capis*', that is chimeres or convocation-style habits and not some tippet or civil hood or anything of the kind. I missed this point in my 'Hargreaves-Mawdsley's *History of Academical Dress* and the Pictorial Evidence for Great Britain and Ireland: Notes and Corrections', *TBS*, 8 (2008), pp. 106–50 (p. 124), https://doi.org/10.4148/2475-7799.1066.

69 *Omnium ordinum habituumque academicorum exemplaria* (Oxford: the engraver, 1674).

70 *Oxonia illustrata* (Oxford: the engraver, 1675), Plate X, nos 10, 17, 18. See also Edmund Eggleston, '*Egregii Procuratores*: The Master of Arts' Full-Dress Gown and its Use by the Proctors and Assessor of the University of Oxford', *TBS*, 17 (2017), pp 84–100 (p. 91), https://doi.org/10.4148/2475-7799.1147.

71 This point is argued by Bruce Christianson in 'A Purple Passion? Queen's College Oxford and the Blood of the Lord', *TBS*, 12 (2012), pp. 63–71 (pp. 66–68), https://doi.org/10.4148/2475-7799.1100.

epiloge or is it a reduced cape or mantle perhaps, like the Cambridge proctor's ruff?[72] Are the Laudian statutes and the 1770 statutes using the term *epomis* for two distinct articles of dress, either because the drafters in 1770 failed to realize that their tippet was not the same as the early-seventeenth-century civil hood or because their tippet had, in a way, replaced it? The civil hood of 1635 and the tippet of 1674 and 1675 had been something worn over or round the shoulder, which is what *epomis* means. I am not convinced that the civil hood (if it is what I think it is) morphed into the tippet of Edwards and Loggan. Was it given up and the cape-like tippet used in its place but, like the full-dress MA and BA gowns, more or less restricted to the proctors and collectors till the noblemen and baronets were given it?

Fig. 12. BA as collector, from Loggan's *Oxonia illustrata* (1675), Plate X, no. 10, with velvet on his facings and lower sleeve and with a tippet covering his left shoulder.

Tippet

What does our writer in 1635 mean by the word *tippet*? It has been used at different periods for different articles of academic dress and indeed Oxford has differed from Cambridge in its usage.[73]

The prescription in 'Different Forms' for the BD has the gown

with facing (if he please) of velvett, plush, Sattin, Taffatie Budge & his hood faced & edg'd with Taffatie, or Sarcenett.

The DD is to have his gown

faced (if he please) with velvett or plush & his Tippett of Taffatie or Sarcenett.

Our document states that a civil hood is worn by BAs when not wearing their other hood and by MAs when not wearing their hood lined with taffeta or miniver. It does not deal with hoods, in the ordinary sense, except here for the BD: it restricts itself to gowns and what might be thought of as their accessories. Could the writer of 'Different Forms' have inadvertently omitted the word 'civil' here and really meant a civil hood 'faced & edg'd with Taffatie, or Sarcenett', that is in contrast to the BA's 'without Taffatie or silke stuffe faceing but of some other stuffe'?

Are we being told that where a BD wears a hood (or civil hood), the DD wears a tippet, whatever that may be in 1635 Oxford? The 1604 Church of England Canon 58 required graduate clergy at certain services to wear their university degree hood and non-graduates to wear 'a decent tippet of black, so it be not silk'.[74] The tippet is there clearly of lower status than the hood, but in 'Different Forms' the higher degree

---

72   Baker, 'Dress of the Cambridge Proctors', pp. 86–91.

73   For the uncertainty about what a tippet is in medieval and early modern texts see E. C. Clark, pp. 95–99; Kerr, 'Layer upon Layer', pp. 54–56.

74   Blunt, p. 398. The distinction actually goes back at least to 1549, when the almuce was discarded and it is recorded that the canons at St Paul's Cathedral put on their university degree hoods instead while the 'petie cannons' put on tippets (see Mayo, p. 89).

has the tippet and the lower degree the hood. The reason is unclear. Is the word being used for a different thing? Incidentally, it should be noted that the word *tippet* does not appear at all elsewhere in the 1604 Canons.

It is quite implausible that it could mean the little cape seen on the left shoulder of proctors and collectors from Loggan's Oxford engravings in the 1670s onwards. That article is not in fact named *tippet* until the eighteenth century. In his diaries Anthony Wood, often a source of information on such matters, uses the word on only one occasion, in an entry in 1663, where it clearly refers to a liripipe on a hood, and not an academic one at that.[75]

Fig. 13. Robert Pink, DD, d. 1647, monument in New College, with horizontal openings at the elbows and a scarf gathered and draped over his gown.

The only item of academic dress that has been reserved at Oxford exclusively for DDs from the seventeenth century on is the scarf, worn by custom if not regulation.[76] I suspect that *tippet* as used in our document means that scarf. The words *scarf* and *stole* do not appear anywhere in the 1604 Canons: it would complicate matters if they did. Pictorial representations of DDs in the early seventeenth century have them with the scarf when wearing the undress gown (see Fig. 13). Hargreaves-Mawdsley establishes that the DD's scarf should be regarded as an academic garment and suggests its superficial similarity to the ecclesiastical stole is coincidental (p. 70). He believes it derives from 'the long piece of stuff to which the roundlet was attached and which was later detached and hung round the neck, being held in place by means of a loop on the back of the collar of the gown.'[77] He writes that 'the stole was a vestment, the scarf simply a symbol of dignity and learning.' He adds (significantly for us) that in the 1522 statutes of Brasenose College 'it is called a "tippet", which implies that it is not regarded as anything particularly ecclesiastical.' The word *tippet* in the 1604 Canon is taken by some to refer to such a scarf, academic like the hood rather than ecclesiastical.[78] If it did, the reversal of status of the BD and the DD in 'Different Forms' against the graduate and the non-graduate in the Canon mentioned above would still remain problematic—unless perhaps we think our writer meant a civil hood for the BD as against a scarf for the DD.

As we have seen, Ward in 1845 translated Laud's *epomis* as 'scarf', but in the previous subsection of this article we established that *epomis* in the 1630s actually refers to a civil

75 Wood, Vol. I, pp. 481–82.

76 See Edwards' and Loggan's engravings; Buxton and Gibson, pp. 33 n. 2, 38; John Venables, *Academic Dress of the University of Oxford*, 9th edn (Oxford: Shepherd & Woodward, 2009), p. 14.

77 Could the antecedent of this scarf be the article, a kind of chaperon, worn over the head by a priest illustrated in a fifteenth-century French manuscript of the *Roman de la Rose* in the British Library? It hangs down to the shoulder on the wearer's left and forms a long, thin pendant on his right. Illustrated in Robinson, Plate I, facing p. 4 <archive.org/details/transactionsofst05stpa/page /4/mode/2up>.

78 See Percy Dearmer, *The Parson's Handbook*, 6th edn (London: Henry Frowde, 1907), pp. 148–55, and *The Ornaments of the Minister*, new edn (London: Mowbray, 1920), pp. 105–08; Mayo, p. 89.

hood. What 'Different Forms' calls a tippet is most probably the scarf, a completely different thing, which has been part of the DD's academic dress down to modern times.

Perhaps it is worth noting that Nathan Bailey defines *tippet* in his *Universal Etymological English Dictionary* in the 1730s as: 'a kind of Kerchief for Womens Necks (commonly of Furs) also a long Scarf which Doctors of Divinity wear over their Gowns.'[79]

Winged plaits/pleats or flaps

In 'Different Forms' a post-holder MA who is not a clergyman may wear a BCL-type gown,
that is a lay gown with a flap collar, embellished with

> winged playtes or flappes behinde the Arme pitt.

The term *wings* (or *shoulder wings*) for 'stiffened and generally decorative bands,
often crescent-shaped, projecting over the shoulder seam' has been used by historians of
dress construction for these features in fashionable dress from the mid-sixteenth to the
mid-seventeenth century.[80] At this period it seems wings were routinely included on academic gowns with sleeves hanging behind the arm (see Figs 6, 7 , 9 and 14) but not necessarily on other lay gowns (see Figs 4 and 5), so that adding them to a BCL-style gown
may have been a distinguishing mark. By the 1670s, as seen in Edwards and Loggan, lay
gowns were invariably provided with wings. The term *wings* is still used in describing such
features on academic gowns: at Oxford all graduate lay gowns, as well as the commoners',
graduate students' and bedels' gowns, have modest wings.[81]

The spelling *playtes* could be for *plates* or for *plaits* in a now obsolete sense of 'pleats';
the latter seems the more likely in the context.[82] Winged plaits/pleats or flaps will be shoulder wings that are made of narrow strips of fabric sewn together giving the appearance of
pleats, as are also present on doublets of the period.[83]

A parallel can be seen in dress at the Bar. In 1557 the Inns of Court legislated 'that
none of the Company except knightes or Benchers [...] weare [...] wynges on ther gownes'
sleeves'.[84] Wings were evidently deemed a sign of superior status and an embellishment not
to be adopted by the ordinary barrister.

Commentary

This commentary does not discuss the frock, the civil hood, the tippet and winged plaits/
pleats or flaps, which have already been considered in the previous section.

Before 1635

The academic gown that evolved from the medieval *supertunica* in England had wide sleeves.
In the last quarter of the sixteenth century gowns with hanging sleeves began to be mentioned
in university regulations and to appear in portraits and on monuments. These must have been
borrowed from civilian and professional dress outside the universities. They were typically

---

79 5th edn (London: Knapton etc., 1731), unnumbered pages.
80 Cumming, Cunnington and Cunnington, p. 294.
81 See Groves, pp. 21, 320; Venables, pp. 20–29, 35–37, 41, 43, 47.
82 *OED*, s.vv. 'Plait', 'Pleat'.
83 Illustrated in, for example, Valerie Cumming, *A Visual History of Costume: The Seventeenth Century* (London: Batsford, 1984), pp. 18, 21, 23, 24.
84 *The Records of the Honorable Society of Lincoln's Inn: The Black Books*, 6 vols (London:
Lincoln's Inn, 1897–1968), Vol. I, p. 320. Also cited by Baker, 'Gowns at the Bar', p. 16.

worn by non-foundationer undergraduates and by graduates in the lay faculties of Medicine and Civil Law and a little later in the faculties of Theology and Arts, except by BAs.[85]

There seems to have been little control over undergraduate dress except where colleges prescribed a livery or laid down their own rules, as they generally did for those on the foundation.[86] A variety of styles for students' gowns is found on the few existing monuments for them in the period leading up to 1635. Some are much as would be prescribed in 'Different Forms', for example, commoner John Pendarves and gentleman-commoner John Walrond (Figs 6 and 7). This is also true of John Bisshop, junior student (scholar and undergraduate fellow) of Christ Church, who died in 1588: he is shown on his brass in the Cathedral in a wide-sleeved gown, still with an upstanding collar.[87] Some, however, would not fit the 1635 specification. Edward Chernock seems to have matriculated at Trinity College as a gentleman-commoner but migrated to Brasenose, where he died at the age of sixteen in 1581. On his brass in St Mary the Virgin Church he is depicted in a gown with hanging sleeves, inverted-T armholes, fur-covered facings and a flap collar—in 1635 he would have needed armholes at the shoulder and sleeves hanging behind the arms.[88] Walter Dotyn, who was a scholar and undergraduate fellow of Exeter College and died in 1603/4, is shown on his alabaster incised-slab monument in St Michael's Church in a gown with hanging sleeves, a horizontal slit at the elbow for the armhole and a tube below, open at the foot (Fig. 15). No doubt this is the kind of gown Laud referred to in 1630 when he complained of freshmen wearing MA-style gowns 'soe as ther is noe distinction by the habit betweene Mrs of Art and undergraduates'.[89]

Fig. 14. Richard Radcliff, DM, d. 1599, brass in St Peter in the East Church (now the library of St Edmund Hall).

At least one BA is portrayed in a gown with hanging sleeves. Nicholas Roope, graduate of Broadgates Hall, died in 1613 and is commemorated by a brass in St Aldate's Church, which shows him wearing one with a horizontal slit for the armhole. He is also wearing a simple-shape hood and so we may be sure the gown is academic.[90] Some MAs after 1580 are shown on their monumental brasses either in coat-style sleeves (so-called trunk sleeves) or their gown is sleeveless—it is sometimes difficult to tell which. Some have gowns with hanging sleeves,

85 Alex Kerr, 'Gowns Worn by MAs in Early-Seventeenth-Century England and the Curious Case of Thomas Thornton's Sleeves', *TBS*, 12 (2012), pp. 72–85 (pp. 75–82) https://doi.org/10.4148/2475-7799.1101.

86 See Hargreaves-Mawdsley, pp. 92–93, 98–99, although his interpretation of details may be questioned.

87 See Church Monuments Society, Oxfordshire <www.churchmonumentsgazetteer.co.uk/Oxfordshire.html>, scroll down to 'City of Oxford—Christ Church Cathedral'.

88 See Edward T. Beaumont, *Academical Habit Illustrated by Ancient Memorial Brasses* (Oxford: privately printed, 1928), figure facing p. 87; Alex Kerr, 'The Turbulent History of Undergraduate Academical Dress', *Burgon Notes*, No. 17 (Summer 2011), pp. 2–3 (p. 2, top right).

89 Quoted in Buxton and Gibson, p. 30.

90 Beaumont, figure facing p. 30; the caption incorrectly gives the date 1603.

horizontal-slit or inverted-⊺ armholes, with or without fur-covered facings, and with either a yoke or a flap collar, in any of the eight combinations of these that are possible. The distinction in the University Archives manuscript of 'Different Forms' between a horizontal sleeve opening for divines and an inverted ⊺ for non-divines does not seem to apply: clergymen are depicted in both styles.[91]

DDs may be shown with hanging sleeves or, like Philip Bisse in his 1612 portrait in Wadham College, with coat-style sleeves. Where the lower part of his gown appears below his convocation habit it can be seen that it has velvet facings.[92] Coat-style sleeves do not figure in our document, but velvet facings as an option for DDs do. At the turn of the seventeenth century lay doctors have a variety of gowns with hanging sleeves, usually with inverted-T armholes. Brasses in New College commemorate Walter Bailey, DM, d. 1592/3, in a gown elaborately trimmed with lace,[93] and Hugh Lloyd, DCL, d. 1601, in a gown that has a small flap collar, a narrow edging round the armholes and the lower part of the sleeve, which is a hollow bag, open at the foot. A brass for Richard Radcliff, DM, d. 1599, in St Peter in the East Church has him in a plain gown with a flap collar, wings and sleeves hanging behind the arms, a style not specified in 'Different Forms' for any graduates (see Fig. 14).

Some gowns with hanging sleeves in the pre-Laudian period have an unexplained feature not mentioned in 'Different Forms'. This is an additional opening halfway down the lower part of the sleeve. It can be seen on several legal and academic gowns in the early seventeenth century.[94] A good example is on the gown of Henry Airay, DD, d. 1616, on his brass at Queen's College.[95] Jerome Keyt's BCL gown on his monument of 1631 (Fig. 4) may have an opening of this kind, but we cannot be sure whether the oval of lace actually surrounds a 'hand-slit' or is, by this time, just ornament.

'Different Forms' and what came later

One aim of the Laudian Code and therefore of 'Different Forms' was to curb any *laissez-faire* practice in academic dress and provide tighter regulation than existed before. After all, Laud had censured the University in the past for a slackness in these matters.[96] With that in mind, several features of the gowns described in our document may surprise the student of academic dress acquainted with Fell's *Orders* and the engravings of Edwards and Loggan, which we take to present a clearly defined scheme of dress with almost no room for deviation. Of course, Fell in 1666, like an earlier vice-chancellor, Paul Hood, in 1660, was concerned to reimpose Laud's requirements after the survival of academic dress had

---

91 Kerr, 'Gowns Worn by MAs', pp. 77–82.

92 Kerr, 'Gowns Worn by MAs', p. 76 n. 22; <weblearn.ox.ac.uk/access/content/group /1803d649-431f-46cd-9428-f1dc63ef43a3/Rare%20Books/bissepoole.html>.

93 Kerr, 'Gowns Worn by MAs', p. 80 n. 32. Also see <www.bridgemanimages.co.uk/en/asset /434809>.

94 J. H. Baker writes in connection with a Bar gown on a 1600 monument of an 'arm-slit' and a 'hand-slit': one at the elbow, the other lower down to allow just the hand to emerge ('Gowns at the Bar', p. 18). He illustrates another Bar gown with the same feature on a monument for Thomas Palmer, d. 1621, in Epping, Essex (ibid., p. 16).

95 See <www.rct.uk/collection/650115/henry-airay-provost-of-queens-college-oxford-1559 -1616>.

96 Buxton and Gibson, p. 30.

been under threat during the Commonwealth.[97] It is striking that 'Different Forms' in 1635 allows the nobleman to choose between a gown with hanging sleeves that have a slit at the elbow and one with hanging sleeves that have armholes at the shoulder (a 'frock').[98] Later regulations at Oxford do not permit wearers to decide which style of gown they prefer.

Fig. 15. Walter Dotyn, d. 1603/4, undergraduate fellow of Exeter College, monument in St Michael's Church.

'Different Forms' allows considerable latitude in the trimmings that may be added to the gowns. The phrase 'if they please' or 'if he please' occurs seven times in this short document of under 850 words.[99] In 1635 material for facings or ornament is often an optional extra or one of two or more from which the wearer may choose (see Appendix A). Our document permits gowns to be made of a very dark brown or blue or of a purple fabric instead of black and the Code specifies they should be of black or a dark colour (*coloris nigri aut subfusci*), alternatives not offered in subsequent regulations.[100]

Choristers are included in Laud's list of foundationers. The pudding-sleeved style of gown specified is unique to this rank and seems not to be found anywhere but in our document. Choristers do not figure in Fell's *Orders* or on Edwards' or Loggan's plates. In the revised statute of 1770 choristers are required, with undergraduate fellows, probationers, scholars, chaplains and clerks, to wear gowns with wide sleeves (not pudding sleeves).[101] Thus, we might expect the same for all of these and indeed only the scholar is included in Grignion's engravings. Like his counterparts in Edwards and Loggan, his sleeves are no more than half the length of the gown. Although this had long been the norm, it is made explicit in the statute in 1770 to distinguish the undergraduate foundationer from the BA, who, no doubt following what had become cus-

---

97 See William Gibson, '"The Remembrance Whereof is Pleasant": A Note on Walter Pope's Role in the Attempt to Abolish Academic Dress during the Commonwealth', *TBS*, 10 (2010), pp. 43–46, https://doi.org/10.4148/2475-7799.1083. Hood issued a decree in October 1660 in which he alleged that the use of academic dress had fallen into 'almost a totall neglect' and his intention was to reinstate it 'with all severity' <quod.lib.umich.edu/e/eebo2/B09630.0001.001/1:1?rgn=div1;view=fulltext>.

Fell's Orders may be consulted at <archive.org/details/in.ernet.dli.2015.157936/page/n49/mode /2up>; Edwards' engravings at <www.britishmuseum.org/collection/search?keyword=george& keyword=edwards&keyword=reverendis> ; and Loggan's plate of Oxford dress at <archive.org/details /gri_33125008536811/page/n51/mode/2up>.

98 A later parallel is found at Cambridge, where DDs may choose between an MA-style gown and a pudding-sleeved gown for their undress.

99 In fact, Fell in 1666 also allows an element of choice: gentlemen-commoners, knights and baronets may opt whether to add ornament to their gowns and noblemen may choose whether to have coloured gowns.

100 Griffiths, p. 143; Ward, Vol. I, p. 151. In the statute this applies, with sons of peers in the House of Lords exempted, to dress in general, not only gowns.

101 *Parecbolae*, p. 167; Ward, Vol. II, p. 10.

tomary by 1770, has longer sleeves reaching the hem of the gown.[102] James Roberts, however, in his 1792 set of watercolours based on Grignion adds a chorister. He gives him the BA-style gown with wide sleeves down to the ankles and tucked up at the elbow, whereas his scholar has the shorter wide sleeves.[103]

Our document's servitors have yokes ('standing capes'), perhaps surprisingly for non-foundationers; Fell gives them 'round capes' and the battelars 'square'. Hargreaves-Mawdsley (p. 100) takes this to mean a yoke for the servitor and a flap collar for the battelar and he may be right. A decade later Loggan has both with flap collars, the servitor with round corners to the flap, the battelar square corners (see Fig. 16). Perhaps that is what Fell intended or perhaps the move from yoke to flap collar had progressed only so far by 1666.

Although scholars' gowns seem to have remained essentially unchanged, Fell requires them to have the sleeves 'turn'd up to the Wrist', unlike the BAs, whose sleeves are 'to hang at length'. Non-foundationer undergraduate gowns shifted to give each rank a style that had previously belonged to the rank above. In 1635 servitors appear to lack any sleeves; in 1666 they (with battelars, not mentioned in 1635) have plain sleeves hanging behind the arm. In 1635 commoners have plain sleeves hanging behind the arm; in 1666 they have ornamented sleeves hanging behind the arm. In 1635 gentlemen-commoners have ornamented sleeves hanging behind the arm; in 1666 they have ornamented hanging sleeves with an opening at the elbow, one of the options previously open only to noblemen. With Fell, baronets and knights and their sons may now have gold or silver buttons, a distinction absent in 1635. Fell's specifications are corroborated by Edwards' and Loggan's engravings.[104]

The BA gown appears to have remained much the same although Fell specifies that the sleeves must not reach 'beyond the Fingers ends, nor above an ell in Compasse'. Sleeves the size of those on a surplice had been brought by Cambridge men migrating to Oxford in 1649 and Fell evidently intended to curb this excess.[105] Edwards gives his BA wide sleeves reaching the hip, the shape of those on an Oxford doctor's full-dress robe; Loggan's BA has more pendulous ones, which almost reach the knees.

'Different Forms' requires that MAs are to have sleeves on their hanging-sleeved gown reaching 'onlye to the lower part of the knees'. This is stated twice, in relation to divines and to non-divines.[106] It suggests that the authorities disapproved of sleeves that were extravagantly long. The pictorial evidence from around 1635 shows hanging sleeves ending just below the knees, but later in the century they lengthen to be more or less down to the hem of the gown. Hollow sleeves that ended in an opening or a cuff give way in Edwards and Loggan to a sewn-up 'boot' that would increasingly take on a crescent shape. Panel sleeves on lay gowns are also sewn shut but remain square-ended. In Edwards and Loggan, as in later texts and pictorial sources, no distinction is made between the sleeves of

---

102 See Grignion's engravings of 1770 (Hargreaves-Mawdsley, Plate 11C).

103 Bodl., MS Top. Oxon. d. 58, fols 82, 73.

104 Fell distinguishes three styles of gown as 'Wide sleeu'd', 'half sleeued' and with 'Sleeues hanging behind the Shoulder'. Perhaps the shifts illustrate a general principle found also elsewhere in the history of academic dress: each rank apes the rank above, and eventually the regulations bow to the inevitable and retrospectively legalize it.

105 Wood, Vol. I, pp. 149, 300.

106 The Magdalen College copy has sleeves to the knees for a divine and to the skirts for a non-divine.

MAs who are divines and those who are not. The same is true in the Laudian Code itself, although it naturally requires clergymen to wear clerical dress.[107]

It looks as though the requirement for the BM and DM to have their sleeves open up to the shoulder was dropped. Although Loggan illustrates gowns for both the medical and legal graduates, there is no discernible difference between them in this regard.

The prescription in 'Different Forms' of a BCL-style gown for MAs holding certain posts if not clergymen is not explicitly stated elsewhere, but it seems this is viewed as a kind of gown of office. This stipulation is not found in later records.[108] However, the Laudian Code has the bedels, not mentioned in our document, in a 'suitable gown of the usual fashion'.[109] Edwards and Loggan have them in BCL-style gowns: the esquire bedels, who since the late fifteenth century had been graduates, have more elaborate ornament (large tassels) than the usually non-graduate yeoman bedels and verger (small tufts).[110] The distinction between the two classes of bedels was abolished in 1856 but the lay gown for bedels and verger, now without ornament, is still in use today.[111]

Fig. 16. Servitor (left) and battelar (right), from Loggan, Plate X, nos 1 and 2. Both have gowns with sleeves hanging behind the arms. The servitor's flap collar appears to have rounded corners and the battelar's square corners. Edwards shows only the servitor, but gives him square corners to his flap collar.

Our document makes no mention of the Student of Civil Law or degrees in music. Perhaps the SCL had no distinctive dress at this date. In Fell, Edwards and Loggan he has a plain hanging-sleeved gown with inverted-T armholes and a flap collar. The BMus was

107 Title XIV §1 (Griffiths, p. 143; Ward, Vol. I, p. 151).

108 John Rouse, MA, Bodley's Librarian 1620–52, was painted in a hanging-sleeved gown with inverted-T armholes, the vertical slit reaching the shoulder, prominent wings and what look like velvet facings, but no ornament (Bodl., LP 116 <digital.bodleian.ox.ac.uk/search/?q =john+rouse>). Wood (Vol. I, p. 414) records a public orator appearing at a ceremony in 1661 in 'a proctor's habit'. Buxton and Gibson (p. 40) comment: 'it is said that it is traditional for the Keeper of the Ashmolean Museum, if not a doctor, to wear a silk [MA] gown on formal occasions.' At Cambridge in 1585 Burghley allowed facings in various silk fabrics for a doctor, a head of a college, hall or hostel, a current or former University orator or proctor, a taxor, and a Regius or Lady Margaret reader (Cooper, Vol. II, p. 411).

109 Title XVIII sect. 2 §2: 'habitu decenti et consueto togatos' (Griffiths, p. 182; Ward, Vol. I, p. 199).

110 On the status of the bedels see Carl I. Hammer, Jr, 'Oxford Town and Oxford University', in History of the University of Oxford, Vol. III, The Collegiate University, edited by James McConica (Oxford: Clarendon Press, 1986), pp. 69–116 (pp. 75–76).

111 Cox, pp. 419–24; Venables, pp. 46–47. In 1814 Uwins shows the esquire bedel with gimp and the yeoman bedel without (Combe, Plate XVII; Jackson, pp. 32, xii–xiii (unpublished Uwins drawings)).

established by 1502 and the DMus by 1511. These degrees have had an almost 'external' or diploma status through much of their existence and did not qualify their holders for membership of Convocation.[112] Loggan illustrates the BMus in a lay gown with small buttons and tufts for ornament like gentlemen-commoners (see below). The DMus is shown in full dress only; he was not expected to be a resident member of the University.

Fig. 17. DM, from Loggan, Plate X, no. 20, with velvet facings and lace with large tassels as ornament.

Facings in materials different from the body of the gown, a feature of many of the 1635 gowns, had apparently been phased out in most cases by the 1670s. Loggan's DM and DCL still do have velvet facings (see Fig. 17), but his DD does not, and that includes the vice-chancellor in procession in a DD undress gown. Of course, this could mean that velvet was still optional or that lay doctors kept it but DDs gave it up. The proctor has velvet facings and his sleeves are now part-covered in velvet, perhaps an extension of a lining turned back and fixed in place as we know happened with the DD's full-dress robe. The collector has the same, whereas in 1635 he had satin or taffeta facings. Only the proctor and the collector (with the later addition of the pro-proctor) kept the velvet on their black gowns right through the eighteenth century.[113]

As for ornament, in 'Different Forms' gentlemen-commoners are to have buttons and loops, the size unspecified, BMs and BCLs what seem to be small buttons, DMs and DCLs large buttons, with post-holder MAs having the same as BCLs. Fell uses the word 'button' to include the accompanying strip of lace and tufts as well as the button itself. He requires commoners (who did not have any ornament in 1635) to have six on each (hanging) sleeve. He gives gentlemen-commoners the option of forty-eight on their hanging-sleeved gown, which now opens at the elbow instead of the shoulder. Noblemen (who in 1635 could choose what ornament they liked) now may have the same number as gentlemen-commoners in gold or silver. These details are followed to the letter in Edwards' and Loggan's plates. However, Edwards' gentleman-commoner has a sizeable tuft with each button; Loggan's has smaller tufts (Fig. 18). Loggan's plate shows a more complex hierarchy for lay bachelors and doctors than set out in 1635. It has the BMus (not acknowledged at all in 'Different Forms') with small tufts, the BCL with similar ornament on the lower sleeve but larger tassels on the upper sleeve, and the BM with the larger tassels on both the upper and lower sleeve. The DM and DCL have the larger tassels, with five or six rows on the lower sleeve (see Fig. 17) while the bachelors have four. If we compare Ed-

112 C. F. Abdy Williams, *A Short Historical Account of the Degrees in Music at Oxford and Cambridge* (London and New York: Novello, Ewer & Co., 1894), pp. 11–19, 40–44, 65–66; Hargreaves-Mawdsley, pp. 77–78, 87–88.

113 See Grignion's engravings of 1770 (Hargreaves-Mawdsley, Plate 11A); Uwins' drawings engraved by Agar in Combe, Plates XIV, XVI (and XV for the pro-proctor with velvet facings on an MA gown); Jackson, pp. 16–32; Eggleston, pp. 85–88, 98.

wards' DM/DCL plate with Loggan's BMus and BCL (nos 7 and 11), it seems that lay doctors have a panel of tassels on the back of the gown but bachelors do not. In the mid-eighteenth century the lace and tuft/tassel ornament was replaced by gimp for graduates in lay faculties and for noblemen and baronets in full dress and by box-pleating for commoners. Gentlemen-commoners kept lace and tufts for a dress gown until the mid-nineteenth century while using box-pleating on an undress version.[114]

In 1666 Fell referred to 'Modells or Patterns [...] allready provided'. Even if Laud's press or chest still existed then, new contents would have been required to accompany the issue of the *Orders* for junior members' dress in what Wood called 'the reformation of gowns and caps (drawne up by the new vice-chancellor)'. A payment of £10 14s. 'to the Tayler for publique Patternes for Gownes' appears in the vice-chancellor's accounts for 1666/7. In 1690 it was reported that the patterns were still kept 'in a Press by the Vestry of the Convocation House, for Recourse to be had unto them upon all Occasions'.[115] In 1770 the new Title XIV referred to patterns engraved on copper (that is Grignion's plates) to be lodged in the chest of the Convocation House; the old sample garments may then have been thought redundant.[116]

Laud's press or chest may be lost but we have brought to light a significant preliminary draft inventory of some of its intended contents. In writing about the changes in academic dress between the Reformation and the publishing of Edwards' plates, Charles Franklyn rightly commented that 'We still do not know all the steps between 1540 and 1674 [...]'.[117] Although this is still true, I hope that this study of 'Different Forms of Gowns for All Sorts of Scholars in their Several Ranks' from 1635 has added to our knowledge of one of those steps.

Fig. 18. Gentleman-commoner, from Loggan, Plate X, no. 5, with lace and small tuft ornament.

114   Tsua, pp. 104–06, 115–16. See also Grignion's engravings of 1770 (Hargreaves-Mawdsley, Plates 11B, 11C, 11D); Uwins' drawings engraved by Agar in Combe, Plates V, IX, X, XI, XV; Jackson, pp. 16–32.

115   Buxton and Gibson, pp. 30–32 and especially p. 31 n. 3; Wood, Vol. II (1891), p. 84, and Vol. IV (1895), p. 69; Oxford, University Archives, Reg. Conv. B b 29, at end. In the 1660s £10 14s. was worth about £1,170 in 2021's money <www.nationalarchives.gov.uk/currency-converter/#>. The vestry or Apodyterium (robing room) of the Convocation House also served as the Chancellor's Court, the name by which it is now known.

116   *Parecbolae*, p. 166; Ward, Vol. II, p. 9. Douglas Veale, writing in 1957, admitted: 'diligent, though intermittent, search during my twenty-eight years as Registrar has failed to locate the chest, though I naturally hesitate to impute negligence to the august persons whose duty it was, under the Laudian Code, to provide it' (Venables, p. 2). It seems clear that one was provided either by Laud's Hebdomadal Board or later by Fell. On the 1957 'Register of Colours and Materials of Gowns and Hoods for Degrees of the University of Oxford' see A. J. P. North, pp. 111–14.

117   *Academical Dress from the Middle Ages to the Present Day, Including Lambeth Degrees* (Lewes: Baxter, 1970), p. 110.

Rank	Sleeves		Collar		Facings				Ornament			Civil hood	Tippet
	wide	hanging	yoke	flap	fur or budge	non-silk material	satin or taffeta	velvet or plush	short laced buttons	long laced buttons	winged plaits/pleats or flaps		
chorister	req (1)		req										
servitor		req (2)	req		alt	alt							
scholar	req		req			req							
commoner		req (3)		req	alt	alt							
gentleman-commoner		req (3)		req	alt	alt			req				
nobleman undergraduate		alt (3)/alt (4)		req	opt	opt	opt	opt	opt	opt			
BA	req		req		req	req						req (7)	
BA: nobleman or compounder	req		req					opt				req (7)	
BA: collector	req		req				req					req (8)	
MA: non-divine	alt	alt (5)	req				opt					req (8)	
MA: divine	alt	alt (4)	req				opt					req (8)	
MA: post-holder	req	req (5)		req				opt	opt		req		
MA: proctor	req		req					opt					
MA: nobleman or compounder	alt	alt (5)	req					opt				req (8)	
BD		req (4)	req		opt		opt	opt					
DD		req (4)	req				opt	opt					req
BM		req (6)		req		alt	alt	opt	req				
DM		req (6)		req				opt		opt			
BCL		req (5)		req		alt	alt	opt	req				
DCL		req (5)		req		alt	alt	opt		opt			

46

Appendix A

Summary table of the provisions in 'Different Forms' in Oxford, University Archives, WPγ/26/1/369

To fit on a single page, the chart appears opposite, with its key below.

Key:

alt = one of alternatives between which to choose

opt = an option ('if he please')

req = a requirement

(1) pudding sleeve
(2) possibly with sleeve hanging behind the arm but more likely sleeveless
(3) with sleeve hanging behind the arm
(4) with horizontal slit
(5) with inverted T
(6) with inverted T up to shoulder
(7) unless wearing 'other' hood
(8) with the wide-sleeved gown unless wearing the taffeta- or miniver-lined hood

Appendix B

Transcription of Oxford, Magdalen College, MS 367 (81).

[ ] = letters supplied by editor to resolve abbreviations.

Different formes of gownes for all sortes of
schollers in there severall rankes.

Stat: tit: 14 §: 2

Choristers

1 Gownes widesleeved but close at the handwrist & standing capes for Choristers.

Servitors

2 ffrockes with standing capes for poore schollers & servitors with faceing of furre or some stuffe [tha]t is not of silke.

Schollers & Probationers:

3 Schollers of Colledges and not Graduates wide-sleeved gownes w[i]th standing capes w[i]thout silke or silke stuffe faceing but of some other stuffe of lesse cost

Undergrad[uates]

4 ffrockes w[i]th falling capes & long hanging sleeves w[i]th faceing of furre or some stuffe [tha]t is not of silke, velvet, or [th]e like & without buttons upon the sleeves, lace or other [th]e like ornament for undergraduates [tha]t are not poore schollers or Servitors vnd[er] the estate & quality of knights or esquires sonnes, in the Matriculation booke.

The sonns of Knights & Esquires

5 The like gownes for fashion & faceing but w[i]th lace or buttons on the sleeves or other fitt places for knights & esquires sonnes [tha]t are undergraduates.

The Nobility

6 The like gownes or w[i]th sleeves cutt above [th]e elbowes w[i]th faceing and ornament to their owne or their freinds likeing & choice, for Lords, Lords sonns, Bishops sonnes, Knight Baronetts, or their sonnes [th]at are not Schollers & fellowes of Colledges.

Bacc: Art:

7 Batchellors of Arts wide sleeved gownes w[i]th standing capes & Civill Hoods sowed fast to their gownes & to bee worne hanging backwards from [th]e left shoulder only without Taffata or silke stuffe faceing but of some other stuffe.
And the like gownes for Batchellors of Artes who are compounders or of birth and quality as in the sixth Article but faced w[i]th velvet, plush or [th]e like if they please, likewise Collectors of [th]e Lent but faced w[i]th Sattin or Taffata or [th]e like

Mri Artis non Theologi

8 Of a standing cape, sleeves cut halfe over above the elbowes and reaching down to the skirts for a M[aste]r of Arts [tha]t is no divine no Batchellor of Physick or Law w[i]thout buttons lace faceing of velvet, plush, or [th]e like costly weare but (if hee please) w[i]th Sattin or Taffata or the like.

Theologius

9 ffor a divine [th]e like gowne but the sleeves to reach only to the knees.

Bacc: Theol:

10 ffor a Batchellor of divinity [th]e like but w[i]th faceing (if hee please) of Velvet Sattin Taffata Budge and his hood faced & edged w[i]th Taffata.

Doct: Theol:

11 A doctor of divinity a gowne of [th]e same fashion but faced (if hee please) w[i]th velvet or plush & his tippet of Taffata or Sarcenett.

Bacc: Med:

12 Of a falling cape w[i]th sleeves open from [th]e shoulders on the outside of his arme with buttons & loopes w[i]thout lace or tuffes or faceing of velvet & plush but of some Stuffe Taffata or Sattin for a Batchellor of Physick.

Doct: Medic:

13 The like but (if they please) w[i]th faceing of velvet plush or [th]e like and w[i]th ornaments of lace and laced buttons for a D[octo]r of Physick.

Bacc: LL

14 The like to [tha]t of [th]e Batchellors of Physick save only w[i]th this difference [tha]t it bee cutt halfe above the Elbowes for a Batchellor of Law.

Doct: LL

15 The like for fashion but (if they please) w[i]th faceing of velvet, plush, or [th]e like and w[i]th ornament of lace or laced buttons for D[octo]rs of Law.

Publick lecturer orator &c.

16 A M[aste]r of Arts [tha]t is a publike Lecturer Custos Archivorum the University publick Orator [th]e cheife Library Keeper and no divine a gowne like to that of a Batchellor of Law but w[i]th ornament of laced buttons & faceing of velvet (if hee please) & w[i]th winged plaites or flapps behind [th]e arme-pit.

> And [tha]t all (except [th]e sonns of Barons [tha]t have place & right of suffrage in [th]e higher house of Parliament & are not schollers or fellowes of Colledges) have their gownes for [th]e color of them black or of some other darke color puke purple or the like

Appendix C

Glossary of terms used in 'Different Forms' to denote the materials employed for facings and ornaments

Based on entries in Cumming, Cunnington and Cunnington and suggestions from Dr Susan North

budge   lambskin with the wool dressed outwards.

buttons   ball, flat disc or toggle shape, either functional with buttonholes or loops, or simply decorative.

fur   animal skin with the hair or wool dressed outwards; here probably a synonym for budge.

lace   narrow woven decoration; what is now called braid.

loops   functional or decorative buttonholes or openings at the end of braid strips.

miniver   a high-status white fur, at this time made from the belly of the European grey squirrel (referred to here only in connection with an MA hood).

plush   a long-pile weave of cotton or wool or silk; here silk is probably intended.

sarcenet   a thin, soft plain-weave silk textile having a slight sheen on the surface, mainly used for linings.

satin   a very smooth glossy weave with either the warp or weft threads predominantly on the surface of the fabric. It uses more thread than a plain weave and is therefore more expensive. Here probably silk satin, although it is possible to have a satin weave in worsted, linen, cotton, etc.

silk   the product of the cocoon of the silk moth, woven into an expensive fabric.

silk stuff a mixture of silk and other fibres such as wool.

taffeta   a plain-weave silk, heavier than sarcenet.

velvet   a weaving technique creating a dense pile, either plain or with decorative effects; in this context used with silk. Until the late seventeenth century, silk velvets were woven only in Italy and had to be imported into England, making them one of the most expensive silk fabrics.

Transactions of the Burgon Society, 20 (2020), pages 52–66

Cap and Gown? Use of Headgear at Graduation in UK Universities in the Twenty-First Century

By Martin J. Hardcastle

Academic headwear, particularly in the form of the square cap or mortar-board, is perhaps the most widely recognised symbol of educational achievement in the world. The square cap in particular is symbolic of universities in iconography world-wide, and has spread from its origins as clerical and then academic dress in the United Kingdom to become a component of graduation ceremonies in many countries that otherwise nowadays have little cultural connection to the UK. It is therefore perhaps surprising that a number of universities in the UK restrict the use of headwear during graduation and that some have adopted schemes of academic dress that do not include it or have abolished it altogether. In this article I aim to survey the current practice at graduation ceremonies in UK universities, to understand whether there are common factors in the use or disuse of headwear, and thus tentatively to explain the wide variation in practice that is seen in the twenty-first century.

Introduction

The square cap, trencher or mortar-board is possibly the most widely recognised symbol of academic achievement in the world. Hargrave[1] traces the historical origin of the cap from the middle ages to the final form that it arrived at in the eighteenth century, and both he and Keenan[2] discuss the fact that in some of the older universities the use of headwear in general and the cap in particular[3] seems to be in decline, in spite of its world-wide recognition. At the same time, new universities in the UK continue to adopt it with enthusiasm, with the effect that stock photos of graduation celebrations, when they are British at all,[4] often represent newer institutions. In practice, the differences are not as simple as hats being used at some institutions and disused at others. I have attended or participated in graduation ceremonies at six UK universities, all of which have treated headwear somewhat differently from any of the rest. Rather than looking at the practices of one institution or a few institutions in detail, it seems worthwhile to establish an overview of the situation throughout the UK.

---

1   S. A. Hargrave, 'The Church and the Trencher: An Examination into How England's Changing Theology and Church Have Influenced the Evolution and Design of the Square Cap Causing its Use as Academic Attire', *TBS*, 14 (2014), pp. 16–34, at <newprairiepress.org/burgonsociety> https://doi.org/10.4148/2475-7799.1116.

2   O. J. Keenan, 'How Can Academical Dress Survive in the Third Millennium?', *TBS*, 10 (2010), pp. 99–125, https://doi.org/10.4148/2475-7799.1086.

3   Throughout this paper I refer to academic headgear in general as 'hats'—this should be taken to include the square cap in its various forms, the round doctor's bonnet and the other less common forms such as the John Knox cap. Where 'cap' is used it refers explicitly to the square cap.

4   Often the UK media use stock photos of North American academic dress, in which the cap tassel hangs from a cord.

In this article I exclusively consider the use of academic dress at graduation ceremonies. All universities in the UK have some form of ceremony in which either degrees are conferred or degree certificates are presented and all either require or strongly encourage the wearing of academic dress—i.e., always the gown, almost always the hood, and sometimes the hat—for students who wish to participate in them. For simplicity I shall use the term 'graduation ceremony' for all of these, and the term 'graduand' for the recipients of degrees, irrespective of whether the participants are actually formally graduating. Outside the ancient universities of England and Scotland, the graduation ceremony will be the only encounter with academic dress for most students (and their families) and quite often the only occasion across the whole university when academic dress is worn. The regulations (or traditions with the same force) that apply in graduation ceremonies become, de facto, the understanding of what academic dress actually is,[5] and may in the end come to affect the rules of academic dress de jure, a point I shall return to later. In the following sections I present my approach to gathering data, a summary of the results and observed relationships between them, a discussion of the obvious groupings among institutions, and some initial conclusions.

Approach

The study of graduation ceremonies has the advantage that they are extremely well documented. In the past few years most universities have moved to live-streaming their graduation ceremonies and of those many make video of the full ceremony available on the Internet via YouTube, Facebook or their own video-sharing sites. Only a few of the older universities have resisted this trend. In addition, information aimed at graduands can usually be found on the public Internet, although the details of academic dress are very often 'outsourced' to the university's official robemaker.

My approach in this article is to look for a combination of written, photographic and video evidence for a particular university's practice regarding graduands. I first checked the university's own description of the dress code for graduation, where available; this often explicitly mentions headgear as a component of the required academic dress, or implies its existence by mentioning head measurements, or in some cases implies its absence by saying that academic dress consists of gown and hood. In a very few cases the use of headgear is explicitly forbidden. In a large number of cases, however, the documentation is not sufficient to establish what the actual practice is, particularly when it consists of little more than a link to the robemakers' website. University graduation websites are almost always illustrated by images of graduands and graduates and if they are shown without hats it is very likely that hats are not used—this is the case for most of the Scottish universities, for example. But neither the written or photographic evidence is always definitive.

I therefore made use, where possible, of the most recent publicly available video evidence of what happens in the ceremony itself. These were usually from 2019, the previous full year at the time of writing, but sometimes only earlier videos were available: very few were from ceremonies earlier than 2015, and when this is the case it is noted in Table 1. The video almost always provides details of practice that are not mentioned in the guidance provided to graduands. Where available, the most recent video of a full ceremony provided by the university itself was used; if none is available, I use either 'highlights' videos or, as a

---

5   At staff robing for Hertfordshire graduation ceremonies I have encountered graduates of Cambridge and Bristol who were surprised to learn that hats were a permitted part of their academic dress.

last resort, unofficial video posted by graduates. I tried to avoid videos of graduation ceremonies in countries other than the UK as the practice there may not exactly follow that of the home institution. For the purpose of this study, the key moment is the presentation of individual graduands to the presiding officer—all graduation ceremonies have this aspect in some form. If graduands are wearing hats at this point, it is safe to assume that they will be wearing them throughout the ceremony. Where the video showed that hats are not worn at the time of presentation, I checked the video in more detail, if possible, to try to establish whether hats are worn at any other stage and, if so, when. Hats are almost universal for senior officials at least at some point in the ceremony, and also widely used by participating academic staff, even in those universities where they are not used by graduands, and I do not generally consider this aspect of the ceremony further.

The universities considered here are all the full degree-granting universities listed in the latest edition of Shaw's Academical Dress—hereafter Groves[6]—or their successors after merger or renaming, currently in existence and located in the United Kingdom. The universities in the Irish Republic listed by Groves are excluded, as are Royal Colleges with degree-granting powers. The use of Groves' list as a starting point allows a comparison between actual practice and the regulations as listed by Groves. In Table 1 I list the 121 institutions meeting these criteria together with the date when they started to award degrees in their own right as given by Groves, the nation of the United Kingdom where they are located, and a numerical categorization of the practices related to headwear at graduation. Notes in the table draw attention to variations in the form of the ceremony or the data available.

Results

Summary statistics

Each of the 121 universities considered in this study can be placed in one of four broad groups, as follows: these are used to categorize institutions in Table 1.

1. Hats do not form part of the academic dress of the university, or by custom are not used at all by graduands (including outside the ceremony), or are optional but normally unused by graduands.

2. Hats form part of the prescribed academic dress but are not worn at all in the ceremony (can be distinguished from (1) if photography outside the ceremony shows hats being worn).

3. Hats are worn as part of the ceremony but not during the presentation of graduands; most commonly new graduates wear them when processing out of the ceremony location, but they may be required to carry them during the presentation as well, or explicitly instructed by the presiding officer to put them on at some point in the ceremony.

4. Hats are worn by all graduands throughout the ceremony.

Of these it is relatively easy to distinguish (4) in video evidence, relatively easy to distinguish (1) from a combination of video, written and photographic evidence, and somewhat harder to distinguish (2) and (3) from each other, since it is possible that hats are being worn off-camera in a ceremony that I class as (2); fortunately there are relatively few institutions that fall into this intermediate category.

---

6 N. Groves, *Shaw's Academical Dress of Great Britain and Ireland*, 3rd edn (London: Burgon Society, 2011).

Table 1. British universities' hat-wearing practices

Nations: England, Wales, Scotland and Northern Ireland.
Category 1 Caps not used. **2** Caps not in ceremony. **3** Caps not at presentation. **4** Caps used throughout.
Evidence: the numbers refer to hyperlinks in the online version of this chart, found at <https://www.extragalactic.info/tbs>
Notes: **C** denotes that 'capping' of graduands is practised in the ceremony and **H** denotes hooding.

Name	Date	Nation	Cat.	Evidence	Notes
Aberdeen	1495	S	3	[1][2]	CH
Abertay	1994	S	1	[3][4]	C
Aberystwyth	2009	W	4	[5][6]	
Anglia Ruskin	1993	E	4	[7]	
University of the Arts, London	2004	E	4	[8]	
Aston	1966	E	4	[9][10]	
Bangor	2007	W	4	[11][12]	
Bath	1966	E	3	[13][14][15]	CH (doctors)
Bath Spa	2006	E	4	[16]	
Bedfordshire	2006	E	4	[17][18]	
Birmingham	1900	E	4	[19][20]	
Birmingham City	1993	E	4	[21]	
Bishop Grosseteste	2008	E	3	[22][23]	
Bolton	2004	E	4	[24][25]	
Bournemouth	1993	E	4	[26][27]	
Bradford	1963	E	4	[28][29][30]	Groves says hats forbidden
Brighton	1993	E	4	[31][32]	
Bristol	1909	E	1	[33][34]	Higher doctors and honorands wear hats
Brunel	1966	E	4	[35][36]	
Buckingham	1983	E	4	[37]	
Buckinghamshire New University	2007	E	4	[38]	
Cambridge	1209	E	1	[39]	No video available. Hats optional.
Canterbury Christ Church	2005	E	4	[40][41]	
Cardiff	2004	W	4	[42]	
Central Lancashire	1993	E	4	[43][44]	
Chester	2005	E	4	[45][46]	
Chichester	2005	E	4	[47][48]	
City	1963	E	3	[49][50][51]	
Coventry	1993	E	2	[52]	
Cranfield	1993	E	4	[53]	

The author maintains links to his sources.
To view them online, go to:
https://www.extragalactic.info/tbs/

Name	Date	Nation	Cat.	Evidence	Notes
University for the Creative Arts	2008	E	4	[54]	
Cumbria	2007	E	4	[55][56]	
De Montfort	1992	E	4	[57]	
Derby	1993	E	4	[58]	
Dundee	1967	S	1	[59][60]	C
Durham	1832	E	1	[61][62][63]	Hats now abolished below higher doctorates. No recent video available.
East Anglia	1963	E	4	[64][65]	
East London	1992	E	4	[66][67]	
Edge Hill	2006	E	4	[68][69]	
Edinburgh	1582	S	1	[70][71][72]	C
Edinburgh Napier	1992	S	1	[73][74]	Hats not listed in Groves
Essex	1965	E	4	[75]	
Exeter	1955	E	4	[76][77]	
Falmouth	2005	E	4	[78][79]	
Glasgow	1451	S	1	[80][81]	C
Glasgow Caledonian	1993	S	1	[82][83]	C Honorands wear hats
Gloucestershire	2001	E	4	[84]	
Greenwich	1993	E	4	[85][86]	
Harper Adams	1996	E	4	[87][88]	
Heriot-Watt	1966	S	1	[89][90]	C
Hertfordshire	1992	E	4	[91][92]	
Highlands and Islands	2011	S	1	[93]	C
Huddersfield	1992	E	4	[94][95]	
Hull	1954	E	4	[96]	
Imperial	2007	E	1	[97]	
John Moores, Liverpool	1992	E	4	[98]	
Keele	1962	E	4	[99][100]	Video of presentation not found
Kent	1965	E	4	[101]	
King's College London	2007	E	1	[102][103]	Hats not part of scheme: Groves
Kingston	1992	E	4	[104]	
Lancaster	1966	E	4	[105]	
Leeds	1904	E	1	[106][107]	PhD graduands wear hats
Leeds Beckett	1992	E	4	[108][109]	
Leicester	1957	E	2	[110][111]	

Name	Date	Nation	Cat.	Evidence	Notes
Lincoln	1992	E	4	[112][113]	
Liverpool	1903	E	4	[114][115]	
Liverpool Hope	2005	E	3	[116][117]	CH
London	1836	E	4	[118]	
University College London	2007	E	4	[119][120]	
London Metropolitan	2002	E	4	[121][122]	
London School of Economics	2007	E	3	[123][124]	Carried
Loughborough	1966	E	4	[125][126]	Instructions to graduands and practice are inconsistent!
Manchester	2004	E	3	[127][128]	
Manchester Metropolitan	1992	E	4	[129]	
Middlesex	1992	E	4	[130][131]	
Newcastle	1963	E	1	[132][133]	H Higher doctors wear hats
Northampton	2005	E	3	[134][135]	
Northumbria	1992	E	3	[136][137]	
Norwich University of the Arts	2008	E	4	[138]	
Nottingham	1948	E	2	[139][140]	
Nottingham Trent	1992	E	4	[141][142]	
Open	1969	E	1	[143][144]	
Oxford	1096	E	3	[145][146]	Hats required in the ceremony but not worn. No recent/ official video available
Oxford Brookes	1992	E	4	[147][148]	
Plymouth	1992	E	4	[149][150]	
Plymouth Marjon	2007	E	4	[151][152]	
Portsmouth	1992	E	4	[153][154]	
Queen's University Belfast	1909	N	1	[155][156]	
Queen Margaret	2007	S	1	[157][158]	C
Reading	1926	E	4	[159]	
Robert Gordon	1993	S	2	[160][161]	CH
Roehampton	2004	E	3	[162][163][164]	
St Andrews	1410	S	1	[165][166]	CH
St Mary's	2007	E	3	[167][168]	
Salford	1967	E	3	[169][170]	
Sheffield	1905	E	4	[171][172]	

Name	Date	Nation	Cat.	Evidence	Notes
Sheffield Hallam	1992	E	4	[173][174]	
South Bank University	1992	E	4	[175]	
Southampton	1952	E	4	[176][177]	
Southampton Solent	2005	E	4	[178][179]	
Staffordshire	1992	E	4	[180][181]	
Stirling	1967	S	1	[182][183]	Hats not part of scheme: Groves
Strathclyde	1964	S	1	[184]	C
Suffolk	2007	E	4	[185]	
Sunderland	1992	E	3	[186][187]	
Surrey	1966	E	3	[188][189] [190]	PhD graduands wear hats
Sussex	1961	E	4	[191][192]	
Swansea	2005	W	4	[193][194]	
Teesside	1992	E	4	[195][196]	
Ulster	1984	N	4	[197][198]	
Wales Trinity St David	2010	W	4	[199]	
Warwick	1964	E	4	[200]	
West London	1992	E	4	[201][202]	
West of England	1992	E	4	[203]	
West of Scotland	2007	S	1	[204]	CH
Westminster	1992	E	4	[205]	
Winchester	2007	E	2	[206]	
Wolverhampton	1992	E	4	[207][208]	
Worcester	2005	E	2	[209][210]	
York	1963	E	4	[211][212]	
York St John	2007	E	3	[213][214]	

A few universities use hats at presentation for PhD graduands (Leeds and Surrey are noted in the table) but not at the level of masters' or bachelors' degrees. Newcastle and Bristol use hats for the presentation of substantive higher doctors (the former caught on video, the latter according to their regulations). As video evidence of the form of even PhD presentations is not easy to find for all universities and higher doctorates are very rare, the results in the table cannot be systematic and I classify universities according to the head-wear allowed for the non-doctoral degrees, while noting that in many cases PhDs and other 'lower' doctorates are treated identically to the lower degrees. The treatment of honorary graduands varies widely and again the table is not intended to be systematic.

Table 2 shows the number of institutions broken down by each category, and the total.

At this point it is worth noting the existence of the practices which I will refer to as 'capping' (where the graduand is lightly tapped on the head with a cap or something ap-

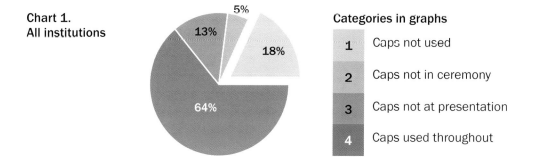

Chart 1.
All institutions

5%
13%
18%
64%

Categories in graphs

1	Caps not used
2	Caps not in ceremony
3	Caps not at presentation
4	Caps used throughout

Table 2 and Chart 2. Numbers of institutions in different categories

Country	Category 1	2	3	4	Total
England	8	5	15	71	99
Scotland	13	1	1	0	15
Wales	0	0	0	5	5
Northern Ireland	1	0	0	1	2
Total	22	6	16	77	121

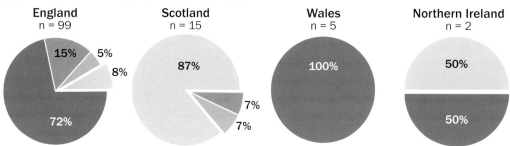

England
n = 99

15% 5%
8%
72%

Scotland
n = 15

87%
7%
7%

Wales
n = 5

100%

Northern Ireland
n = 2

50%
50%

Table 3 and Chart 3. Practices of English universities by date of foundation

Date range	Category 1	2	3	4	Total	Cats 2–4 (per cent)
Ancient (1000–1800)	1	0	1	0	2	50.0
Pre-war (1801–1944)	3	0	0	5	8	62.5
Post-war (1945–1991)	2	2	4	16	24	91.7
Post-'92 (1992–2019)	2	3	10	50	65	96.9
Total	8	5	15	71	99	91.9

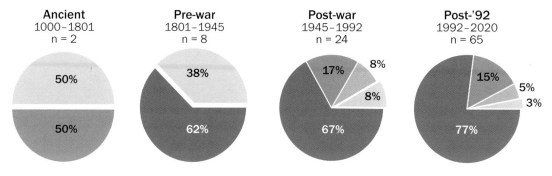

Ancient
1000–1801
n = 2

50%
50%

Pre-war
1801–1945
n = 8

38%
62%

Post-war
1945–1992
n = 24

17% 8%
8%
67%

Post-'92
1992–2020
n = 65

15% 5%
3%
77%

proximating a cap) and 'hooding' (where the graduand arrives on the stage carrying, not wearing, their hood and has it placed over their head before being greeted by the presiding officer). These are very widespread in Scotland and much less common in the rest of the UK.

Practices by nation and foundation date

There are too few universities in Wales and Northern Ireland to draw conclusions: broadly they seem to follow the same practices as England. All universities in Wales use hats throughout the ceremony.

However, there are very obvious differences between Scotland and the rest of the UK. Scottish universities almost universally do not use hats; the only exceptions are the two universities in Aberdeen, where hats form part of the dress but are not used during the presentation ceremony (categories 2 and 3). Thus 87 per cent of universities are in category 1. In the rest of the UK, 72 per cent of institutions are in category 4 and only 8 per cent in category 1—clearly a significant difference.

Practice is more variable in England than in any other nation of the UK (there are of course many more universities in England than in the other nations) and so it is interesting to break the English universities down further. The obvious subdivision is by date of foundation (as independent degree-awarding bodies that host their own graduation ceremonies), and this is shown in Table 3.

Although the numbers of older universities are small compared to the explosion of post-'92 institutions, it is clear that generally older universities are more likely to have abandoned the use of headwear at graduation altogether. The two post-'92 institutions that do not use hats at all are King's College and Imperial College, London, and these are only post-'92 in the technical sense that their independent degree-awarding powers date only from the twenty-first century. I return to this point below.

Notes on some institutions

In this section I provide some additional notes on the practice of individual institutions where the categorization is doubtful or needs to be clarified.

Oxford (category 3). The instructional video provided by Oxford and linked from the table shows that graduands do not wear hats in the Sheldonian when being presented for their degrees; nor do they wear them when returning in the gown and hood of their new degree. However, they are required to have the caps with them and to 'cap' the academic procession as it leaves the Sheldonian. On the basis that graduands would not be admitted to the ceremony without having the cap I have placed Oxford in category 3. There would be an argument for placing it in category 2.

Cambridge (category 1). As with Oxford, caps should be carried rather than worn by graduands in the Senate house, but, unlike the case at Oxford, caps are not a required part of academic dress for undergraduates. They may be carried by graduands, but the form of the Cambridge graduation ceremony makes this inconvenient, as discussed in more detail below, and in practice few if any graduands use them. For this reason it seems most appropriate to place Cambridge in category 1.

Durham (category 1). A full set of headwear is listed by Groves, but Durham has effectively abolished hats for degrees below higher doctorates in their current regulations.[7]

7   Durham University Calendar, at <www.dur.ac.uk/university.calendar/volumei/academic_dress/> [retrieved 7 February 2021].

Assuming that this was not the case at the time of compilation of the 3rd edition of Groves around 2011, this must have happened in the past decade, and is the only case that I am aware of of an English university removing hats from its formal definition of academic dress, as opposed to never including it in the first place (e.g., King's). Most universities' academic dress regulations are not available on line and so this cannot be investigated systematically.

Bradford (category 4). Groves states that Bradford 'does not permit' the use of the square cap in graduation ceremonies by the regulations, but they are clearly used throughout recent ceremonies and figure strongly in the university's promotional material. Again, assuming that this was not the case in 2011, Bradford must have changed its practice in the last decade.

Men and women

In all the institutions whose graduation ceremonies I have been able to view men and women are treated equally. Formerly there were traditional differences reflecting the different social rules for headwear for the sexes[8] but these seem almost entirely to have died out, although they were alive and well in the Republic of Ireland at least until recently.[9] Although the evolution of these differences towards the current position of complete uniformity would be an interesting topic for historical study, the present paper focuses on the situation at the present day and so I do not consider them further, other than to comment below on their relevance for some present-day urban myths.

Discussion

Why does the practice vary so widely between institutions? I will consider the variation based on the natural groups that emerge from Tables 2 and 3.

Ancient English universities

The forms of the graduation ceremony in Oxford and Cambridge can be seen from illustrations to have changed relatively little since the late nineteenth or early twentieth century. Although a more detailed examination of the historical evidence would be interesting, it seems that (male) graduands have gone bare-headed continuously for at least a century and probably much longer. The practices we see now are quite natural in the context of, say, the late nineteenth century, which differed from that of the early twenty-first in three key respects:

1. Academic dress was, much more than it is today, 'uniform' for members of the university and cap and gown would have been worn in the streets;

2. All adults would have been familiar with a much wider range of formal headwear than most of us use today but also, crucially, with the etiquette for when it should and should not be worn;

---

8   See, e.g., S. Wearden, 'How Academic Dress Is Mobilized in Degree Ceremonies and to What Effect', *TBS*, 15 (2015), pp. 14–29, at p. 24 for a discussion of a very recent change at Lancaster, doi.org/10.4148/2475-7799.1131.

9   See, e.g., E. Brauders, 'Hats off!', *The University Times*, 16 January 2015, at <www .universitytimes.ie/2015/01/hats-off/> [retrieved 8 June 2021]: the history of the urban myths surrounding the Irish practice would also be an interesting topic for investigation.

3. The graduation ceremony was then actually, as it still is in form at these universities, not a celebration of graduation but a collective request on the part of the graduands to be permitted to graduate, reflecting the origin of graduation ceremonies as 'quality control' for the medieval university.

Traditional hat etiquette is not quite as simple as the rule that it is often reduced to: 'men should remove their hats indoors'. The removal of a hat is a sign of respect or submission (which is why senior officials in these ceremonies do not remove hats[10]). But in the context of graduations it would be entirely normal for the graduands, who were making a humble request of the whole university[11] to be allowed to receive their degrees, to remove their caps in the Sheldonian or the Senate House, putting them back on again when they left. Oxford preserves this almost completely;[12] Cambridge has lost it to the extent that caps are no longer required with the gown in general[13] but preserves it in that caps, if brought into the Senate House, must be carried and not worn.

It is tempting to suggest that the change in Cambridge regulations in so far as they cover graduation, and in practice where not covered by regulations, is a pragmatic one. The form of the Cambridge graduation (in which the graduand kneels, bare-headed, and offers both his or her hands to be clasped by the Vice-Chancellor) means that a hat would have to be placed on the floor of the Senate House.[14] A graduand in this ceremony has a hard enough job to avoid tripping over the hem of the gown on rising without having to remember to pick up a hat as well. It is possible there has been some relaxation of the Cambridge practice back towards the use of hats—in the 1990s my college firmly instructed graduands not to bring them to the ceremony, whereas now it is made clear that they are optional—but both tradition and convenience point in the same direction here and it seems unlikely that they will ever make a full reappearance.

---

10 Long-established practice: see Joseph Wells, *The Oxford Degree Ceremony* (Oxford: Clarendon Press, 1906), p. 4.

11 See for example the wording of the 'grace' that introduces the presentation of graduands at Cambridge: 'Supplicant reverentiis vestris viri mulieresque ... ut gradum quisque rite petivit assequatur'; '[These] men and women beg your reverences ... that they may proceed to the degrees for which each has applied according to the regulations'.

12 The different rules for wearing what used to be called the Oxford women's soft cap, now rare and in principle allowed irrespective of gender, preserve the different hat etiquette for women.

13 *The Statutes and Ordinances of the University of Cambridge*, (Cambridge University Press, 2019), chapter 2, specify under 'headdresses': 'with all other gowns, for residents the square cap: provided that an undergraduate shall wear either the square cap or no headdress.' The 'provided that' stems from amendments first made due to a materials shortage during the Second World War, but made permanent in 1953: see Keenan, p. 102. In practice, although the wording here covers only undergraduates, the carrying of a cap in the Senate House by resident graduates is not enforced.

14 As can be seen in the 1904 drawing by Sydney Hall from the Graphic reproduced by A. Kerr, 'Academic Dress on Picture Postcards Published by Davis's of Oxford, their Rivals and Successors', *TBS*, 18 (2018), pp. 75–106, at p. 90, https://doi.org/10.4148/2475-7799.1157, though here the position of the hat is surely artistic licence; the graduand has just finished holding the praelector's finger with his right hand and so the cap should be on the floor to his left. Those Cambridge graduands wishing to take a cap into the Senate House are currently instructed that it should be carried in the left hand.

Scotland

The Scottish universities have almost universally rejected headwear at graduation—only the two universities in Aberdeen make any use of hats. The remaining 12 institutions, which do not use them at all, include the remaining three ancient Scottish universities as well as some very modern foundations, some of which (Stirling is mentioned by Groves and Edinburgh Napier is implied) have never included hats in their scheme of academic dress. Dickson[15] describes how, in the case of Glasgow, a scheme of academic dress on the English model was initially imposed from outside in the nineteenth century—it is clear from Dickson's account that hats never had a very secure part in the resulting scheme in practice and they have now been abolished, except for senior officials, in the cause of bringing the regulations in line with tradition. It is plausible that the same is the case for Edinburgh, though not for St Andrews where hats are apparently still used outside graduation along with other aspects of traditional academic dress.[16] For all the ancient Scottish universities we would expect considerations similar to those for Oxford and Cambridge, discussed above, to have governed the historical form of the ceremony in terms of when headwear would be appropriate. In addition, all but two of the Scottish institutions practice 'capping', as mentioned above, and four of them also make use of 'hooding': these would be both impractical and also slightly absurd if the graduand were wearing a hat at presentation.[17] At Glasgow 'capping' pre-dates the reintroduction of hats, and has survived their abandonment.[18] The complete absence of hats outside Aberdeen in the new universities may have something to do with the use of capping but is more likely an intentional conformation on the part of the university authorities to the locally prestigious norm set by St Andrews, Glasgow and Edinburgh. (The different approach taken by Robert Gordon University must surely be a result of the practice at the University of Aberdeen.)

Modern English universities in categories 1–3

It is interesting first of all to consider the remaining English universities that do not allow headgear at all, or restrict it to doctors or to higher doctors. Durham's tradition of not using hats at graduation presumably has similar origins to the practices of Oxford and Cambridge, but has taken a stronger form. Hats were still in use in the 1960s but, as noted above, have now been formally abolished even up to the level of PhDs. The reason for this is most likely to be have been, like Glasgow, a desire to bring the regulations in line with the practice at graduation—with the implicit assumption that academic dress regulations are only relevant to graduation ceremonies held at Durham. Newcastle is the offspring of Durham and inherited many of its traditions related to graduation, such as the dress of senior officials: it seems likely therefore that Durham had largely abandoned the use of hats by the mid-1960s when the first Newcastle students would have been graduating.

Newcastle is one of the few universities to provide an explanation for its practice, on its website:

---

15 N. Dickson, 'Tradition and Humour: the Academic Dress of the University of Glasgow', *TBS*, 12 (2012), pp. 10–35, doi.org/10.4148/2475-7799.1097.

16 Hargrave, p. 21.

17 Newcastle, which is one of the few English universities to use hooding, does combine it with hats in the case of higher doctors, at great risk to the dignity of all involved.

18 Dickson, p. 14

> Most academic dress at Newcastle University does not include a mortar board, by tradition. The story goes that when Newcastle became an independent university in 1963, students celebrated freedom by throwing their traditional hats into the River Tyne.
>
> Since then, Newcastle University academic dress has not included a mortar board.[19]

This story is, of course, an urban myth that is very unlikely to contain any truth at all, as is the story told at Durham that students threw their caps into the river at the time of the admission of women to Durham (in 1881!), and similar stories that circulated at Bristol and Cambridge in my time there.[20] While unfortunately I have not been able to date this more precisely, it does not seem implausible that the change in attitude to headgear at Durham and Newcastle dates from the 1960s, a decade not just of social change but of changes in non-academic fashion. The Open University, founded in 1969, owes its long-standing tradition of using no headgear at all, which continues to surprise students to this day, to its foundation in the same decade and the intention of its founders to break away from the practice of the older universities.[21] Of the other older institutions in category 1, only Leeds provides an explanation for its practice in its publicly available regulations,[22] and this simply attributes it to tradition:

> Those being awarded diplomas, first degrees and masters degrees at the University's degree ceremonies wear academic dress: they do not, through long established University custom and practice, wear the cap (mortar-board) prescribed as part of full academic dress.

By contrast Bristol's custom, which denies hats to 'lower' doctors at graduation as well, is directly inconsistent with their regulations which specify that graduates 'shall wear' a cap or bonnet. Bristol, Leeds, and Queen's University Belfast, as early twentieth-century institutions, passed through the same social transition as Durham—but so did Liverpool and Birmingham, of similar date, and they retain (or have reintroduced?) the use of headgear at graduations. Detailed historical work would need to be done to understand why these institutions followed such different paths.

The case of the two 'twenty-first-century' institutions that do not allow hats is an interesting one. As is well known, King's College London designed an entirely new form of academic dress on starting to award its own degrees; it is perhaps not surprising that this did not include hats since it constituted an intentional and publicly stated break with tradition.[23] However, Imperial's scheme, which is much more traditional, does not allow

---

19 Newcastle University Congregations, at <www.ncl.ac.uk/congregations/before/gownhire/> [retrieved 7 February 2021].

20 The 'protest at the admission of women' story may have its origin in the differences between etiquette for men and women, discussed above, in which men would remove their hats indoors but women would not; if so, it must have arisen some time between the period when these were alive and well socially, and would have been understood as social rules by those participating in the ceremonies, and the period when the universities moved to a gender-neutral position in their regulations.

21 Hargrave, p. 16; Wearden, pp 21–23; Goff, Philip, 'Blithering Nonsense: The Open University and its Academic Dress', *TBS*, 19 (2019), pp. 7–37, doi.org/10.4148/2475-7799.1160.

22 Leeds University General Regulations, Section 1, Academic Dress, at <www.leeds.ac.uk /secretariat/general_regulations.html>, [retrieved 7 February 2021].

23 Comparable to the unsuccessful, and now largely reverted, redesign of headgear for the University of East Anglia: see discussion by Groves.

hats at graduation except for honorands (Groves suggests that they are specified in the regulations, but these are not available online). In establishing a 'tradition' that hats are not worn at graduation, did Imperial intend to contrast with the post-'92 universities discussed below and link to the tradition of other Russell Group institutions like Durham, Bristol, Leeds and Queen's?

We can now consider institutions in categories 2 and 3—that is, universities where graduands get hats as part of their (normally hired) academic dress but do not wear them at all during the ceremony, or do not wear them until some specified stage in the proceedings after presentation. One new university, Worcester, in category 2, provides an explanation for its practice in material provided to graduands: 'In order to respect the wishes of the Dean and Chapter of Worcester Cathedral you are requested to remove your mortar board whilst inside the Cathedral.'[24] This is interesting, since a number of institutions use cathedrals for their graduation ceremonies, including Coventry, Liverpool Hope, Winchester and York St John, all of which are in categories 2 or 3 (but see below for more discussion of York St John). However, other institutions use cathedrals and appear to have no problem with hats being worn throughout (Canterbury Christ Church and Hertfordshire being two examples)—presumably the requirements of the cathedral authorities are different in different cases. The practices of Leicester and Nottingham, both pre-1960s foundations that prescribe hats but don't allow graduands to wear them during the ceremony, have no obvious explanation unless they are adhering to a version of the Oxford tradition.

A small number of post-'92 institutions have a tradition of hats not being worn until the end of the ceremony, e.g., when new graduates follow the academic procession out of the venue. Some, including York St John (as seen in the linked video) and Sunderland, have the graduates don their hats at a specific instruction from the presiding officer, the idea presumably being to mark the transition from graduand to graduate. From a historical perspective, this makes little sense—if anything the hood, rather than the hat, has been the mark of the graduate since at least the seventeenth century.[25] As a piece of ceremonial, though, it seems quite effective. One can imagine that other institutions, both in England and in the wider world, may over time develop their own interpretation of the meaning and function of academic dress in general and the wearing of headgear in particular. However, it is hard to see in the present climate any English university that has moved to hat-wearing throughout the ceremony stepping away from it again.

Modern English and Welsh universities in category 4

As we have seen, a substantial majority of English universities—and all the Welsh ones—take the very simple approach of having the graduands wear the full academic dress appropriate to their degree throughout the ceremony. The proportion doing this is 71 per cent overall, and 77 per cent among the post-'92s.

---

24 University of Worcester Awards Ceremonies 2019, at <www2.worc.ac.uk/registryservices/documents/graduation-info-2019.pdf> [retrieved 7 February 2021].

25 Wells, p. 73, laments the fact that the cap has ceased to be the marker of the highest degrees, presented with high ceremonial at inception ceremonies, and has descended to mere undergraduates and choristers.

As discussed above in the context of the ancient universities, from a historical point of view it is this practice that is anomalous, but in practical terms it is now the norm in England and Wales. It is interesting to ask why this has come about, but probably many factors are at play. One may be the fact, intentionally ignored up till now, that many graduation ceremonies do not in fact involve graduation—the degrees have already been conferred in absentia. Thus the graduands actually are graduates, and the element of supplication that was historically present no longer is. Certainly, this is relevant to the former polytechnics in the UK, where degrees were awarded by the CNAA before a presentation ceremony for the new graduates at their institution. However, I would argue that the state of affairs as we see it in the twenty-first century arises principally from a radically different perception of the nature of academic dress from the historical one. From a 'uniform' commonly worn by all members of a university, with differences that depend on status and occasion, academic dress in most universities has become 'graduation attire', which many people will wear only once in a lifetime, and it is then natural for graduands to want to wear what is perceived as full academic dress[26] and to ignore a complex etiquette for the wearing and removal of hats with which few of them are now familiar. In practical terms, new universities will design their schemes of academic dress in close collaboration with the robemakers,[27] the robemakers will presumably suggest hats as part of the scheme for an English or Welsh university, and institutions will generally wish to adopt practices that align as closely as possible with the perceived prestigious historical tradition of academic dress[28] in order to emphasise their own credentials—just as they largely adopt other aspects of graduation ceremonial such as official dress, processions, maces and the like.[29] Hats, gowns and hoods for all graduands are one of many ways in which a new university states its continuity with the perceived historical university tradition, and in this respect perception is far more important than the details of past practice.

Summary and conclusion

We have seen that the use of academic headwear at graduations through the United Kingdom varies widely by nation and by date of foundation, and I argue that the relationships between these can be understood in terms of direct descent from a historical tradition on the one hand and of a modern interpretation of what constitutes a locally prestigious standard of academic dress on the other. All these practices are governed by tradition (often unwritten, sometimes in contradiction to the supposed written regulations) but in some cases institutions are adhering to a genuine historical tradition, in others re-interpreting the tradition to suit the needs of a twenty-first-century university; even the recently invented traditions may no longer be clearly understood by the students and staff of the university

26 Wearden, p. 24.

27 For a discussion of the process for one post-'92 institution, see P. Goff 'An Inside Job: Reflections on Designs of Academical and Official Dress for the University of the Arts London (formerly the London Institute)', *TBS*, 18 (2019), pp. 7–31, dx.doi.org/10.4148/2475-7799.1154.

28 I.e., in England and Wales, the use of caps and bonnets; in Scotland, the adoption of other traditions of the ancient universities such as capping.

29 S. Wearden, 2017, The perpetuation of degree ceremonies, PhD thesis, University of Lancaster.

at which they are observed. A survey such as this cannot do more than scratch the surface of the historical detail needed to understand each institution's choices.

Acknowledgements

I am grateful to Dr Sandra Wearden for a number of very helpful suggestions on earlier drafts of this paper, to the examiners of the Burgon Society dissertation on which it was based for constructive remarks, and to Professor Bruce Christianson for a supportive review of the article.

Transactions of the Burgon Society, 20 (2020), pages 67–93

The Evolution of Undergraduate Academic Dress at the University of Cambridge and its Constituent Colleges

By Brian Newman

This article is the product of a number of years of research and of assembling a collection of prints and other images of the undergraduate dress of members of the various colleges of the University down the years. This collection has been augmented by those of others.

Specifically, I have researched a number of publications, from the Burgon Society and others, accessing the archive at the Cambridge University Library and making enquiry of the archivist of each of the colleges as well as of those few remaining robemakers that supply members of the University.

The University Library archive was short on detail, consisting very largely of correspondence with Heads of Houses and others about whether undergraduates should still be required to wear gowns on certain occasions (e.g., to lectures, to examinations) and very little about the actual design of the dress. Similarly, the response from the college archivists yielded very little; what I could glean is repeated later in this paper. I did however receive some images of interesting entries from very old Ede & Ravenscroft ledgers, but unfortunately the archivist was unable to date them for me. These also feature later, in the Appendix.

Introduction: from class to college

This paper charts the development of the distinctive academic costume worn by undergraduate members of England's second oldest university, Cambridge.

It follows the evolution in undergraduate academic dress from differentiation based upon social class and wealth (and regulated as such by the University) to one of differentiation, in most historical cases at least, by the college of which undergraduates are members, about which the University's only current stipulation is that gowns should be knee-length.[1] This is unlike the evolution from a similar class-based and wealth-based scheme at the University of Oxford to one based on academic achievement, a commoner's attire being very distinctly different from that of a scholar, or (in some cases) an exhibitioner. As a consequence of the abolition of entrance awards to Oxford, the sole wearers of a scholar's gown in a cohort of undergraduate fresh-men and women at matriculation are now the chapel musicians, the choral and organ scholars! Whereas at both Cambridge and Oxford

I would like to acknowledge the encouragement that I have received from Fellows of the Burgon Society in this endeavour, especially Dr Alex Kerr, whose knowledge of, in particular, the images of academic dress is nothing short of encyclopaedic.

1 Cambridge University Ordinance relating to Academical Dress created under Statute B, VI,1, adopted by Grace of the Senate, 13 June 1889, relating to all dress for graduates and may also contain this stipulation for undergraduates. However, Dr Alex Kerr informs me that it does not appear in the Ordinances up to 1911 that he has viewed. It does appear in the *Cambridge University Reporter* of 17 May 1932.

the University regulates the academic dress of its respective graduates, both show little interest in regulating undergraduate attire, being left over the years largely to colleges and robemakers and at Oxford 'entirely governed by precedent',[2] the exception at Cambridge being headdress.

The early classes of undergraduate were as follows:

- nobleman, heir to a peerage
- fellow-commoner (if younger son of a peer or heir to a baronetcy then a 'hat' fellow-commoner)
- pensioner (if a scholar then a foundationer)
- sizar

Today this is reduced to pensioner, scholar and exhibitioner, with, in some colleges, the term sizar relating to those with significant bursaries.[3] The title fellow-commoner still exists in some colleges, but is now an honorary award of status, similar to but junior to the award of honorary fellow.

The requirement to wear academic dress on specific occasions has also altered over the years, very notably over the last sixty or so. Until the early 1960s it was required for members of the University to wear gowns after dark when out of college in the town. All Arts faculties required gowns to be worn for lectures and examinations, and all colleges required it likewise when visiting one's Tutor, Director of Studies, the Dean or the Master. It was required attire for dining in Hall every evening and for attending Chapel. Some colleges, for example King's, required the wearing of a surplice for Chapel rather than a gown.

Today, some more liberal colleges hardly require gowns to be worn at all, let alone surplices.[4]

Origins

Academic dress in England is a direct descendent of the medieval dress of those in, or preparing for, holy orders. This consisted of a closed, narrow-sleeved garment, not dissimilar to a cassock.[5] In addition, undergraduates also had a small, unlined hood, important in winter as often their heads were tonsured. Figure 1 shows Chaucer's Clerk of Oxenford wearing this type of clothing. Some students also wore a tabard over this *supertunica*.[6] Many of the students, but by no means all, were destined for holy orders; there is an interesting modern parallel of Roman Catholic seminarians wearing garb similar to priests, namely clerical collar and multi-button cassock, or black suit, even though not themselves ordained.

---

2   Andrew James Peter North, 'The Development of the Academic Dress of the University of Oxford 1920–2012', *TBS*, 13 (2013), pp. 101–41 (pp. 117–18) at <newprairiepress.org/burgonsociety> https://doi.org/10.4148/2475-7799.1111.

3   For example, Churchill College, a twentieth-century foundation, offers sizarships for promotion of music, theatre and visual arts. See <www.chu.cam.ac.uk/student-hub/resources /financial-support/sizarships/> [retrieved 10 June 2021].

4   At a recent formal dinner in my own college, Sidney Sussex, whereas everyone at High Table, where I was dining, wore academic gowns, many of the undergraduates did not.

5   W. N. Hargreaves-Mawdsley, *A History of Academical Dress in Europe until the End of the Eighteenth Century* (Oxford: Oxford University Press, 1963), pp. 4–6.

6   Alex Kerr, 'The Turbulent History of Undergraduate Academic Dress', *Burgon Notes*, 17 (Summer 2011), pp. 2–3 (p. 2).

Towards the end of the fourteenth century, scholars of King's Hall (founded in 1317 by Edward II, and absorbed into the later foundation of Trinity College by Henry VIII) were ordered to wear a long outer garment, the *roba talaris*.[7] This ankle-length gown, similar to that worn at Oxford, would be specified also for wear at Henry VI's foundations at Eton College (1440) and King's College, Cambridge (1441), together with a short tabard and a cloth hood.[8] This most ancient form of hood was 'that which was sewed or tied to the upper part of a coat or gown, and brought over the head for a covering, in the same manner as a cowl: but when caps were introduced the hoods became an ornament of the shoulders and back; they were then enlarged and lined with skins.'[9]

Fig. 1. Chaucer's Clerk of Oxenford.

Early in the fifteenth century we see evidence of the 'class' distinction evolving in undergraduate academic dress, which was to persist into the nineteenth century and that based on wealth into the twentieth century. By an enactment of the University Congregation in 1414 for the regularizing of the dress of noblemen members of the University, it was laid down that whilst adhering to the general *talaris* scholars' dress, noblemen were permitted silk facings, similar to masters gremial (in residence at the University).[10]

The sixteenth century

After 1500, the tabard was left off and the *roba talaris* tunic evolved into the early open gown. The sleeves were no longer tight like a cassock, but widened into a bell shape.[11] By the 1530s all college gowns were black, with a cloth hood to match. However, with the founding by Henry VIII of Trinity College in 1546, this was to change. The College's Foundation Statutes indicate that gowns should be blue, but probably violet was originally intended.

In 1549, scholars on the foundation were ordered by parliamentary visitors to wear square caps to differentiate them from non-foundationers, who were wearing round caps, as worn at the time by the general populace and having no particular academic significance. Apart from some future stipulations on head-dress, most notably in the eighteenth century, thereafter undergraduate costume is largely left to the colleges, and to the town's tailors.[12] This is in distinct contrast to the dress of graduates which was, and still is, closely regulated by the University.

---

7   Hargreaves-Mawdsley, p. 131, referencing T. Rymer, *Foedera*, 9 vols (London: A. and J. Churchill, 1709), Vol. VII (1373–97), p. 242.

8   Foundation Statutes, King's College, (De habitu Sociorum et Scholarium 1441); see also Martin Lewis, 'Weaving the Fabric of Success: Exploring Academic Attire at Eton College from 1440', *TBS*, 18 (2018), pp. 107–21 (pp. 110–12), https://doi.org/10.4148/2475-7799.1158>.

9   Christopher Wordsworth, *Social Life at the English Universities in the Eighteenth Century* (Cambridge: Deighton, Bell & Co., 1874), p. 487.

10   Hargreaves-Mawdsley, p. 128, referencing Cambridge University Library, Enactment of a Congregation in 1414, MS 4.47, §176, fols 271 (65)ff.

11   Kerr, 'The Turbulent History', p. 2.

12   Hargreaves-Mawdsley, pp. 132–33.

In 1557, Cardinal Archbishop Reginald Pole, who had the honour of being not only the Chancellor of the University but at the same time was also Chancellor of Oxford, published his Statutes. He was himself of noble birth, being a great-nephew of both Edward IV and of Richard III. He permitted noblemen and their sons to wear at the University any manner of dress that they liked, the logic being that they were living entirely at their own expense.[13]

Gonville Hall, which had been founded in 1348 and was the fourth oldest college, was re-founded in 1557 by Dr John Caius, also spelled Keys, hence the pronunciation. In 1558 Caius instructed all College members *in statu pupillari* (that is, undergraduates and those with the Bachelor of Arts degree who had yet to proceed to Master of Arts) to wear a *vestis*, a long ankle-length gown, with full sleeves and having a standing collar. This was to be made of black or violet cloth, or some colour between the two.[14] This move away from black would doubtless have annoyed the fellows of Trinity, and would resonate again nearly four hundred years later when the College authorities chose a very distinctive undergraduate gown design in the 1830s. In sympathy with the Catholic revival under Queen Mary, who died in November of 1558, Dr Caius required students to wear a cassock (*tunica*) under this gown, whether or not the wearer was in holy orders.[15]

The University statutes of 1560 permit the wearing of a distinctive mourning dress. This is a 'sad coloured' gown of priestly shape as an alternative to normal academic dress;[16] the square cap has wide black ribbons across its diagonals with a black rosette at the intersection. In addition to mark the death of the Chancellor or a member of the royal family, the skull cap part of the hat was decorated with small black bows of ribbon. However, its use was abused by undergraduates as it gave commoners the look of graduates. As we shall see later, in the following century its use was greatly restricted as a consequence. This square cap is being worn by the Master of Arts with his hood squared in Figure 16.

Cardinal Pole ceased to be Chancellor in 1559 and was succeeded by Sir William Cecil, who had entered St John's College at the age of fourteen, but never took a degree—not unusual for someone not destined for the Church. Seven years after becoming Chancellor, he instructed that noblemen's academic dress should be brought into line with those of other undergraduates though the garments could be altogether richer.[17] By 1570, the prescribed dress for pensioners was the same that lasted for nigh on two hundred years, and in the case of some colleges even longer: a gown was worn down to the ankles and a round bonnet with a band and large brim—similar to lay hats of the period. This lay type of gown, similar to the commoner's gown today at Oxford, but to the ground, was the dress of all colleges with large pensioner populations. Those colleges with mainly fellow-commoners and other foundation members, namely King's, Queens', Peterhouse and Trinity Hall, had a gown similar to the Bachelor of Arts gown. Furthermore, a scholar was forbidden 'to wear a plumed hat, except he be unwell'. Those not noblemen were also 'forbidden from wearing a camisia or plaited ruff about the neck.'[18]

13 Hargreaves-Mawdsley, p. 132, referencing J. Heywood, *A Collection of Statutes of the University and Colleges of Cambridge* (London: Clowes, 1840), pp. 241–43.

14 Ibid., p. 132, referencing *Documents Relating to the University and Colleges of Cambridge*, 3 vols (1852), Vol. II, pp. 258–60, ¶27 (De Vestitu).

15 Ibid., p. 132.

16 Ibid., p. 136, referencing C. H. Cooper, *Annals of the University of Cambridge*, 5 vols (Cambridge: Warwick, 1842–53), Vol. II, pp. 161–62.

17 Ibid., p. 129, referencing C. H. Cooper, Vol. II, p. 230.

18 Wordsworth, *Social Life*, pp. 459–60.

To illustrate the rapid way that religious sentiment was changing in Cambridge at this time, in the year that Cecil was created Baron Burghley by Queen Elizabeth, 1571, the wearing of the almuce by priests, a cape covered in fur and an alternative to an academic hood, was forbidden in Cambridge. This was a mere thirteen years after Dr Caius had prescribed Catholic-leaning attire at his college at the very end of Queen Mary's reign.

In 1585, and repeated in 1588, Chancellor Lord Burghley made an order for the apparel of undergraduates:

> They might walk in cloake and hatt to and fro the fields. Also within his College, Hall, Hostell or Habitation it was lawful for any student to wear a gowne, or gaberdyne of playne Turkye fashion with a round falling cape without garde, welte lace, cutt or silke except one cutt in the sleeves therrof to putt out his arms onllye … … Also that everie graduate wearing the above gown and gaberdyne within the Universitie or Towne out of his Chamber or lodging doe weare withal in the day tyme a square cap and none other, no hatt to be worn except for infirmities sake with a kerchiffe about his head, or in going to an fro the fieldes, or in the street or open ayre when it shall happen to rayne, hayle or snowe; the hatt which shal be worne to be blacke, and the band or lace of the hatt to be of the same colour, playne and not excessive in bigness, without feather brooche or such lyke uncomelye for Students. And the gowne sleeves in all these tymes and place to be worn over and upon his armes (except he walke in his cloake and hatt to and from the fieldes).[19]

Thus, scholars and those on the foundation should wear the round cap, but allowing noblemen to have them made from velvet, in other words richer in line with his earlier edict for noblemen (this would appear to be at odds with the stipulation of the parliamentary visitors in 1549, that foundationers should be distinguished from other undergraduates by wearing a square cap). Graduates, however, would be distinguished, *inter alia*, by having the square cap. The 1588 edict also for the first time refers to the position of a sizar, one who was from a poor background and therefore contributed toward his board and studies by waiting at table, helping in the kitchen and so forth.

By the beginning of the reign of Elizabeth I, the statute dress for undergraduates had become a dark coloured gown with a cloth hood to match.[20] However, by the end of her reign, in 1603, marking the end of the Tudor period, the wearing of hoods by undergraduates had gone out of fashion.[21]

The seventeenth century

Dr Cosin, the Master of Peterhouse, wrote in 1636 to Archbishop Laud 'that at Trinitie and otherwise at Caius,' his order for wide-sleeved gowns was kept, but informed him also that 'others all that are undergraduates, wear the new fashioned gowns of any colour whatever, blue or green or red or mixed, without any uniformity but in hanging sleeves.'[22] Whether this 'all' referred to noblemen who were undergraduates—which would seem reasonable— or to all undergraduates is not clear.

The priestly almuce having been banned in 1571, in 1603 the University, however, reinforced that surplices were to be worn in chapel by all members of the University on

---

19 C. H. Cooper, Vol. II, p.411
20 Hargreaves-Mawdsley, p. 132.
21 H. P. Stokes, *Ceremonies of the University of Cambridge* (Cambridge: Cambridge University Press, 1927), p. 45.
22 Wordsworth, *Social Life*, p. 513.

Sundays and major Feasts. This was in accordance with the Canons of the Church of England, which stated that:

> ALL Masters and Fellows of Colleges or Halls, and all the Scholars and Students in either of the Universities, shall in their Churches and Chapels upon all Sundays, Holy-days and their Eves, at the time of Divine Service, wear Surplices according to the Order of the Church of England: and such as are Graduates, shall agreeably wear with their Surplices such Hoods as do severally appertain unto their Degrees.[23]

However, in 1643 the Long Parliament ruled that members of the University could opt out of the wearing of a surplice if they so decided.[24] This led to its almost total abandonment, and especially during the barren years of the Commonwealth. In a further *volte face*, following the Restoration of the Monarchy in 1660, the wearing of surplices was once again insisted upon. This remained so in certain colleges well into the twentieth century.[25]

In 1651 Oliver Cromwell replaced Edward Montagu, Earl of Manchester, as Chancellor with Oliver St John, a friend of Cromwell's father-in-law. With the Restoration he in turn was supplanted and the Earl of Manchester returned to office. It would seem that following the dismal days of the Commonwealth, there was an over-reaction by members of the University. In 1662, the University sent a detailed statement to Dr Whitgift, the Archbishop of Canterbury:

> 'Disorders tending to the decaye of learning and other dissolute behaviours.' Specifically, it was complained that the academical habit of members of the university was disused and the 'Scholars now goe in their Silkes and Velvets liker to Courtiers then Schollers.'[26]

It goes on to complain to the Archbishop about the specific apparel of 'Ecclesiastical Persons' indicating that night caps should only be black (but nevertheless in silk, satin or velvet!) and 'that they wear not any light-coloured stockings'.[27]

As above, we learn that undergraduates had for some time been misusing the privilege of wearing mourning dress as it meant that they could be taken for graduates. In 1681 the Vice-Chancellor of the University finally forbade the wearing of mourning dress for anyone below the rank of Master of Arts.[28]

During this century the various grades of undergraduate student appear to have fully matured. This, as I mentioned earlier, was more about rank in society and wealth than academic prowess, although, in some cases, scholar and exhibitioner appear to be distinguished from pensioner. A similar pecking order existed at Oxford and at Trinity College, Dublin, and in a simpler form at the ancient Scottish universities.[29]

The list is as follows:

- nobleman or heir
- hat fellow-commoner, being either a baronet or a younger son of a noblemen

---

23 Canon XVII of the Church of England, 1604.

24 Hargreaves-Mawdsley, p. 136, referencing C. H. Cooper, Vol. III, p. 336.

25 Indeed, strictly speaking, until the adoption of a complete new set of Canons by the Convocation of Canterbury in 1964, all members of Cambridge colleges should have been wearing surplices in chapel on the aforementioned Sundays and major Feasts.

26 A. G. Almond, *Gowns and Gossip* (Cambridge: Bowes & Bowes, 1925), p. 9.

27 Ibid.

28 Hargreaves-Mawdsley, p. 136.

29 Kerr, 'The Turbulent History', p. 2; Hargreaves-Mawdsley, pp. 91–101, 148–49; Jonathan C. Cooper, 'The Scarlet Gown: History and Development of Scottish Undergraduate Dress', *TBS*, 10

Fig. 2A. Five undergraduates depicted by Loggan, *Cantabrigia Illustrata*, 1690.

- fellow-commoner
- pensioner (if a scholar or exhibitioner then called a foundationer)
- sizar
- subsizar

As a constituent of his *Cantabrigia Illustrata* series published in 1690 in Cambridge, David Loggan depicts in 'Habitus Academici in Universitate Cantabrigiensi' the dress of members of the undergraduate population as well as of graduates (see Fig. 2A). This was copied in 1707 by publisher Pieter, or Pierre, Van der Aa of Leiden for a plate 'Habits ordinaires des personnes qui composent l'Université de Cambridge' in James Beeverell's *Délices de la Grand' Bretagne et de l'Irlande*.

This shows the dress of five different undergraduates:

- Firstly, an undergraduate of unspecified college, whose gown to the floor appears to have hanging sleeves with an armhole at the shoulder, decorated their full length with horizontal decoration and wearing a circular wide-brimmed hat.
- Secondly, a student of King's College and certain other foundations. This shows what would appear to be a very long gown with bell sleeves and a square cap with a tump or pompom.
- Thirdly, an undergraduate student of Trinity College, wearing a gown similar to the second but specified as being violet in colour.[30] With the cap pushed back we cannot see if once more there is a tump on the board.
- Fourthly, a fellow-commoner, in a very elaborate long gown, with long hanging sleeves with a slit at the elbow, very generously decorated at the shoulder and all down the sleeve. He is wearing a 'regular' circular hat with a wide brim.
- Finally (in another part of the plate), a nobleman, also in an elaborate state gown with sleeves to the ground, the upper parts of which are richly decorated, with patterns

(2010), pp. 8–42 (pp. 18, 23–25, 34, 38), https://doi.org/10.4148/2475-7799.1082.

30 Hargreaves-Mawdsley suggests that the undergraduate gowns of King's College, Queens' College, and Trinity Hall are shorter than those at Trinity College. Dr Alex Kerr in his article critiquing the work of Hargreaves-Mawdsley correctly observes that they are no different in length ('Hargreaves-Mawdsley's *History of Academical Dress* and the Pictorial Evidence for Great Britain and Ireland: Notes and Corrections', *TBS*, 8 (2008), pp. 106–50 (p. 140), https://doi.org/10.4148/2475-7799.1066).

Fig. 2B. Engraving of figures after Loggan, The *Universal Magazine*, March 1748.

lower on the sleeve Although not clear from this black and white image the gown is probably made from fine coloured silk. He, like the fellow-commoner, is wearing a 'regular' circular hat with a wide brim.

The silk undress gowns of noblemen (different from that depicted in Loggan), as also of the fellows, specifically of King's College, were enhanced by 'bishop's sleeves', so called as they were gathered at the wrist like a bishop's rochet.[31]

The 'other foundations' would seem to be Peterhouse (the University's oldest college), Queens', and Trinity Hall. These colleges admitted primarily fellow-commoners who paid full fees and were of such a status as to sit for meals in Hall with the fellows rather than with the other pensioner undergraduates. At other colleges, which admitted fewer fellow-commoners but mainly pensioners and sizars, undergraduates continued to wear the first gown show by Loggan, which later lost its sleeves and was nicknamed 'the curtain.'

31 William Gibson, 'The Regulation of Undergraduate Academic Dress at Oxford and Cambridge, 1660–1832', *Burgon Society Annual 2004*, pp. 26–41 (p. 29) at <newprairiepress.org/burgonsociety> https://doi.org/10.4148/2475-7799.1027, referencing J. R. Tanner (ed.), *The Historical Register of the University of Cambridge* (Cambridge: Cambridge University Press, 1917), p. 197.

Interestingly Loggan and Van der Aa both depict the sons of noblemen as being shorter than others—at this time many came up to the University in only their early or mid-teens. This had been the case since the early sixteenth century.

The eighteenth century

We are fortunate that in the eighteenth century a number of wealthy undergraduates, noblemen and in particular fellow-commoners, had their likenesses painted in portraits or miniatures. For the first time we can see for ourselves the bright-coloured and heavily decorated gowns sported by noblemen. There are also some more modest images in black and white of 'ordinary' undergraduates.

John Byrom, the polymath, is pictured in Figure 3 in 1707 as an undergraduate of Trinity College. What appear to be buttons down the facings of his gown may simply be his coat underneath. His headgear is not the traditional square but a John Knox Cap and he is wearing academic bands.

Painted in 1736 by William Hogarth, Figure 4 illustrates a portrait of Thomas Western, a fellow-commoner of Clare College. This shows a full-length gown with long, closed sleeves, much decorated with gold embellishment at the shoulder, down the sleeves and around the hem and a square cap with gold tassel.

The *Universal Magazine* published an article in March 1748 together with the plate shown in Figure 2B. Whilst it is fifty-eight years after Loggan, it is clearly copied from his engraving. Interestingly, however, whereas Loggan illustrated an undergraduate of King's College, this image is now entitled 'A scholar of a perticular [*sic*] foundation' and Loggan's nobleman has become 'a nobleman's son' who, as in Loggan, is noticeably shorter in stature than the other figures shown.

The American Ralph Wormeley V, of Rosegill, Virginia, was painted in 1763 wearing his robes as a fellow-commoner of Trinity Hall. This illustrates well how lavishly decorated they were with gold braid (Fig. 5).

Most noblemen appear to have favoured a lavish gown in blue or violet. Viscount Fitzwilliam was painted, by Joseph Wright of Derby, in his nobleman's gown when he was an undergraduate at Trinity Hall (1761–64). Figure 6 shows him in a gown of pink (as in 'hunting pink') with decorations of gold. The gown has inverted-T armholes and appears also to have pink strings.

By the middle of this century the distinction between the two grades of fellow-commoner, as opposed to a nobleman, was now clear. The eldest sons of, and therefore heirs to, a baronet or younger sons of noblemen, were as fellow-commoners permitted on other than formal occasions to wear a normal hat. They therefore became known as 'hat fellow-commoners'. Ordinary fellow-commoners were required at all times to wear the academic square. At the same time a University regulation ordered those *in statu pupillari* (all except noblemen and fellow-commoners) to wear clothes of 'grave colour' without lace, fringe or embroidery and without bright colours.[32]

In 1769 the University changed the cap of all remaining undergraduates from round to square. Why? It is suggested that this was a campaign led by Charles Farish to petition

---

32 Gibson, p. 35, referencing Christopher Wordsworth, *The Undergraduate: From Dr. Christopher Wordsworth's 'Social Life at the English Universities in the Eighteenth Century'*, rev., abridged and rearranged with an introduction by R. Brimley Johnson (London: Stanley Paul, 1928), p. 119.

Heads of Houses on behalf of those pensioner undergraduates who wanted removal of the class distinction in headgear.[33] At the same time a letter was sent to the Duke of Grafton by Alexander Clere of Corpus Christi College, requesting him to obtain the Government's consent so that a form of dress more decent and becoming might attend his Grace's installation as Chancellor.[34] The request for change was granted.[35] However, the foundation scholars and exhibitioners continued with the round hat with the tump and no tassel. Sizars and sub-sizars had the same caps as pensioners except no tassel on the square cap. Previously their headgear had been a black cloth bonnet with a brim of prunella (worsted twill) or silk.

A number of portraits were painted in the last decade of the century by the artist Silvester Harding, which show us exactly how fellow-commoners were attired. Among these, and painted c. 1790, is a watercolour of Marmaduke Dayrell, a fellow-commoner of Christ's College. He is shown in an ankle-length gown with closed sleeves and inverted-T armholes. The sleeves are decorated by a gold band around the end of the sleeve about one inch in from the bottom. From shoulder to armhole the gown is lavishly decorated with gold braid, and the gown also appears to have external padded shoulders, also lavishly decorated in gold braid. Dayrell is wearing an academic square with a gold tassel, which appears to fall both to left and to right at the front. In 1794 the artist painted another watercolour of a fellow-commoner, this time of J. T. Nottage of Trinity College. His gown, as would be expected of a member of Trinity is not black but blue (originally specified as violet, but at some time clearly blue became preferred). The gown is similar in style to that of Marmaduke Dayrell's, but the decoration is of silver rather than gold braid. There is also the very characteristic 'Trinity' wavy pattern of braid down each of the facings. Once again, the tassel on the academic square appears to divide right and left but, as with the gown, it is silver rather than gold. Unfortunately, because of the current access restrictions it has not been possible to obtain copies of these images from the Fitzwilliam Museum in Cambridge, and there are no photographic images in their archive.

Harding painted a miniature of Charles Douglas of Jamaica in 1793. Figure 7 shows him attired as a fellow-commoner of Pembroke College, in a black gown, heavily decorated with gold lace, similar to that in the portrait of Ralph Wormeley. Although not dated, Figure 8 shows Francis Alexander Halliday, a fellow-commoner of Trinity College. His gown is in the distinctive blue of Trinity rather than black, much decorated in silver, rather than gold with a glimpse of the characteristic wavy pattern down the facings. Finally, we can see Harding's miniature painted in 1795 of J. N. Ord in the gown of a pensioner of Trinity College in Figure 9. This is clearly shown as the distinctive blue colour with black facings.[36]

33 Gibson, p. 36, noting that Farish was also campaigning for the University to allow fellows to marry; see also Wordsworth, *Social Life*, p. 511, referencing Farish's *Toleration of Marriage in the Universities Recommended to the Attention of the Heads of Houses* (Cambridge: Hodson, 1799), p. 44.

34 Stokes, p. 47.

35 Hargreaves-Mawdsley, p. 134, referencing C. H. Cooper, Vol. IV, p. 355.

36 The miniatures are watercolours commissioned by Sir Busick Harwood. They are in the collections of Downing College (DCPP/HAR/4) and can be viewed in the University of Cambridge Digital Library at <cudl.lib.cam.ac.uk/view/MS-DCPP-HAR-00004/3> [retrieved 10 June 2021].

Fig. 3. Etching of John Byrom, as an undergraduate at Trinity College, 1707.

Fig. 4. Thomas Western, fellow-commoner of Clare College by Wm Hogarth, 1736.

Virginia Museum of History and Culture

Fig. 5. Ralph Wormeley, fellow-commoner of Trinity Hall, 1763.

Fitzwilliam Museum, Cambridge

Fig. 6. Viscount Fitzwilliam in nobleman's gown, by Joseph Wright of Derby, c. 1764.

Fig. 7. Miniatures by Silvester Harding. Charles
Douglas of Jamaica, fel-
low-commoner of Pem-
broke College, 1793.

Fig. 10. Pensioner, by Richard Harraden, 1805.

Fig. 11. Pensioner of Trinity
College, by Richard Harraden, 1805.

Fig. 8. Francis Alexander
Halliday, fellow-common-
er of Trinity College, n.d.

Fig. 12. Nobleman, by R.
Ackermann, 1815.

Fig. 14. Fellow-common-
er of, possibly, St John's
College, by R. Ackermann,
1815.

Fig. 9. J. N. Ord, pensioner at Trinity College.

Figs 7 – 9: The Master, Fellows, and Scholars of Downing College in the University of Cambridge

Fig. 13. Nobleman and fellow-commoners of Emanuel [*sic*] and Trinity Colleges by R. Ackermann, 1815.

Fig. 15. Pensioner wearing the sleeveless gown, with velvet facings by R. Acker-mann, 1815.

Fig. 16. A pensioner of Trinity College and a sizar with an MA in squared hood and mourning cap, by R. Ackermann, 1815.

Fig. 17. A pensioner of Trinity Hall, by R. Ackermann, 1815.

The nineteenth century

The new century opened with the founding of Downing College in 1800. This was the first college foundation since the founding of Sidney Sussex College over two hundred years earlier in the reign of Elizabeth I, in 1596. It would appear from the start that this was to be a college for only fellow-commoners, and no pensioner undergraduates.

The next few decades saw the publication of a number of sets of engravings depicting Cambridge academic dress, which give us a clear idea of how undergraduates were attired in the first half of the century, and in particular illustrate significant changes that were made to gowns in the 1830s.

In an early set of prints by Richard Harraden from 1803, *Costume of the Various Orders in the University of Cambridge*, we have confirmation of the attire of a pensioner at the turn of the century. This is a full-length sleeveless black gown. There appear to be no streamers, and the headgear is a standard black square (see Fig. 10). There were exceptions to this design. In 1805 Harraden states 'The pensioners of Trinity College are distinguished from all others by a blue gown with full sleeves made of Princes stuff (Fig. 11). The gowns of pensioners at Peterhouse, Queens', Trinity Hall and King's are nearly all the same as Trinity except that the former are all black'.[37] We can safely assume that, with these five exceptions, at the turn of the century all other pensioners wore the sleeveless pensioners' gowns, with, except for sizars, velvet facings and collars.

The series of excellent prints by John Samuel Agar after Thomas Uwins, published in 1814–15 by Rudolph Ackermann in his *History of the University of Cambridge*, is a wonderfully detailed record of undergraduate (and graduate) dress at this date.[38] The series contains the following of interest here:

• A nobleman (see Fig. 12). The image of the noble gentleman has been hand-coloured in blue (sometimes they were hand-coloured in violet) with very large gold embellishments on the long sleeves, shoulders and facings. Another is shown (see Fig. 13) in non-formal dress of black gown with short bell sleeves and a top hat.

• Fellow-commoners (see Fig. 13) of Emanuel [*sic*] College and Trinity College. The former wears a black gown heavily decorated in gold on the sleeves, shoulders and back, with a black velvet collar and carrying a top hat, signifying he is the son and heir of a baronet or younger son of a peer. The latter wears the characteristic blue gown of Trinity, richly decorated in silver and once again featuring the twisting silver braid on the facings. He is wearing the black square with a silver tassel.

• A fellow-commoner of, it would seem, St John's College, given the two horizontal gold strips of gold braid at the extremity of the sleeves, is also featured (see Fig. 14). The black of the gown could be in dispute, but it is heavily adorned with gold, and appears to have velvet facings. He wears a square with gold tassel.

• Three pensioners are shown. Figure 15 depicts a member of a college at that time still wearing the old-style pensioner's gown. The facings and flap collar are covered in black velvet. In Figure 16 we see a pensioner of Trinity College in a blue gown with slit bell sleeves and black facings. It appears that the inside edge of the blue sleeves is lined to about three inches in black. A standard black square lies on the floor beside him. The third is from Trinity Hall

---

37 Almond, p. 17, referencing R. Harraden, *Costume of the Various Orders in the University of Cambridge* (Cambridge: Harraden, 1805), unnumbered pages.

38 See Nicholas Jackson (ed.), *Ackermann's Costumes of the Universities of Oxford and Cambridge* (London: Burgon Society, 2016), pp. 33–64.

(see Fig. 17). This is the 'basic' long open-sleeved gown also worn by members of Peterhouse and Queens'. Trinity Hall's gown is later split partway up the arm and secured by a cord and button.[39] This is not clear from the Ackermann print and must be a later modification.

• Figure 16 also shows a sizar. He wears a very basic black sleeveless gown, with no velvet trimming.

Etchings from 1824, by the unknown 'R.A.R' (see Fig. 18), illustrate a nobleman in dress (here called 'State Robe') very similar to that as depicted in Ackermann's image of only a decade earlier, also in blue rather than violet, with hanging sleeves decorated in gold.

A second image (see Fig. 19) depicts a number of fellow-commoners. Those of St John's and Emmanuel Colleges appear very similar, save that there are three strips of horizontal gold at the base of the long, closed sleeve of the Emmanuel gown whereas the Ackermann print show only one. That for St John's College is shown with two. Both are wearing academic squares with gold tassels. The fellow-commoner of Trinity College is in the characteristic blue gown, with silver adornment, and the wavy pattern on the facings and at the base of the closed sleeve.

The Downing College black gown is heavily adorned on the sleeve, shoulder, back and facings, with black braid and tassels, quite different from the gold and silver trimmings of the other colleges.[40] The hat is square with a gold tassel.

The final member of the group is a bit of an anomaly. It is a 'Married' fellow-commoner, wearing a very plain black mourning gown with full sleeves gathered at the wrist and a plain square with what appears to be a grey tassel. He also rather poignantly is wearing very glum expression—probably a joke at his loss of single state!

Harraden's son, Richard Bankes Harraden, published a further two plates of engravings entitled 'Costume of the University of CAMBRIDGE' in around 1830. One depicts nine UNDER GRADUATES (see Fig. 20) and its companion GRADUATES (not here included) featuring the Chancellor and eight graduates holding different degrees. In the Undergraduates image we see noblemen in 'dress' and 'undress' gowns, the former in blue with elaborate gold decoration and black square with gold tassel, the latter a plain black gown with full sleeves gathered at the forearm and a top hat. Whilst an elaborate black gown with considerable braid-and-tassel decoration, the Downing College fellow-commoners' gown nevertheless is not adorned with silver or gold, as are the other fellow-commoners depicted here from Trinity College, Emmanuel College (now once again showing a single horizontal gold strip at the base of the blind sleeve) and an unnamed college but, based on the earlier Silvester Harding portrait, almost certainly Christ's College. The Downing College square hat is nevertheless distinctive by having a gold tassel.

More interesting here are the pensioners' gowns. For St John's College it is the sleeveless 'curtain' at this date; the blue, long open-sleeved gown of Trinity College; but most particularly the very new design of gown for Corpus Christi (Benet's) College. This was the first of a new set of undergraduate gowns for those colleges which up until now wore the sleeveless black gown. It is black with open sleeves, similar to the basic Peterhouse design, but the facings are in black velvet. Unlike the Ackermann image, here we can see the gathered sleeve.

---

39 Almond, p. 18.

40 See Charles Rupert Tsua, 'A Study of the History and Use of Lace on Academical Gowns in the United Kingdom and Ireland', *TBS*, 12 (2012), pp. 103–27 (pp. 116, 118), https://doi.org/10.4148/2475-7799.1103.

Up until this time, the dress for scholars and exhibitioners, unlike at Oxford, conform to that of pensioners. The exceptions were scholars of King's College, Rustat Scholars of Jesus College, Patchett Scholars and Duchess of Somerset Exhibitioners of St John's College all of whom wore a bell-sleeved black gown of fine 'costume' cloth. Arms appear through gashes in the middle of the upper arm of the sleeve. Westminster scholars of Trinity College wore a black (not the usual Trinity blue) bell-sleeved gown with a violet button and loop at the bottom of the forearm sleeve.[41]

As mentioned above, the undergraduate gown of Corpus Christi College was the first of the old sleeveless gowns to be replaced by something similar to those worn at Peterhouse and Queens' College. In 1828 the undergraduates sent a petition to the College fellows requesting a more becoming gown. The minutes of a fellows' meeting of 27 November 1828 record that it had been 'Agreed that the gown which had commonly been worn by undergraduates of this college, be changed for one of the same gown as that commonly used by Bachelors of Arts, with the distinction of velvet facings. This change to take place at the beginning of next term'.[42] This therefore dates the Richard Bankes Harraden print to later than 1828 and, although undated, is believed to be 1830.

A further minute from a Corpus Christi fellows' meeting, of 14 December 1835, reports, 'Agreed that in compliance with the order of 27th November 1828, the gown worn by fellow-commoners of this College be changed for one of the same form as that commonly used by Bachelors of Arts and that it be made of silk with facings (of gold).'[43] This design is confirmed by later images by Whittock and Hyde (Fig. 21) and others and was still in use in the 1960s.[44]

A Clare College order of 18 May 1836 stated 'That the undergraduates of the college, having applied to be allowed to change the form of gown at present worn by them, the Master be requested to make application to the Chancellor of the University for his permission, the new form of gown being approved by the Master and Fellows in College'. It is understood that the wife of the then Master, William Webb, designed the new gown, by incorporating three velvet chevrons on the sleeves. These were mimicking the chevrons on the College's coat of arms.[45]

In Gonville and Caius College there is a record dated 13 May 1837 'To adopt a new gown of the pattern agreed upon'.[46] There can be little debate but that the Caius gown is the most elaborate and decorative of any, blue with the whole forearm seam open, and with a strip of black velvet either side of the open seam. The facings and yoke are covered in black velvet. The blue colour harks back to the re-founding of the College by Dr Caius.

There would appear from my research with college archivists to be no other easily accessible records of fellows' meetings at which in the years 1835–37 all remaining colleges

---

41 Hargreaves-Mawdsley, p. 135, referencing Tanner, p. 196.

42 Almond, p. 19, having been permitted by Dr Pearce, when Vice-Chancellor, to see the College minutes.

43 Almond, *loc. cit.*

44 In 1969, Francis Davey, MA of New College, Oxford, who taught me the little Latin that I know, and went on to become Headmaster of Merchant Taylors' School, held a one-term teacher fellow-commonership at Corpus Christi College, and wore just such a gown when at Corpus, not himself being a Cambridge graduate. See also George W. Shaw, *Cambridge University Academical Dress, with Notes on Oxford Academical Dress* (Cambridge, Cambridge University Press, 1992), pp. 27–29.

45 Almond, pp.16–17.

46 Almond, p. 14, referencing the Caius Bursar having turned up the record, and then Dr Venn in his history of Caius states that use of the 'blue gown' commenced in 1837.

D.D.   Esq. Bedell.   Mus.D.   D.D.   Nobleman.   D.D.   L.L.D.   M.D.
In Surplice.   In Congregat. Robe.   State Robe.   Scarlet Robe.   Congregation Robe.

Fig. 18. Etching with hand colouring showing, third from right, a nobleman in a State Robe, by 'R.A.R.', 1824.

R.A.R. del.   Marraret   S.t John.   Emmanuel   Trinity.   Downing.
FELLOW COMMONERS.

Fig. 19. Etching with hand colouring showing six fellow-commoners, by R.A.R., 1824.

Nobleman.   Trin.Coll.   Down.g Coll.   Fellow Commoners.   Eman.Coll.   S.t Johns Coll.   Trin. Coll.   Corpus Coll.
                                                                     Pensioners.

Fig. 20. Nine undergraduates, by Richard Bankes Harraden, c. 1830.

agreed a variation of the Peterhouse and Queens' College gown. Whilst it was clearly not a matter for the University authorities, it is unclear whether the fellows had a hand in it, or simply delegated the 'customizing' to one of the tailors in the town. But by 1837 St John's, St Catharine's, Pembroke, Magdalene, Emmanuel and Sidney Sussex Colleges had all also adopted their own distinctive gowns for undergraduates, as had Downing, which heretofore since 1800 had made provision only for fellow-commoners.

Such large-scale changes to the undergraduate gowns brought forth several pocket-sized directories, in accordion-fold or folded-map format:

• *The Costumes of the Members of the University of Cambridge*, published *c.* 1843 by Nathaniel Whittock of London and Cambridge;

• *The Costumes of the Members of the University of Cambridge*, published *c.* 1850 by H. Hyde of No. 34 Richard Street, Islington, and sold by B. Stiel, Paternoster Row, London, and all Book and Printsellers in Cambridge (copied from Whittock, but a superior production—see Fig. 21).

• *Costumes of the University of Cambridge*, published 1862 by W. Metcalfe of Green Street, Cambridge (also copied from Whittock, but a much inferior production).

As well as details of the dress of the Chancellor and Vice-Chancellor and of those with various degrees, and a nobleman, for each college these show a picture of a fellow-commoner and a pensioner.

Specifically, the changes to the pensioners' gown unique to each of the colleges as depicted in the three sources above and hitherto not elsewhere described, are:

St John's	four black velvet bars horizontally across each unslit sleeve
Jesus	unslit sleeve gathered in pleats and velvet strip from the pleats to top of forearm seam
Pembroke	unslit sleeve gathered and held by cord and button (as Trinity Hall)
Emmanuel	basic gown with slit sleeves and box pleats on the facings
St Catharine's	basic gown with slit sleeves facings in long vertical pleats
Magdalene	sleeve gathered in pleats
Sidney Sussex	four pleats in the sleeves
Downing	basic gown

Several colleges adopted a fellow-commoners' gown much in design like the pensioners' gowns but with trimmings in gold rather than black (as Downing College).

Whittock and Hyde show the fellow-commoners' gowns for Emmanuel and Sidney Sussex Colleges with gold trimming while Metcalfe shows it in black—this, however, looks like a fault in the printing. All three booklets have the undress gown of a nobleman with 'bishop's sleeves' in contrast to the earlier Ackermann image with short bell sleeves, and R. B. Harraden's with a gathered short sleeve.

There were some further changes to the distinctive pensioner gown designs after the 1830s. For example, Sidney Sussex College changed from four pleats on the closed sleeve to pleats in chevrons either side of the slit in the sleeve in the late 1870s.[47] At some point the Downing gown changed to an unslit sleeve with six broad pleats held by three black cords and buttons and also Trinity Hall, where the sleeve below the slit is left open and held across by two buttons and a cord.

---

47 Almond, p. 18, referencing the 'oldest maker of robes in Cambridge' as stating this change.

Apart from velvet trimmings on some gowns, the cloth of these pensioner gowns, whether black or blue, was 'Prince's stuff', the sole exception being King's which were 'costume cloth', as were some of the scholars' gowns. The former is made from a yarn of wool and silk, used at the time in making clerical gowns and mourning attire, whereas costume cloth is altogether heavier. Fellow-commoners' gowns were typically made of silk.

Six new institutions were founded towards the end of the century. The year 1869 saw the founding of Girton College, the first college in Cambridge for women, followed two years later in 1871 by the second women's college, Newnham. Two new men's colleges followed, Selwyn College in 1882 and in 1887 the formalizing of the Non-Collegiate Students' Board as Fitzwilliam Hall (later Fitzwilliam House and now Fitzwilliam College).

In addition, Hughes Hall, founded in 1885 for the postgraduate training of teachers, and St Edmund's House, founded in 1896 for admission for the first time of Roman Catholic students, became full colleges of the University only in 2006 and 1996 respectively; they are mainly for postgraduate students, who wear gowns appropriate to that status, but now both also admit mature (older than 21) undergraduates.

Homerton College was originally founded in London in 1695 for the education of Calvinist ministers, as English dissenters were barred by law from Cambridge or Oxford. In the early nineteenth century, it was, for a time, affiliated to the University of London, but this ended when theological teaching was transferred to New College, London. Thereafter it was re-founded solely for the training of men and women teachers for Board schools. It moved to Cambridge in 1894 to escape the industrialization of London's East End, and immediately became women-only, a mixed college being anathema to an all-male University at that time. It first re-admitted men in 1976, the year it also became an 'Approved Society' of the University, and students were awarded the Cambridge Bachelor of Education degree. It became a self-governing college of the University on 2010, offering study in all subjects. Gowns for these 'adopted' colleges are discussed in the next section.

The Selwyn and Fitzwilliam gowns are both distinctive. Selwyn is the 'standard' Peterhouse gown but with blue facings, Fitzwilliam with a velvet strip either side of the sleeve slit. Strangely, neither of the respective college archivists has been able to unearth any record of when or why these designs were arrived at. It might simply be that they also delegated the design and subsequent supply to one of the tailors in the town.

The twentieth century

With all of the changes occurring in society at large, gone now is the distinguishing academic dress for noblemen, although noblemen's sons and daughters still attend the University—but with greater anonymity than previously; indeed two of the present Queen's sons studied at the University and are Cambridge graduates. Whilst the title sizar has remained in a limited way, linked to very specific bursary support, the role of the sizar as little more than a servant 'working his passage' to a degree finally ceased in 1902.[48]

Undergraduate gowns of 1862 are shown by Metcalfe as full-length, following Whittock and Hyde. The depiction of undergraduates of Trinity and Clare Colleges in the set of cards published in 1908/09 (with the Duke of Devonshire and Arthur James Mason pictured as Chancellor and Vice-Chancellor respectively) (see Fig. 22) show gowns reaching only to the knee.[49] At what date and why this shortening first took place I have annoyingly

48 Gibson, p. 33.
49 See Alex Kerr, 'Academic Dress on Picture Postcards Published by Davis's of Oxford,

Fig. 21. Undergraduates from *The Costumes of the Members of the University of Cambridge*, by H. Hyde, *c*. 1850.

Fellow Com^{er}.   Pensioner
TRINITY COLLEGE.

Fellow Commoner
TRINITY COLLEGE

Pensioner   Fellow Com^{er}.
MAGDALEN COLLEGE.

Fellow Com^{er}.   Pensioner
QUEENS COLLEGE & PETERHOUSE.

Pensioners   Fellow Com^{er}.
JESUS COLLEGE.

Fellow Com^{er}.   Pensioner
CORPUS CHRISTI COLLEGE.

Fellow Com^{er}.   Pensioner
CLARE HALL.

Dress Gown.   NOBLEMEN   Undress Gown.

87

Fig. 22. Under-graduates of Clare and Trinity Colleges from set of cards published by Davis's of Oxford, 1908/09.

not been able to establish completely beyond doubt with the University Registry. The regulations regarding the dress of graduates were adopted by Grace of the Senate on 13 June 1889. It seems possible therefore that the simple regulation, 'Undergraduate gowns shall reach to the knees', was first formally adopted then also, certainly fitting the timeframe between 1862 and *c.* 1900, albeit not appearing in the regulations up to 1911 as noted earlier.

The photograph in Figure 23 taken, judging by the attire, at the turn of the previous century, clearly also shows undergraduates in gowns only to the knee. Interestingly too all of these undergraduates are either wearing or carrying squares, today never seen except at graduation ceremonies.

In 1931 a subcommittee was established by the University authorities to examine academic dress and its use. A. G. Almond, a leading tailor and robemaker in the town, wrote to the subcommittee in response to their initial report of 3 August 1931 that 'the undergraduate gowns of different colleges should be kept distinct ... and their due use should be insisted upon by University and College authorities'.[50] Furthermore, Prof. E. H. Minns, Master of Magdalene College, wrote, 'The committee suggests that in certain colleges where the undergraduate gown has little to distinguish it from those of other colleges the present enquiry offers an opportunity for the adoption of new differences in design'.[51] The final report adopted these proposals, encouraging colleges to adopt uniquely distinctive gowns. Very little would appear to have come of this. The *Cambridge University Reporter* of 17 May 1932 simply states that undergraduate gowns should be of the form prescribed by the

their Rivals and Successors', *TBS*, 18 (2018), pp. 75–106 (pp. 86–87), https://doi.org/10.4148/2475-7799.1157.

50 Letter to the sub-committee from A. G. Almond, 7 August 1931, held in the archives in the University Library.

51 Letter to the sub-committee by Prof. E. H. Minns, Master of Magdalene College, 14 October 1931, held in the archives of the University Library.

Fig. 23. A group of undergraduates, *c.* 1900.

several colleges and that the gown should reach to the knees. The *Cambridge University Reporter* of 6 February 1934 restates that undergraduate gowns should 'reach to the knees'. No more than that.

Women were not formally members of the University until 1947, although they had attended lectures and supervisions and sat examinations prior to that. At a roll dinner in Girton College on 3 July 1948 Dr Helen Cam in a speech reminded the ladies present that 'Miss Wodehouse [Mistress of Girton 1931–42] led us in the tentative, but I think profitable practice of exercising our hitherto unused privilege of wearing academic dress when engaged in academic work; a practice which became general in the conduct of examinations during the war.'[52] This implies therefore that some time before 1947 the governing body of Girton College had arrived at a suitable gown for the female undergraduates, but nothing has been found in the College records of meetings.

By contrast, the Newnham College Governing Body record in 1947 that 'a specimen was exhibited of the type of gown suggested for women students. This differed from the type worn by men students in that the slits in the sleeves had been sewn up to prevent the exhibition of bare arms by students wearing short-sleeved dresses'.[53] So, whilst the slits in the sleeves of their gowns were indeed sewn up, the lower twelve inches for Girton and four inches for Newnham of the seam respectively were left open. Girton ladies could therefore reveal eight inches more of forearm than their Newnham counterparts!

Today, most undergraduates will not even possess a square and will wear one for the first time at graduation, and often not even then. Why and when did this important part of undergraduate academic dress cease to be seen? The carrying of a square by undergraduates was dispensed with in April 1943, supposedly because of wartime shortages.

---

52 *The Girton Review*, Michaelmas Term 1948.
53 Newnham College, Governing Body meeting minutes, 28 November 1947.

In November 1947, the Senior Proctor wrote to the Registrary that 'wearing of the square was originally a privilege granted to the undergraduate body at its own petition in the 18th century [see above]. This privilege has by custom become a requirement. Police and proctors are in favour of the square being worn, and not simply carried, to aid undergraduate recognition.' However, this was never again insisted upon and following the Second World War they were made compulsory, but only for graduation ceremonies in the Senate House. In 1953 even this was deemed to be optional. That said, no other form of head covering is permitted when wearing a gown.[54]

Another example of how the use of undergraduate dress changed rapidly in the twentieth century, reflecting the change in respect for tradition and the old order in post-war society generally, was the wearing of gowns after dusk in the town. In July 1962 the Proctors and all but five colleges had ruled that wearing of gowns after dusk should continue. However, by November 1963, a proctorial syndicate resolved that after dusk wearing of gowns was no longer necessary[55] and this was ratified overwhelmingly by Heads of Houses in 1964.[56]

After the Second World War, there was pressure to increase student numbers at Cambridge and in particular to make greater provision for postgraduate study and for mature students, often with families. This led to the founding of seven completely new colleges and the incorporating of three other learning institutions.

The three new colleges whose members included undergraduates, graduates and fellows were New Hall (subsequently re-named Murray Edwards) for women only, in 1954, Churchill College in 1960 and Robinson College in 1977. There appear to be no records of how the colleges determined what undergraduate dress should be and indeed checking with foundation fellows of Robinson still today on the fellowship they have no recollection that the matter was ever discussed. Perhaps therefore unsurprisingly, Churchill and Robinson, by default, have adopted the basic (Peterhouse) gown and New Hall, being a women's only college, adopted the Newnham version of the women's gown.

The mid-1960s saw the founding of four graduate only colleges, Darwin (1964), Lucy Cavendish (1965), Wolfson (1965) and Clare Hall (1966). In addition, Hughes Hall, St Edmund's House (now College) and Homerton College became full colleges of the University. Once again there appears to be no written record of how their gowns for undergraduates came to be selected. Perhaps, by default, because Homerton was training women teachers (although now with male and female members, as is Girton) the gown used is the Newnham model, with no split in the sleeve and the bottom four inches of the seam left open.

I am disappointed not to have discovered the origin of the undergraduate gown used by all of the other new colleges as they all use an identical design. Strictly Darwin and Clare Hall being graduate colleges only do not require academic dress for undergraduates as their students, if not Cambridge graduates, are all entitled to a BA gown or, if aged 24 or over, an MA gown, in both cases without strings. The design is the basic gown but with a gathered, unslit sleeve, held in place by a blue cord and blue button. It is described as

54 Cambridge University Heraldic and Genealogical Society, 'The Square Cap', at <cuhags.soc .srcf.net/gowns/squares.html> [retrieved 10 June 2021]; Wikipedia, 'Academic Dress of the University of Cambridge', at <en.wikipedia.org/wiki/Academic_dress_of_the_University_of_Cambridge> [retrieved 10 June 2021].

55 Proctorial syndicate resolution, 11 November 1963.

56 Heads of Houses vote, 27 November 1964.

'the undergraduate gown for the graduate colleges',[57] which, in truth, is what it is! It would seem to bear a remarkable similarity to the gowns worn in earlier days by the Westminster Scholars at Trinity College, as described earlier, albeit with violet rather than blue button and cord, but this is probably simply a coincidence.

The future

The transition over hundreds of years from undergraduate academic dress design as an indicator of wealth and position to one which in some but by no means all cases, can indicate your college is now complete. Gone are the noblemen's gowns. Colleges of modern foundation have no fellow-commoners and at the older colleges the award of a fellow-commonership is an honorary title similar to but junior to honorary fellowships. Most fellow-commoners will wear an MA gown, but a few have a special gown with echoes of their nineteenth-century predecessors.[58]

Should there in the future be further foundations of new graduate only or undergraduate/graduate colleges, given the recent apparent apathy of founding fellows in the matter of specifying a distinguishing undergraduate academic gown, it is likely that any such new colleges would adopt one of only two styles, namely the basic (Peterhouse) design, as did Churchill and Robinson Colleges, or the 'undergraduate in graduate colleges' design. It is hardly conceivable that any further women's only colleges will be founded, so the 'women's gown' will not proliferate.

For so long as the wearing of undergraduate gowns is specified by the University when receiving a BA degree (or four-year taught master's equivalent) their future is probably safeguarded. Even on that most formal of occasions a square is not mandatory, although many graduands wear or carry one for the first time in their Cambridge lives! However, there has been a gradual reduction in the requirement to wear gowns since the middle of the twentieth century (no longer required to be worn: 'after dusk' in town, for lectures or examinations, very few anyway attend college chapel services, self-service college meals and even not being required for 'formal hall'). So, it would seem, that undergraduate dress at the University of Cambridge could, after eight hundred, years, become an endangered species.

---

57 Hughes Hall, 'What You Need to Wear' <www.hughes.cam.ac.uk/student-centre/academic/graduation/what-you-need-to-wear/> [retrieved 10 June 2021].

58 Shaw, pp. 27–29; Tsua, p. 118.

Appendix
Historic ledgers at Ede & Ravenscroft—robemakers

I am indebted to Gemma Field, the Archivist and Record Collections Manager, at Ede & Ravenscroft for nine images of extracts from their ledgers, giving descriptions of the construction of the following gowns:

- nobleman's gown (two separate entries)
- fellow-commoner's gown (four separate entries)
- undergraduate's gown
- sizer's [*sic*] gown (two separate entries)

Where there are duplicate entries for a particular type of gown there are minor differences between how they are described (e.g. number of loops, buttons, length of lace etc.). For ease of reading, here below are one of the entries for a nobleman's gown and one for a fellow-commoner's gown (Figures 24 and 25 show how the actual ledger entries appear). These are followed by the entry for an undergraduate's gown (clearly for a pensioner of Trinity College) and one of the entries for a sizer's gown.

A Noblemans Gown for Cambridge
Is made either of Scarlet, Purple, Crimson, or Skye Blue rich flowered Damask, the body and Sleeves cut the same as Kings Council's Gown with a Back Slit. Trimmed as Pattern, a rich Gold lace all round the Bottom. The common Gown is made of rich Armazeen Silk and Oxford Crape the body and Sleeves cut and made the same as a Clergyman's Gown only the sleeves shorter there is a Pattern to cut the sleeves by ———
   Refer to Lord Powis's account.
   The Noblemans cushion is of crimson Velvet a yard long and the Width of the Velvet the under part of the cushion is of crimson Silk a rich broad Gold Lace to cover the seams the same lace that Goes on the Robe.[59]———

Fellow Commoners Gown
of fine Princes Stuff faced down the front with Blk Velvet, and Velvet Cape, the back cut as pattern and trimd in the fullest manner, on the top of each sleeve 2 Dozn black and gold loops, 1 Dozn black & gold buttons, 1 Dozn of the loops are made with holes in, 1 Dozn long loops & buttons at the bottom of the sleeve, 10 long loops & buttons behind, no back slit, 7 long loops & buttons on each side seam, the sleeve to be trimd as pattern. Black Velvet Cap with Gold Tassel
   4 Dozn small loops 2 Dozn of them made with holes to button.
   4 Dozn long
   6——— buttons
   6½ Yds lace

---

59 This matching cushion is the ultimate academic dress fashion accessory! I am indebted to Timothy Milner, Ceremonial Officer of the University of Cambridge, for his suggestion, having also consulted a learned colleague of his, that it was perhaps for sitting on in Chapel or at Great St Mary's for University Sermons. A sort of place-marker perhaps!

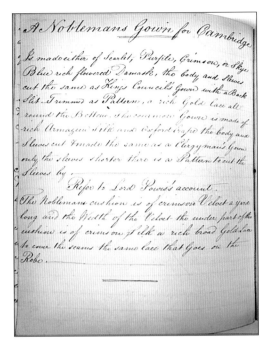

Fig. 24. Specification for a nobleman's gown for Cambridge. Extract from an undated document in Ede & Ravenscroft's archive.

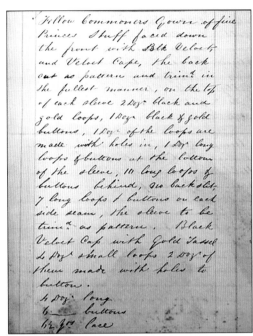

Fig. 25. Specification for a fellow-commoner's gown for Cambridge. Extract from an undated document in Ede & Ravenscroft's archive.

Under Graduate's Gown. Blue Camlet faced with Black, cut as B.A. hem of Sleeve faced with   Black Stuff 3 inches wide   3 Gnas

Sizer's Gown, Princes Stuff with Facings ½ a quarter wide, Cape the same as [no] sleeves, Cloth Cap

Unfortunately, Gemma Field was unable to date these entries for me. However, the descriptions of two of the four fellow-commoners gowns add the phrase 'which is worn at any of the Colleges of Cambridge except Emanuel [*sic*] and Trinity Colleges', which therefore dates them prior to the 1830s. There is an adjacent reference in the ledger to what peers (not noblemen undergraduates) were wearing at the funeral of George II, so would date that entry after 1760. Furthermore, the reference to Lord Powis seems likely to refer to the 1st Earl of Powis, who as Baron Clive, son of Clive of India, was elevated to an earldom in 1804. We can presume that he would have ordered a gown for his son and heir, who was a nobleman at St John's College, 1803–06, and so the entry for a similar gown for another customer would have been soon after that.

In summary there would appear to be material here for some further fruitful research.

Transactions of the Burgon Society, 20 (2020), pages 94–106

A Grave Decent Gown: The 1690 Glasgow Gown Order

By Neil K. Dickson

In the year 1690, in the midst of a turbulent period in its history, the University of Glasgow ordered gowns for two of its officers. I had been aware of that for some years[1] but was recently surprised to learn through social media[2] that the invoice for these gowns is in the University's archives.[3] The invoice (Fig. 1) enables us to examine the designs of the gowns in detail, to see how they influenced academic dress at the University right down to the present day, and to understand the political statement they made at the time, when newly appointed officers were seeking to exercise their authority in the context of a changed national political scene.

The Gown Order

On 11 December 1690 the Senate of the University of Glasgow 'Ordered that a grave decent gown be made for the Deans of faculty of this university to be kept peculiarly for them to be worn on solemn occasions, and the gown now worn by the Rector to have on it some marks of distinction becoming a magistrate.'[4]

The University had—and still has—a single post called variously over time the dean of faculty or dean of faculties. This order is therefore for an official gown for the exclusive use of the person holding the post of dean of faculty in 1690 and his successors. It also tells us that there already existed an official gown for the rector, which was to have embellishments added to it 'becoming' (appropriate for) a magistrate.[5] The rector was indeed a magistrate: he presided over the Rector's Court that dealt with disciplinary cases, and also at that date still claimed jurisdiction over criminal and civil cases involving members of the University to the exclusion of the local magistrates.[6]

---

1   I referred to it on p. 24 of Neil Dickson, 'Tradition and Humour: The Academic Dress of the University of Glasgow', *TBS*, 12 (2012), pp. 10–35, at <newprairiepress.org/burgonsociety> https://doi.org/10.4148/2475-7799.1097, where I cited as source Cosmo Innes (ed.), *Munimenta Alme Universitatis Glasguensis: Records of the University of Glasgow, from its Foundation till 1727*, 4 vols (Glasgow: Maitland Club, 1854), Vol. II, p. 350. Innes is available in electronic form from the National Library of Scotland <www.nls.uk> [retrieved 17 October 2020] and the original records to which it refers are in University of Glasgow Archives and Special Collections.

2   Tweet by Robert MacLean on 13 November 2019: <twitter.com/bob_maclean/status /1194700447245832200?s=20> [retrieved 17 October 2020].

3   GB248 GUA43599. (All reference numbers in this article beginning GB248 are for items in University of Glasgow Archives and Special Collections.)

4   Innes, Vol. II, p. 350.

5   For other evidence of the existence of a gown for the rector at that date and earlier see p. 52 of Jonathan C. Cooper, 'The Dress of Rectors at the Scottish Universities', *TBS*, 12 (2012), pp. 46–62, https://doi.org/10.4148/2475-7799.1099.

6   James Coutts, *A History of the University of Glasgow from its Foundation in 1451 to 1909* (Glasgow: James Maclehose & Sons, 1909) p. 13; J. D. Mackie, *The University of Glasgow 1451–1951* (Glasgow: Jackson, Son & Company, 1954) p. 205; Roger L. Emerson, *Academic Patronage in the*

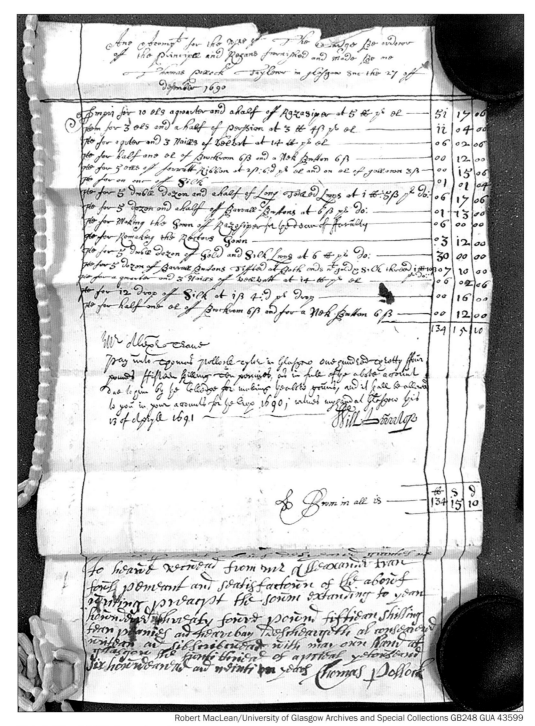

Robert MacLean/University of Glasgow Archives and Special Collections GB248 GUA 43599

Fig. 1. The 1690 gown invoice.

The order having been placed, work on the gowns proceeded quickly, and the invoice is dated 27 December 1690. Thomas Pollock the tailor was however kept waiting for payment. The invoice is endorsed with an instruction to pay by Principal William Dunlop dated 13 April 1691 and a receipt from Thomas Pollock dated 23 April 1691. The payment is also recorded in Principal Dunlop's accounts, where it is described as 'for making ane black goun for the Deans of Faculty and for charging the Rectors goun with gold buttons silke stuffe and other furnishing'.[7]

The designs of the gowns

A transcription and analysis of the invoice are in Appendix A and Appendix B at the end of this article. From these it is clear that the gowns had matching designs with velvet collars, the main difference between them being that the ornamentation on the rector's gown was mostly gold (appropriate for a magistrate) while the ornamentation on the dean of faculty's gown was entirely black silk.[8] The neck buttons suggest that both gowns were intended to be worn closed, that is fastened at the neck. The quantity of ornamentation is surprising: the rector's gown has five dozen (sixty) ornaments which I shall call frogs, consisting of a barrel-shaped button with loops either side of it, and twelve drops, while the Dean's gown has sixty-six frogs.

The University of Glasgow's portrait of John Orr of Barrowfield, who was elected rector in 1731, is of assistance (Fig. 2).[9] The gown he is wearing could be the gown made in 1690. It certainly fits the description. We can see the velvet collar. We cannot see if there is a neck button because it would be beneath his scarf, nor can we see if there are any drops, the problem being that the invoice implies they were black which could make them difficult to see on a black gown. We can, however, clearly see large numbers of gold frogs—seventeen on the right sleeve alone. Indeed, given the configuration of them on the front of his gown, there could easily be more than sixty in total.

The influence of the gowns

The 1690 gowns have influenced academic dress at the University of Glasgow right down to the present day.

The current rector's gown is a direct descendent of the 1690 rector's gown. Over time the gold frogs have become larger in size and fewer in number. They have also changed shape and materials. A sketch of *c.* 1840 shows the rector's gown as having twenty-eight frogs (seven on the left and right fronts of the gown and on each sleeve) and instead of barrel-shaped buttons with gold loops the frogs appear to be strips of gold braid with tassels.[10] A sketch of 1868 (Fig. 3) shows the frogs as gold rectangular panels with tassels.[11] The gold

Scottish Enlightenment: Glasgow, Edinburgh and St Andrews Universities (Edinburgh: Edinburgh University Press, 2008) p. 22.

7   Innes, Vol. III, p. 582; GB248 GUA26749.

8   See Cooper, pp. 48–49 for a discussion of the ornamentation considered appropriate for a magistrate.

9   This is the portrait referred to in Cooper, p. 52.

10   University of Glasgow, Special Collections, MS Murray 593, which is reproduced in Cooper, p. 47.

11   Fig. 3 is a sketch by an unknown artist of the Prince of Wales receiving an honorary degree on 8 October 1868 reproduced in David Murray, *Memories of the Old College of Glasgow* (Glasgow:

Historic Environment Scotland (SCRAN image 000-000-145-808-R)

Fig. 2. John Orr of Barrowfield (Rector) 1732.

Artist unknown

Fig. 3. The Prince of Wales Receiving an Honorary Degree 1868.

rectangular panels evolved into the current fairly plain design by 1899.[12] The 1868 sketch and 1899 photograph also show that the velvet collar had greatly increased in size and prominence, and had acquired a gold fringe, but *c.* 1908 the collar was replaced by the current design, which is a square flap collar. It is made of the same material as the body of the gown, edged in gold, and matches the design of the collar on the vice-chancellor's gown.[13]

The current gown of the dean of faculties (as the post is now styled) is a direct descendent of the 1690 gown of the dean of faculty. In examining the changes over the years it is

Jackson, Wylie & Co, 1927), opposite p. 594. The rector is fourth from the left.

12 Photograph of Lord Rosebery and Robert Story <www.universitystory.gla.ac.uk/images /UGSP00385.jpg> [retrieved 17 October 2020].

13 Dickson, 'Tradition and Humour', p. 24.

also necessary to consider the gowns worn by the principal and professors in the eighteenth and nineteenth centuries, which were of the same general design, and which I discussed in a previous article.[14] This raises a question. Was the design of the 1690 dean of faculty's gown influenced by the gowns that the principal and professors were wearing at that date, or was it the other way round with the designs of the principal's and professors' gowns developing from the 1690 dean of faculty's gown? The problem is that no detailed evidence has yet come to light as to what gowns the regents, professors and principal were wearing around 1690, other than that they appear to have been black.[15]

Portraits, engravings and photographs do, however, show how the designs of the gowns of the dean of faculty, principal and professors developed. As with the rector's gown, the frogs became larger in size, fewer in number and changed shape and materials. A series of photographs taken in 1870 shows considerable variation in the number of frogs on the principal's and professors' gowns, from none at all to approximately forty in the case of Principal Barclay's gown, which is far short of the sixty-six on the 1690 dean of faculty's gown.[16] As Principal Barclay's gown is densely covered by the frogs this gives some indication of the increase in their size.

The velvet collar on the gowns of the dean of faculty, principal and professors was quite small and neat in the middle of the eighteenth century but by 1870 had greatly increased in size and prominence. From 1868 onwards the professors gradually abandoned their traditional gowns and wore instead graduate gowns and hoods. A new style of gown was created for the principal *c.* 1900. However, the dean of faculties, as he had become, continued to wear his traditional gown and still does so today, complete with frogs and large velvet collar.[17]

Figure 4 shows the dean of faculties in 1891.[18] Close examination of it shows that the frogs on the front and sleeves of the gown have an unusual spacing. Instead of being evenly spaced, they are in pairs: two very close together then a large gap before the next pair. The current gown also has that feature. Perhaps that spacing was intended as a way of distinguishing the dean of faculty from the principal and professors whose frogs seem always to have been evenly spaced—but no evidence has yet been uncovered to prove or disprove that.

All the available illustrations of rectors, deans of faculty and professors from the eighteenth century onwards show them wearing their gowns open at the front as is standard practice in Britain today. This suggests that the neck buttons fitted to the 1690 gowns were a feature that was quickly discontinued. It also seems likely that the drops on the 1690 rector's gown were omitted from later versions of the gown as the frogs increased in size.

14 Dickson, 'Tradition and Humour', p. 12.

15 Response of the University to the parliamentary Commission in 1695: Innes, Vol. II, p. 517.

16 Dickson, 'Tradition and Humour' contains a selection of the photographs; the count of the frogs on Principal Barclay's gown was made using the official photograph of the Senate leaving the Old College in 1870 reproduced in Coutts opposite p. 432; these photographs are also accessible at <universitystory.gla.ac.uk> [retrieved 17 October 2020].

17 Dickson, 'Tradition and Humour', pp. 24, 25. The statement there that 'there is no evidence of a special design being created' for the dean of faculty has been overtaken by the discovery of the 1690 gown invoice.

18 This is an image of a photograph in William Stewart (ed.), *University of Glasgow Old and New* (Glasgow: T. & R. Allan & Sons and James Maclehose & Sons, 1891) supplied by University of Glasgow Archives and Special Collections (GB248 fUh.12).

The political context of the gowns

1690 was a time of political and religious turmoil. In 1688 the unpopular King James VII of Scotland and II of England, who was a Roman Catholic, fled to France. The English parliament, and then the Scottish parliament, declared that King James had abdicated and invited William of Orange and his wife Mary (daughter of King James), who were both Protestants, to become joint sovereigns of England and Scotland. Both parliaments moved quickly to entrench their own supremacy, the Protestant religion and a requirement that future kings and queens must be Protestant. In Scotland there was a further issue regarding the governance of the church. Since the Scottish Reformation in 1560 there had been considerable strife over whether the reformed Church of Scotland should be Episcopalian (governed by a hierarchy of bishops and archbishops) or Presbyterian (governed by assemblies of ministers all of whom had equal status).[19] In 1690 the Scottish parliament abolished the Episcopalian structure then in place and entrenched Presbyterianism.

In 1690 the Scottish parliament also appointed a Commission which held office for more than five years. The Commission's principal function was to inspect all schools, colleges and universities and ensure that all teachers and teaching conformed to current political and religious thinking.[20] University staff were required to take an oath of allegiance to King William, not just as actual ruler but also as rightful ruler, and to subscribe to the Westminster Confession of Faith, which is a declaration of belief in Protestant Presbyterianism.[21]

University of Glasgow Archives and Special Collections GB248 fUh.12

Fig. 4. Robert Berry (Dean of Faculties) 1891.

---

19 This simplified description of the differences between Episcopacy and Presbyterianism greatly understates the deep and complex differences that affected the whole relationship between king, parliament, the church, its clergy, its members and local landowners.

20 The Commission also issued instructions regarding academic dress: see Dickson, 'Tradition and Humour', p. 12, and Jonathan C. Cooper, 'The Scarlet Gown: History and Development of Scottish Academic Dress, *TBS*, 10 (2010) pp. 8–42 (p. 14), https://doi.org/10.4148/2475-7799.1082.

21 Coutts, pp. 163–68, explains these developments in the context of the University of Glasgow.

At the University of Glasgow this led to what has been described as the *Purge of 1690*, but was in fact a much more orderly and civil handover than that name implies.[22]

In 1690 the University of Glasgow was run as a university with one college. The College was governed by the seven academic staff comprising the principal (James Fall), four regents (William Blair, John Boyd, George Sinclair and John Tran), each of whom took a group of students through the entire Arts curriculum, one professor (James Wemyss) who taught his specialist subject and one person (Thomas Gordon) who was both a regent and a professor.[23] The University was run by the seven academic staff plus the chancellor, rector and dean of faculty. This structure caused these three officers to act in effect as external supervisors of the College. Before the Reformation and during Episcopalian government of the church after the Reformation, the archbishop of Glasgow was *ex officio* chancellor of the University. The rector and dean of faculty were elected positions, with elections being held annually—and with the re-election of the existing occupant of a post being permitted and frequently occurring.

By early 1690 the University was taking steps to adapt to the new order. George Sinclair, who had previously been forced to resign as a regent in 1666 because of his political and religious views,[24] had already been reappointed. Thomas Gordon, who was a Jacobite,[25] resigned. However, the most significant development was what happened at the annual election of the rector, which was delayed by a month from 1 March to 1 April 1690. Recent rectors had generally been Episcopalian clergymen.[26] The new rector was a layman, David Boyle of Kelburn, who was a prominent politician and became the first Earl of Glasgow in 1703.[27] His appointment started a trend: he was the first of a long line of public figures who were elected as rector.[28] The post of chancellor was vacant because the conversion of the church from Episcopalian to Presbyterian government had abolished the post of archbishop of Glasgow. (A new chancellor was not appointed until 1692 when John Carmichael, second Baron Carmichael and later first Earl of Hyndford, was appointed. He was a member of the parliamentary Commission, and chaired the visit of the Commission to the University mentioned below.)[29] The annual election for the dean of faculty, normally held in June or July was postponed, and the post treated as if it was vacant. (The outgoing dean of faculty was an Episcopalian clergyman.) When the election was held on 11 December 1690 the new dean of faculty was Patrick Simpson, a Presbyterian minister with strong political links.[30]

The parliamentary Commission visited the University in August 1690. The members of the Commission explained the requirements regarding the new oaths and the Westminster Confession of Faith and instructed the academic staff to appear before them in

22 Emerson, pp. 26–34.

23 In 1690 the University's teaching arrangements were in transition from the regent system that dated back to its foundation to the professorial system that is currently in use.

24 Innes, Vol. II, pp. 336, 337; GB248 GUA26626, GB248 GUA32002.

25 The term Jacobite is used for a supporter of King James VII and II and his Roman Catholic descendants.

26 Innes, Vol. III, pp. 324–28.

27 Emerson, p. 29.

28 For a complete list of Rectors see <universitystory.gla.ac.uk>.

29 Emerson, pp. 28–29.

30 Emerson, p. 33; Innes, Vol. III, pp. 357, 358.

Edinburgh in September 1690. At that meeting in Edinburgh, Principal Fall explained his unwillingness to take the new oaths and was deposed. He was, however, publicly thanked by the Commission for his work and the University paid him six months' salary in compensation for the loss of his post.[31] One of the regents (William Blair) and the professor (James Wemyss) also declined to take the new oaths and were deposed. William Blair received six months' salary in compensation.[32] The three other regents (John Boyd, George Sinclair and John Tran) took the new oaths and were confirmed in post.[33]

At this point Thomas Gordon asked for compensation, claiming that although he had resigned as regent he had not resigned as professor. He sought payment of 600 merks a year for three and a half years. After some negotiation, he submitted a further resignation letter and received 1,000 merks.[34]

A new principal (William Dunlop) was speedily appointed and inducted into office on 11 December 1690.[35] Steps were also taken to fill the other vacancies and to reduce the number of regents and increase the number of professors.[36]

In December 1690 the University of Glasgow therefore had new men in charge. It had a new rector, a new dean of faculty and a new principal, all with strong involvement with, or connections to, the new national political regime. The rector and the dean of faculty had very different backgrounds from their predecessors. Both of them would have been fully aware of their differences from their predecessors, their external supervisory role in relation to the college, all the upheavals that had taken place, and the expectations of the political regime. I suggest that in these circumstances both of them would have been keen to establish their positions and exert their authority, and that the gowns ordered for them were designed to provide visual support for that. I suggest that it is no coincidence that the gowns were ordered on 11 December 1690, the very day on which the recently elected new rector was joined by the newly elected dean of faculty and the newly inducted principal.[37]

Summary and Unanswered Questions

The gowns purchased in 1690 for the rector and the dean of faculty made a political statement and have influenced academic dress at the University of Glasgow right down to the present day.

---

31 £880 13s. 4d. Scots: Innes, Vol. III, p. 595; GB248 GUA26630; converted to sterling in Coutts, p. 168. It was the custom of the University to pay six months' salary to any principal, professor or regent who resigned 'excepting the case of censure': Innes, Vol. II, p. 324. Therefore, the University in making the payment was generously treating him as if he had resigned in normal circumstances.

32 £660 Scots: Innes, Vol. III, p. 595; GB248 GUA26630. As explained in the previous footnote, this was treating him as if he had resigned in normal circumstances. One would expect James Wemyss to have been treated in the same way: Coutts, p. 168, states he was but Innes is silent.

33 Coutts, pp. 166–68.

34 A merk or mark was 13s.4d., that is two thirds of a Scots pound. Therefore 600 merks equals £400 Scots. Innes, Vol. II, p. 348, Vol. III, pp. 595, 596; GB248 GUA34786, GB248 GUA26630.

35 Principal Dunlop was regarded as a loyal supporter of the new national political regime: Emerson, p. 28.

36 For example, George Sinclair demitted office as regent to become the first professor of Mathematics in 1691: Coutts, p. 170; Innes, Vol. II, p.349; GB248 GUA31997.

37 The attendance list for the meeting of Senate that ordered the gowns was the rector, the principal, the dean of faculty and the three regents then in post (John Tran, John Boyd and George Sinclair), the six of them being listed in that order, which presumably reflects their view as to seniority: Innes, Vol. II, p. 350.

Principal Dunlop's accounts record other purchases of items for use in formal ceremonies around 1690. There are payments for a black velvet pileus (academic cap), and a gown for the bedellus,[38] but there appears to be something missing. One would have expected that, when the new chancellor was appointed in 1692, he would have been provided with a new gown to match the gowns of the rector and dean of faculty. Was he? What did it look like? Was this the point when the black gown with frogs and white fur facings (used by chancellors and vice-chancellors in the nineteenth century) was designed?[39] We do not (yet) know the answers.

Acknowledgements

This article could not have been written without the active assistance of Robert MacLean (Assistant Librarian, Archives and Special Collections, University of Glasgow) and Dr Susan North, FBS (Senior Curator, Fashion, Textiles and Furniture Department, Victoria and Albert Museum, London). Robert MacLean noticed the invoice in the Archives inventory, decided to publicise it on social media, photographed it, provided the transcription, assisted in identifying relevant Archives items and drew my attention to Emerson's book. Susan North's professional expertise enabled her to provide detailed analysis, interpretation and insight into the gowns. I am most grateful to both of them for their assistance and for permitting me to include their work on the invoice.

I am very grateful to Robert MacLean's colleagues in Archives and Special Collections, University of Glasgow who most efficiently provided me with images of relevant items in spite of all the restrictions imposed on them by the coronavirus pandemic.

I also thank Rev. Dr Graham Deans, FBS, for explaining to me the complex differences between Episcopalianism and Presbyterianism, and the University of Glasgow and Historic Environment Scotland for permission to include Figures 1, 2 and 4.

---

38 In 1693 and 1694 respectively: Innes, Vol. iii, pp. 584, 585; GB248 GUA26749.

39 Fig. 3 shows the vice-chancellor wearing such a gown in 1868. (He is the fourth from the right in that picture.) See Dickson 'Tradition and Humour' for photographs of a surviving gown of that design (p. 33), and for references to nineteenth-century photographs and a portrait of such gowns (footnote 90 on p. 25). These nineteenth-century photographs and portrait are also accessible at <https://universitystory.gla.ac.uk> [retrieved 17 October 2020].

Appendix A: Transcription of the Invoice[40]

This transcription retains the original spelling, which is inconsistent and often phonetic. Abbreviations have been extended in square brackets. Uncertain words with possible reading have been placed in square brackets with a question mark. For clarity, the items relating to the dean of faculty's gown, which come first, have been separated by a space from the later items that relate to the rector's gown.

	£	s	d
Impri[mis] for 10 els a qwarter and a half of Razasiper at 5 [pounds] p[e]r el –	51.17.06		
Item for 3 els and a half of perssian at 3 [pounds] 4 [shillings] p[e]r el –	11.04.00		
Ite[m] for a qrter and 3 nails of velvat at 14 [pounds] p[e]r el –	06.02.06		
Ite[m] for half ane el of Bwckram 6 [shillings] and a Nek Bwtton 6 [shillings]	00.12.00		
Ite[m] for 5 ells off forratt Ribbon at 2 [shillings] 6 [pence] p[e]r el and an el of gallown 3 [shillings]	00.15.06		
Ite[m] for on [ounce?] off Silk	01.01.04		
Ite[m] for 5 dwble dozon and a half of Long Tailled Lwps at 1 [pound] 5 [shillings] p[e]r do[zen]	06.17.06		
Ite[m] for 5 dozon and a half of Barrall Bwttons at 6 [shillings] p[e]r do[zen]	01.13.00		
Ite[m] for making the Gown off Razasiper	06.00.00		
Ite[m] for Remaking the Rectors Gown	03.12.00		
Ite[m] for 5 dwble dozon off Gold and Silk Lwps at 6 [pounds] p[e]r do[zen]	30.00.00		
Ite[m] for 5 dozon off Barrall Bwttons Tiffted at Both ends w[i]t[h] gold & silk threed 1 [pound] 10 [shillings] p[e]r do[zen]	07.10.00		
Ite[m] for a qwarter and 3 naills off vellvat at 14 [pounds] p[e]r el	06.02.06		
Ite[m] for 12 drop off Silk at 1 [shilling] 4 [pence] p[e]r drop	00.16.00		
[Ite]m for half ane el off Bwckrom 6 [shillings] and for a Nek Bwtton 6 [shillings]	00.12.00		
	134.15.10		

---

40 Courtesy of Robert MacLean.

Appendix B: Analysis of the Invoice[41]

Prices are believed to be in Scots pounds, shillings and pence. There was a fixed exchange rate: £12 Scots equalled £1 sterling. Scots pounds were divided into twenty (Scots) shillings which in turn were divided into twelve (Scots) pence, just like pounds sterling. The symbols £sd were used for both Scots and sterling pounds, shillings and pence.

A Scots *ell* was 37 inches (93.8 cm), a *quarter* was a quarter of a yard, that is 9 inches (22.7 cm) and a *nail* was a sixteenth of a yard, that is 2.25 inches (5.7 cm).

Materials

Barrel buttons Buttons shaped like a barrel (broader in the middle than at the ends).

Buckram Coarse linen or hemp, gummed and calendered,[42] used for stiffening. (This was probably used here to stiffen the yoke, collar and shoulder wings.)

Drop of silk A decorative element made of silk covering a wooden core.[43]

Forratt Probably ferret, which was a stout cotton tape or silk ribbon (the latter being more likely here).[44]

Gallown Galloon or woven lace, what we would now call braid, often wide with a decorative weave structure, sometimes with metal thread.[45]

Lwps Loops. The loops for the rector's gown are gold and silk; the long-tailed loops for the dean of faculty's gown were probably of braided silk. Dwble dozon is double dozen, that is a dozen pairs of loops or twenty-four loops. The quantities of loops and barrel buttons on both gowns suggest there was a loop on each side of each button, as does the statement that the barrel buttons on the rector's gown are tifted (tufted) at both ends with gold and silk thread.

---

41 Courtesy of Dr Susan North.

42 'Calendered' is the name given to a process for finishing the surface of a cloth by pressing it in a machine with rollers, using a combination of moisture, heat, and pressure.

43 Annabel Westman, *Fringe, Frog and Tassel: The Art of the Trimmings-Maker in Interior Decoration* (London: Philip Wilson Publishers, 2019), p. 241.

44 C. W. and P. Cunnington, *Handbook of English Costume in the Sixteenth Century* (London: Faber & Faber, 1954), p. 218. The word forratt or ferrett also occurs in another invoice by Thomas Pollock: GB248 GUA78181. That invoice, dated 1694, is addressed personally to Principal Dunlop and is for clothing for himself and his family. A transcription accompanying that invoice in the Archives interprets ferret as fur from the animal of the polecat family known as a ferret, which is now believed to be a misattribution.

45 Florence Montgomery, *Textiles in America 1650–1870: A Dictionary Based on Original Documents, Prints and Paintings, Commercial Records, American Merchants' Papers, Shopkeepers' Advertisements, and Pattern Books with Original Swatches of Cloth* (New York: W. W. Norton & Company, 1984), p. 245.

Neck button   Given its price, this was presumably a large decorative button to fasten the gown together at the top of the front of the gown just below the neck of the wearer.

Ounce of silk   Silk when measured by weight (one ounce equals twenty-eight grams) is usually silk thread for sewing.

Perssian   A thin plain silk, principally used for linings in coats, petticoats and gowns, originally from Persia but copied in Britain.[46] This was probably used here to line the sleeves and part-line the body of the gown—the yoke at the back and the front to below the arm holes.

Razasiper   Probably the French silk raz-de-St-Maur, often rendered in English as radzimir or rasdimore. This was a serge (twill-weave) fabric of silk, or silk and fleuret (fine wool), or a wool warp and silk weft, dyed black. It was well known in the eighteenth century and into the nineteenth; Queen Victoria wore it for mourning.[47] The 10 ells, quarter of an ell and half of a quarter of an ell of Razasiper give a length of about 384 inches or 9.75 metres. Silk was traditionally about 20 inches (51 cm) wide. Roughly seven widths would be needed to make the gown (one for each front, one for each sleeve and three for the back (gathered into the yoke). This makes each panel about 54 inches (137 cm) long. The back panels were likely shorter and the sleeves shorter still, leaving some extra for the collar, shoulder wings and yoke.

Velvet   A cut pile-weave silk.[48] This was probably used here to 'face' (cover the upper surface of) the collar.

The work on the rector's gown is described as 'remaking' the gown, and the list of materials consists only of embellishments (loops, buttons, velvet and drops) and buckram. This suggests that the tailor may have 'turned the gown', that is unpicked all the seams and turned the pieces inside out on the principle that the inside of the silk would be in better condition than the outside (a technique that only works for reversible fabrics). The gown would then be sewn back together with the fresh buckram, a velvet facing on the collar, and the addition of the loops, buttons and drops.

---

46 Montgomery, p. 321.
47 Montgomery, p. 330.
48 Montgomery, p. 270.

Transactions of the Burgon Society, 20 (2020), pages 107–142

Reaping the Whirlwind:
American Degree and Subject Colours (1962–Present)

By Kenneth L. Suit, Jr

> For they sow the wind,
>   and they shall reap the whirlwind.
> The standing grain has no heads;
>   it shall yield no flour;
> if it were to yield,
>   strangers would devour it.
>   Hosea 8.7 (ESV)

It was supposed to be so very simple.

A committee of representatives from several East Coast universities called the Intercollegiate Commission on Academic Costume standardized the American system of academic costume in 1895. The keystone of the cap and gown standards the Commissioners designed was the hood. In its shape, edging, and colours the American academic hood was to be

> a plain badge of the degree, be it Bachelor, Master or Doctor; of the department of learning, be it Arts, Philosophy Law, Theology or other; and of the institution granting the degree or with which the holder was then connected.[1]

This basic semiotic system of hood design became the most important part of the committee's Intercollegiate Code of Academic Costume, which included eight colours 'distinctive of the Faculty to which the degree pertains' that were used to encompass all of the degrees conferred at the universities that had sent representatives to serve on the committee.

These eight degree colours were conceived both specifically and broadly, so for instance the brown of Fine Arts would not only indicate the Bachelor and Master of Fine Arts degrees but also the Bachelor of Painting, Bachelor and Master of Architecture, and Bachelor and Master of Design degrees, among other degrees in the fine and applied arts. Likewise, the golden yellow of Science would indicate the Bachelor, Master, and Doctor of Science degrees but also the Doctor of Chemistry degree as well as the Bachelor and Master of Engineering degrees.

But almost immediately some universities began to request special colours to represent subsets of these broadly defined degree colour categories. Bachelor, Master, and Doctor of Engineering degrees, for instance, were later assigned orange; Bachelor, Master, and Doctor of Education degrees were separated from the Liberal Arts white and given light

---

1   Gardner Cotrell Leonard, *The Cap and Gown in America, to which is Added an Illustrated Sketch of the Intercollegiate System of Academic Costume* (Albany: Cotrell & Leonard, 1896), p. 11.

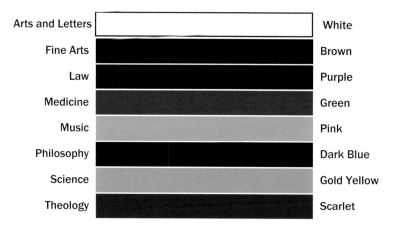

Arts and Letters	White
Fine Arts	Brown
Law	Purple
Medicine	Green
Music	Pink
Philosophy	Dark Blue
Science	Gold Yellow
Theology	Scarlet

Fig. 1. The original degree colours authorized by the 1895 Intercollegiate Code of Academic Costume.

blue; and Doctor of Dentistry and Doctor of Pharmacy degrees were respectively granted lilac and olive so as to be distinct from the green of the Doctor of Medicine degree.

The 1895 committee had left the authorization of new degree colours like these to the Intercollegiate Bureau of Academic Costume, a clearing-house for information about academic costume that was affiliated with the largest academic costume manufacturing company in the US, Cotrell & Leonard.[2] In 1903 the Regents of the University of the State of New York[3] appointed the IBAC to maintain a collection of records and documents about academic costume and to assign new colours to degrees authorized by that state. The Intercollegiate Bureau engaged in these tasks with great vigour, so by 1918 there were a total of twenty-two official degree colours the Bureau had authorized.[4]

The Intercollegiate Bureau of Academic Costume felt these new colours were justified because they represented graduate degrees being conferred by new 'faculties' (that is, schools or colleges within a university, rather than departments within a school or college)—and importantly, these degrees had titles that included the name of that faculty (Master of Public Health, Master of Education, Doctor of Pharmacy, etc.). Most of these new degrees were not traditional liberal arts or research degrees like the standard Master of Arts, Master of Science, or Doctor of Philosophy degrees, but were instead vocational graduate degrees with degree titles that identified the profession. The Intercollegiate Bureau could not have foreseen the problems this steady expansion in the number of professional programmes would bring to the Code, but even in 1911 critics were arguing that the 'multiplication of degrees has been carried to an extreme in this country accompanying in

---

2   The Cotrell & Leonard company was said to be the 'depository' for the Intercollegiate Bureau of Academic Costume.

3   The Regents of the University of the State of New York are the state-accrediting organization for all educational institutions in New York, including public and private primary and secondary schools as well as public and private colleges and universities.

4   For a more detailed history of early American degree colours, see Kenneth L. Suit, Jr, 'The Iridescent Web: American Degree Colours (1895–1935)', *TBS*, 15 (2015), pp. 41–74, at <new prairiepress.org/burgonsociety> https://doi.org/10.4148/2475-7799.1133.

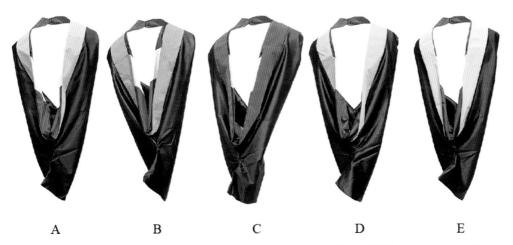

Nevada Wolf Shop: www.nevadawolfshop.com

Fig. 2. Time for a pop quiz. These hoods from the University of Nevada, Reno, are for Master's degrees in Agriculture (maize), Engineering (orange), Nursing (apricot), Science (golden yellow), and Social Work (citron). Which one is which?[5]

extent the opportunities for specialization in the different studies. [...] The increase in the number of degrees is of recent growth, dating perhaps from the middle of the last century'.[6]

Possibly as an expression of resistance to the proliferation of these 'boutique' degree titles, the Intercollegiate Bureau significantly slowed the pace of new degree colour authorizations after World War I, but even so, by the late 1950s the situation had got out of hand. By that point the IBAC was receiving an excessive number of requests for new degree colours and felt that the large number of official colours was already making the precise identification of the shades of existing colours difficult. Among the twenty-seven degree colours the Intercollegiate Bureau had authorized by 1958 were a half dozen or more that were difficult to distinguish from each other, and some of the degree colour categories the IBAC had created were rather obscure. The crimson of Humanics was easily confused with the scarlet of Theology, for example, but one would be lucky to find a college or university that conferred a bachelor's, master's, or doctor's degree in Humanics ... or anyone who knew what that degree was!

With the Intercollegiate Bureau's help, an association of college and university presidents called the American Council on Education had already updated the 1895 Intercollegiate Code between 1932 and 1935 without making significant changes to the list of twenty-two IBAC degree colours, so to address some of the colour problems the Intercollegiate Bureau of Academic Costume was encountering in the late 1950s, this 1935 Academic Costume Code was revised again between 1959 and 1960, with a few additional 'subject colors' added at that time and in 1961. For American degree colours, this mid-century revision was nothing short of disastrous.[7]

---

5 Answers: A = Social Work (citron); B = Nursing (apricot); C = Engineering (orange); D = Science (golden yellow); E = Agriculture (maize).

6 'Degrees', *A Cyclopedia of Education*, ed. Paul Monroe (New York: Macmillan, 1911), pp. 285–86.

7 For a more detailed history of this revision, see Kenneth L. Suit, Jr, 'Conforming to the Es-

'Degree colors' become 'subject colors'

The Intercollegiate Bureau of Academic Costume and the American Council on Education revised the 1935 Academic Costume Code in the late 1950s because there had been a sharp increase in the number of degree titles American colleges and universities were using after World War II. Since the degree title determined the degree colour used on the hood, and because the eight broad degree colour categories in the 1895 Code had been extensively subdivided during the sixty years thereafter, the Intercollegiate Bureau had run out of distinctive shades of colours to assign to these new degrees.

American colleges and universities were using a greater variety of degree titles because professional degrees were becoming more popular with students—many of whom were veterans of World War II attending college under the GI Bill. The way American institutions distinguished between a traditional liberal arts (or research) degree in a particular subject and a new professional (or technical) degree in the same subject was to have separate degree titles for each pedagogical approach. For instance, as part of a traditional liberal arts education, an agriculture programme might require coursework in history, literature, philosophy, and so on. Or, as part of a technical education, an agriculture programme might primarily require vocational training and coursework in the profession and science of agriculture, with very few (if any) courses in the liberal arts. Both programmes would confer a degree in agriculture, but to reflect the different pedagogical approaches to the subject, colleges and universities assigned a different degree title to each. The Master of Science degree with a major in agriculture would be a traditional liberal arts degree, whereas the Master of Agriculture degree would be a professional or technical degree. Thus the wording on a student's diploma would indicate which pedagogical approach the student had taken, either liberal arts or professional.

Because it used a semiotic 'code of signals'[8] by which the degree title determined the degree colour used on the hood, the 1895 Intercollegiate Code of Academic Costume was able to visually distinguish between these liberal arts and professional degrees: the Master of Science degree in agriculture would use a hood edged golden yellow (for Science) and the Master of Agriculture degree would use a hood edged maize (for Agriculture). This was the foremost reason the Intercollegiate Bureau had subdivided many of the original eight degree colours from 1895: the Bureau needed to distinguish between the degree titles of traditional liberal arts degrees and these new professional degrees.

But to better define a liberal arts degree's major (the primary subject of one's coursework), in the 1930s some colleges and universities began to 'tag' some of their Bachelor or Master of Science degrees (and to a lesser extent, their Bachelor or Master of Arts degrees) with the pedagogical focus of the degree. So the 'Master of Science' degree in agriculture mentioned above might be relabelled a 'Master of Science in Agriculture' degree, the tagged degree thus displaying on the student's diploma the faculty of the degree (Science) and subject area (Agriculture). By the late 1950s tagged degrees had become epidemic. So an important question for the Intercollegiate Bureau and the American Council on Education became: which part of the tagged degree title would determine the degree colour: the faculty or the tagged subject?

tablished Standards: American Degree Colours (1936–1961)', *TBS*, 17 (2017), pp. 39–75, https://doi.org/10.4148/2475-7799.1144.

8   'Albany Bureau of Academic Costume: Caps, Gowns and Regalia for American Colleges Originate Here', *The* [Albany, N.Y.] *Argus*, 27 July 1902.

The root of this problem lies in the nomenclature of American degree titles. By the end of the nineteenth century, American colleges and universities had begun to standardize the degree titles for liberal arts degrees as degrees in Arts, Science, or Philosophy. There was quite a bit of overlap in the curricular requirements for these degrees, which is why the BA, BS, MA, MS, and PhD degrees were conferred by departments that were becoming consolidated (at larger institutions) into schools or colleges of Arts and Sciences (traditionally called Philosophy and Natural Philosophy).[9] But what did these degree titles mean? Was a Bachelor of Science degree a bachelor's degree in science? Not necessarily. In American nomenclature, a Bachelor of Science degree was (in most cases) becoming a liberal arts degree without a foreign language requirement, or a liberal arts degree with a few more required courses in general science. But the BS degree could be conferred in a non-science discipline, like history, literature, or theology.

In 1906, a grumpy professor wrote:

> It is, indeed, practically impossible that a degree should indicate exactly the scholastic attainment or training of its holder. But there was a time, not so long ago, when there was an idea in America that the degree ought to designate very exactly the nature of the academic training of the holder. Hence the degree Ph.B. was given to men who had not studied Greek and other degrees were invented for other special needs. But few people know what was the outcome in fact, as also in logic. In Emerson's College Year Book of ten years ago is a list of degrees given by American Colleges [with] over two hundred different degrees. Most of them are such as people in general have never heard of: M.P.L. means Master or Mistress of Polite Literature, M.B.Sc. means Master of Business Science, D.O. means Doctor of Oratory. No one could remember what such things indicate. The effect is just the same as with the university hoods used to indicate the [wearers'] degrees. There is no one, except the agent of the furnishing shop who can tell what they mean. At any great university occasion, a part of the fun consists in asking, What is that green and white hood with the orange border? The variety of hoods and colors certainly makes an attractive sight, but it conveys no information. Nor does the variety of college degrees. And if we reduce the variety to unity, the case is not bettered. The degree does not and cannot be made to serve as a true indication of the academic training of its holder.[10]

Tagged degrees were invented as a way to address this problem. A tagged degree clearly stated the area of academic concentration (or major) of the person possessing it.

Fine. But so that the visual distinction between liberal arts and professional degrees would be maintained, the Intercollegiate Bureau of Academic Costume said that the primary degree title determined the degree colour, not the tagged subject of the degree or the major. To clarify this matter, a late 1920s booklet from the IBAC said that the velvet trim should be in the 'proper width to indicate the degree and of a color signifying the department to which the degree pertains', helpfully providing customers with an example of the system in practice:

> It is important to note that the reading of the degree, and not the department in which major work was done, governs the color proper for the velvet of the hood. Thus a degree conferred as 'Bachelor of Science in Engineering' requires the gold yellow of Science and not the orange of Engineering.[11]

---

9   By the early twentieth century the PhB and PhM were a dying breed of degree, as was the DSci degree.

10   Edward E. Hale, Jr, 'The Abolition of Academic Degrees', *The Bookman*, 23 (5) (July 1906), p. 563.

11   John Erwin, *The History of Academic Costume in America* (Albany, N.Y.: Cotrell & Leonard

An IBAC catalogue from 1948 said nearly the same thing: in selecting the velvet degree colour trim for a hood, the Bureau privileged the degree faculty over the degree subject or major.[12] Thus a Master of Science in agriculture and a Master of Science in Agriculture—both liberal arts degrees—would use hoods edged in golden yellow (for Science). But a Master of Agriculture degree—a professional degree—would use a hood edged with maize (for Agriculture).

The American Council on Education was less sure. In their 1935 Academic Costume Code (an update of the 1895 Intercollegiate Code of Academic Costume which was written with the help of the Intercollegiate Bureau of Academic Costume), the ACE said that the coloured edging of the hood and the trim on the doctoral gown

> should be distinctive of the Faculty or subject to which the degree pertains, as indicated by the wording of the diploma[13]

which meant the Master of Science degree would use golden yellow to indicate the faculty (Science), but the Master of Science in Agriculture degree could ignore the faculty (Science) and use maize to indicate the subject (Agriculture) if desired. Under the 1935 Academic Costume Code, then, the visual distinction between a liberal arts degree in agriculture and a professional degree in agriculture began to be defaced. This problem can be illustrated thus:

Type of degree	Degree title	Degree or Subject colour	
		IBAC (1895)	ACE (1935)
Liberal arts degree	'Master of Science' in agriculture	golden yellow	golden yellow
Liberal arts degree	'Master of Science in Agriculture'	golden yellow	golden yellow or maize
Professional degree	'Master of Agriculture'	maize	maize

When the 1935 Academic Costume Code was revised between 1959 and 1960—again with the help of the Intercollegiate Bureau of Academic Costume—the American Council on Education rewrote the description above to state that the coloured velvet of the hood edging

> should be distinctive of the subject to which the degree pertains. For example the trimming for the degree of Master of Science in Agriculture should be maize, representing agriculture, rather than golden yellow, representing science.[14]

Note something important here. The phrase 'as indicated by the wording of the diploma' in the 1935 Code was excised from the 1960 Code, which meant the degree title no longer mattered. The ACE intended any degree in agriculture to use a hood edged with the 'subject color' of maize:

for the Intercollegiate Bureau of Academic Costume, n.d. but c.1928), pp. 11, 14.

12 O.J. Hoppner, *Academic Costume in America* (Albany, N.Y.: Cotrell & Leonard for the Intercollegiate Bureau of Academic Costume, 1948), p. 11.

13 *An Academic Costume Code* (Washington, D.C.: American Council on Education, 1935), p. 4. Also Clarence Stephen Marsh, ed., *American Universities and Colleges*, 3rd edn (Washington, D.C.: American Council on Education, 1936), p. 1065.

14 'Memorandum' including 'Appendix II: An Academic Costume Code and Academic Ceremony Guide' (12 October 1959), and also 'Appendix II: An Academic Costume Code and Academic Ceremony Guide' (29 October 1959), both in Hoover Institute Archives, American Council on Education Collection, Box 468, Folder 8 (henceforth Hoover ACE). Also Mary Irwin, *American Universities and Colleges*, 8th edn (Washington D.C.: American Council on Education, 1960), p. 1135.

Type of degree	Degree title	Degree or Subject colour	
		IBAC (1895)	ACE (1960)
Liberal arts degree	'Master of Science' in agriculture	golden yellow	maize
Liberal arts degree	'Master of Science in Agriculture'	golden yellow	maize
Professional degree	'Master of Agriculture'	maize	maize

Changing the degree colour to a 'subject color' indicating the major subject of study marked a radical change to the semiotic system the Intercollegiate Bureau and the American Council on Education had been using to that point, because if one's area of specialty determines the colour of the edging on one's hood, an observer is not able to identify one's degree title by looking at the hood. As a 1965 guide to the American doctoral degree explained,

> What is important in determining the proper subject color is the field of concentration of the study for the degree, not the degree itself. For example, all doctorates in agriculture (whether Ph.D., Ed.D., Sc.D., D.Agr., or other) have a subject color of maize. This would apply to a wide variety of fields of concentration such as agricultural education, vocational agriculture, animal husbandry, agronomy, dairy science, and horticulture.
>
> All doctorates in engineering (whether Ph.D., Sc.D., Eng.D., or other) have a subject color of orange. Again a sizable number of fields would be included, examples being aeronautical engineering, ceramic engineering, chemical engineering, electrical engineering, and mechanical engineering. All doctorates in the sciences (whether Ph.D., Sc.D., or other) have a subject color of golden yellow. Included here would be the fields of biology, chemistry, geology, mathematics, and physics. Some would want to include psychology.[15]

Minutes from the meetings of the American Council on Education committee that produced the 1960 Academic Costume Code show that the committee wanted to endorse a 'subject color' approach so that American academic hoods would 1) more precisely indicate the graduate's primary area of study and 2) make commencement ceremonies a more colourful affair. This was because the Intercollegiate Bureau's 1895 Code caused most edging on academic hoods in the US to be either white (for the MA including tagged MA degrees), golden yellow (for the MS including tagged MS degrees), or dark blue (for the PhD), reflecting the overwhelming popularity of these three degrees. The subject colour approach of the 1960 Code would thereby create more hood edging colour variety among graduates, and indicate more precisely their academic specialties.

The ACE now found itself between a rock and a hard place.

One of the things that brought that ACE committee together in 1959 was a complaint that there were too many degree colours. But if the 1960 Code suddenly allowed the graduate's major to determine the hood edging, the committee would have had to significantly increase the number of authorized subject colours to incorporate the hundreds of different academic majors available at American colleges and universities. But it did not. The committee only increased the 1935 list of twenty-two 'faculty and subject' colours to twenty-six 'subject' colours by the end of 1961 (for the ACE; the IBAC used a slightly longer list of twenty-nine colours).[16]

---

15 George K. Schweitzer, *The Doctorate: A Handbook* (Springfield, Ill.: Charles C. Thomas, 1965), pp. 66–67. David A. Lockmiller, a member of the ACE committee that wrote the 1960 Academic Costume Code, described the new subject colour policy in a similar fashion; see his *Scholars on Parade* (New York: Macmillan, 1969), p. 191.

16 The Intercollegiate Bureau officially used the twenty-six subject colours of the 1960 Academic Costume Code. See, for instance, O. J. Hoppner, *Academic Costume in America* (Albany, N.Y.:

Nor did the committee proactively rename or combine some of the colour categories in the 1895 and 1935 Codes so as to better incorporate the plethora of academic majors in American colleges and universities. Some of the narrow subjects in the 1935 Code were not merged in the 1960 Code into broader categories (Physical Education was not folded into Education, for instance). Thus, by privileging some subject colours that had been authorized between 1895 and 1961 and at the same time ignoring others that had been left out, it was as though the ACE committee perversely said: 'Graduates, you may now wear a color that represents your major ... but we're not going to give most of you a color that represents your major. Tough luck.'

For example, if a student with a Master of Science degree majored in journalism, he or she would get to wear a hood edged crimson because the ACE assigned Journalism that colour in 1959. But a student with a Master of Science degree who majored in radio-television would wear ... what? White (for Arts, Letters, and Humanities)? Golden yellow (for Science)? Silver grey (for Speech)? Brown (for Fine Arts)? The American Council on Education had nothing to say about this problem because it never authorized a subject colour for radio-television. Now, if the ACE wanted one's hood edging to represent the major of one's degree but did not want to increase the number of colours, the ACE committee could have enlarged some of the existing subject categories, so that crimson became not only the colour for journalism alone, but also the colour for all majors in Mass Media (including Journalism). Or better yet, the ACE could have taken the existing colour for Speech (silver grey) and enlarged it to become Communication and Mass Media, which would have allowed crimson to be retired. But that is not what the American Council on Education did. Instead, it authorized only three new subject colours in 1959 and one in 1961. And then the ACE stopped, leaving the muddled thinking behind their 1960 Code to bedevil American academic costume thereafter, leading to what can only be called 'semiotic incoherence' among American academic hoods today.

After 1961 the Intercollegiate Bureau of Academic Costume and the American Council on Education washed their hands of the 'subject color' system they had created. There is a strong sense that they knew it was broken, that the 1960 revision of the Academic Costume Code was confusing, and that the best thing to do in these circumstances was to whistle past that graveyard and hope for the best.

In revising the elegantly simple degree colour policy of the 1895 Intercollegiate Code of Academic Costume so that the major 'subject' of the degree determined the colour of one's hood edging, not the prepositional 'faculty' in the degree title, the American Council on Education had first in 1935 and then in 1960 sown the wind. The Intercollegiate Bureau of Academic Costume had agreed to this folly. Now they would both reap the whirlwind. The seeds of the 1960 Academic Costume Code would yield only a feeble and sickly crop, and strangers (primarily academic costume manufacturers, universities, and professional organizations) would devour the last grains.

Cotrell & Leonard, n.d. but *c.* 1965), p. 7. But privately, the IBAC included three additional degree colours in the list they provided for potential clients: Optometry (seafoam green), Podiatry (Nile green), and Social Science (cream). See, for instance, the degree colour lists the Bureau supplied to Kevin Sheard in *Academic Heraldry in America* (Marquette: Northern Michigan College Press, 1962), p. 7; Hugh Smith and Kevin Sheard in *Academic Dress and Insignia of the World*, 3 vols (Cape Town: A. A. Balkema, 1970), Vol. II, p. 1529; and to George W. Shaw and the other authors of *Degrees and Hoods of the World's Universities and Colleges* (Lewes, Sussex: W. E. Baxter, 1972), p. 116.

Stagnation and confusion

After the American Council on Education and the Intercollegiate Bureau of Academic Costume agreed to adopt the 1960 Academic Costume Code and added an additional subject colour for Home Economics in 1961, both organizations lapsed into a lethargic state of academic costume ennui that has lasted more than a half century. Both the ACE and the IBAC lacked the will and energy to supervise the American systems of academic costume they each had played a part in creating, mainly because the number of professional degrees and academic majors had increased so much in the US that the degree and subject colour systems of the IBAC and ACE had become unwieldy, and neither organization was willing to update or manage these systems in a clear and unambiguous manner.

The Intercollegiate Bureau of Academic Costume's degree colour list was slightly longer than the subject colour list of the ACE because the IBAC was obligated to assign colours to new degrees authorized by the Board of Regents of the University of the State of New York, and so the Bureau briefly tried to keep up with those changes. But O. J. Hoppner, the director of the Intercollegiate Bureau, was ready to throw in the towel. In 1961 a reporter from an Elmira, New York, newspaper explained why.

Fig. 3. O. J. Hoppner, the President of the Intercollegiate Bureau of Academic Costume and General Manager at Cotrell & Leonard, on 28 April 1949. Hoppner served as an adviser to the American Council on Education committees that wrote the 1935 and 1960 Academic Costume Codes.

A velvet trimming adorning the hood forms a yoke about the neck and represents the field of study. That trimming can be one of 25 colors. It's here the problems begin.

The rainbow has run dry, as far as Hoppner and his employer, Cotrell & Leonard, are concerned.

Years and years ago, the matter of degrees was less complicated. The areas of study were divided simply: medicine, science, theology, law, and the arts.

Today there are 33 separate fields in which degrees are awarded. The 25 colors, approved under an intercollegiate code, overlap in a few instances.

As specialization expands, there are new requests for colors. Hoppner says there'll be no more.

'Look at the greens,' Hoppner said pointing to the chart. A degree in medicine is represented by green. Physical education is a sage green and surgical chiropody is a Nile green.

'Or you tell me what color apricot is? What is apricot to you may not be apricot to me,' Hoppner said. Under the code, apricot is for a nursing degree.[17]

17 Robert Markowitz, 'Rainbow Robes: Doctorate Gowns Lose Drabness', *The Sunday Telegram: Elmira* (N.Y.) *Star-Gazette Sunday Edition*, 21 May 1961. Note that Hoppner refers to Surgical Chiropody, which was an official degree colour only in the IBAC list, not the ACE list. Parsing the numbers quoted in this article is difficult, but it appears that the '25 colors' in the article referred to the ACE list of authorized subject colours from early 1961, and the '33 separate fields in which degrees are awarded' referred to all of the degree colours the IBAC had officially approved since 1895, including colours for two degrees (Humanics and Philanthropy) the IBAC had removed from its list and colours for four degrees to which the IBAC had either recently assigned a colour (Social Science) or had considered assigning or briefly assigned colours in the late 1950s (Naprapathy, Political Sci-

115

This interview with Hoppner was made only weeks before the IBAC and ACE approved the maroon colour for Home Economics, bringing the final total number by the beginning of 1962 to twenty-six subject colours for the ACE and twenty-nine degree colours for the IBAC. But after that Hoppner held his ground and the Bureau did not approve another new degree colour until 2001, a year after he died at age 101.

After maroon for Home Economics was authorized in 1961, the American Council on Education and the Intercollegiate Bureau of Academic Costume fielded numerous requests for new subject (i.e., major) colours. This desire for more colours was due in part to the ACE's ossified subject colour list, which included broad subject categories like Science, Fine Arts, Engineering, Medicine, Education, and so on, as well as very narrow subject categories like Physical Education, Economics, Home Economics, Journalism, Forestry, and Library Science. Other specific majors and subjects were left out. So—the argument for new subject colours went—if Education and Physical Education had each been given their own separate subject colours, why should mathematics have to use the same golden yellow colour as biology, physics, and chemistry? Why not authorize separate colours for each of these majors, as the 1960 Code permitted? The obvious rebuttal was that there are so many academic subjects and majors in existence that assigning distinctive colours to each one would be impossible and impractical.

In 1967 the American Council on Education attempted to silence some of these requests by proposing a new section to the Code entitled 'Additional Guidance on Costume'.[18] As this guidance was finally worded when first published in 1973, the ACE stated that 'adaptations' to the Code

> are entirely acceptable as long as they are reasoned and faithful to the spirit of the traditions which give rise to the code. They are not acceptable when they further subdivide the recognized disciplines and designate new colors for such subdivisions. The spectrum of colors which manufacturers can utilize and which can be clearly identified as distinct from other colors is for practical purposes exhausted. Problems may arise with emerging broad interdisciplinary areas; it is recommended that these be resolved by using the color of the discipline most nearly indicative of the new area. New disciplinary designations for colors traditionally assigned would not be readily recognizable nor useful.[19]

The Council then attempted to provide several examples of how an 'emerging interdisciplinary field' might employ a subject colour for its hoods. In what Stephen L. Wolgast describes as 'astonishingly vague information' within a 'ridiculous framework',[20] the ACE stated that the hood trim for physical therapy degrees and similar subjects

---

ence, and Retailing). Home Economics would be added to the Bureau's list before the end of the year, bringing to thirty-four the total number of degree colours either officially authorized or considered for authorization by the Intercollegiate Bureau from 1895 to 1961.

18 See the memo in the Columbia University Archives entitled 'Regulations Affecting Academic Costume' (9 November 1967) from the Commission on Academic Affairs of the American Council on Education to member institutions.

19 W. Todd Furniss, ed., *American Universities and Colleges*, 11th edn (Washington, D.C.: American Council on Education, 1973), pp. 1757–58. This was also the edition of American Universities and Colleges that first allowed degrees in Commerce, Accountancy, and Business to use the alternative colour of sapphire blue (see below). In other words, the ACE could not be counted upon to follow its own new subject colour ban.

20 'The Intercollegiate Code of Academic Costume: An Introduction', *TBS*, 9 (2009), p. 30, https://doi.org/10.4148/2475-7799.1070.

Author's collection

Fig. 4. Two Ohio University PhD hoods from the 1960s. On the left is the academic hood of Virginia Marie Branson, who, in 1961, was the first woman to graduate from Ohio University with a Doctor of Philosophy degree. Her dissertation was entitled 'An Investigation of the Possible Existence of a "Better" Ear in Normal Hearing Young Adults'. Because neither the American Council on Education nor the Intercollegiate Bureau of Academic Costume had created a subject colour for 'speech and hearing therapy', Ohio University decided that the subject colour for Dr Branson's hood would be white, the colour the 1960 Code assigned to majors in 'Arts, Letters, Humanities'. One can only guess why the university selected white, as silver grey (Speech), golden yellow (Science), green (Medicine), or salmon pink (Public Health) were available subject colour categories. As a result, Dr. Branson's hood becomes impossible to read with any kind of semiotic precision, except to say that it is a hood for a doctoral degree of some sort.

On the right is the academic hood for Catherine McQuaid Steiner, who earned a PhD in 'comparative arts' from Ohio University in 1967. If the university had used the subject colour approach of the 1960 Academic Costume Code, the velvet edging of this hood would have been white. Instead, it is dark blue. Evidently, Ohio had by this point abandoned the 1960 Code and returned to the 1895 Intercollegiate Code, whereby the velvet edging indicated the degree title—in this case, dark blue for Doctor of *Philosophy*.

Both hoods were manufactured by the C. E. Ward Company of New London, Ohio, at that time the official supplier of academic dress for state colleges and universities in Ohio. The Intercollegiate Bureau had assigned Ohio a hood lined olive green with a white chevron. The shade was supposed to be dark, to match the official shade of dark olive green used by the university, but Ward inaccurately used a lighter shade of olive green in their hoods, as shown here. The university did not seem to mind—the inaccurate shade continued to be used without change on the hoods Ohio University ordered from Ward until 1968, when the company was purchased by Oak Hall.

should be white if the degree is awarded in arts (BA or MA), golden yellow if in science (BS or MS). Interdisciplinary doctorates should be distinguished by the colors of the principal field under which the degree is awarded. Thus, urban affairs may be distinguished by copper (economics), peacock blue (public administration), or another field already assigned a color above. Multiplication of color assignment is impracticable.

So did the subject colour indicate the degree title (as in the 1895 Code) or the subject of the major (as in the 1960 Code)? 'Yes', the ACE's 1973 Academic Costume Code seemed to say.

Thus by 1973 the American Council on Education had declared a moratorium on new subject colours and had given contradictory advice about new degrees and subjects, which left institutions to splutter and splash in this muddied water. Most chose to stay with the 1895 Intercollegiate Code and its degree colour system. In a 1985 article called 'Academic Colors ... Academic Confusion', S. Mark Strickland and John L. Fluitt pointed out that the 1960 Code 'clearly ... [specifies] that *the color of the subject area to which the degree pertains* and not that in the title of the degree should be used in hood trimmings.'[21] But they were sad to report that this was not the way everyone was interpreting the Code. A year earlier, Strickland and Fluitt had conducted a survey of 452 colleges and universities, asking each one to describe the colour of the velvet trim on its Master of Arts, Master of Science, Master of Education, Doctor of Education, and Doctor of Philosophy hoods. Most of the 300 institutions that responded and were tallied used the degree colour (white for the MA, golden yellow for the MS, light blue for the MEd and EdD, and dark blue for the PhD). Conversely, depending upon the degree, only 16 per cent to 31 per cent of these institutions used colours that indicated the subject or major of the degree. 'It seems apparent from these totals', Strickland and Fluitt observed,

> that in practice the name of the degree is the major factor in determining the color of the hood trimming prescribed by a large majority of institutions. This is true for every type of degree, and especially the Doctor of Philosophy. Of course, some of the selections of the color of the subject in the title of the degree [more accurately: the 'faculty' in the title of the degree] might actually be subject area color choices since in many instances the subject area studied is the same as that in the title of the degree. However, it seems improbable that this could be the case for the Doctor of Philosophy degree, and it is in this degree where the largest majority of institutions use the academic color of the subject ['faculty'] in the title of the degree.
>
> A review of the literature suggests that it is likely that this wide-spread current use of the color of the subject ['faculty'] in the title of the degree rather than that of the subject studied for the degree reflects earlier practices.[22]

Indeed. Old habits die hard. Ever since the Intercollegiate Costume Code was written in 1895 most American colleges and universities had been using degree colours to indicate the 'faculty' in *the wording of the wearer's degree*. The 'subject color' dictum of the American Council on Education's 1960 Academic Costume Code had not significantly changed this practice because American faculty are very much aware that some degrees are research or liberal arts degrees and some degrees are professional degrees—and research degrees are more respected in the collegiate environment.

---

21 Emphasis in original. In *College and University: The Journal of the American Association of Collegiate Registrars*, 61.1 (1985), p. 27.

22 Ibid., p. 29.

Put bluntly: egos are involved. A faculty member with a PhD in Agriculture wants an academic costume that shows that he has done the stringent and time-consuming research that is required to earn a Doctor of Philosophy degree, not a vocational, less-rigorous Doctor of Agriculture degree. Therefore, he wants dark blue hood trim, not maize coloured trim, thank you very much. It is of no concern to him what the 1960 Code says about it.[23]

Not long after Strickland and Fluitt published their research, the American Council on Education waved the white flag, at least in the case of the Doctor of Philosophy degree. The Council's 1987 edition of *American Universities and Colleges* makes an exception to the subject colour policy of the 1960 Code, allowing hood and gown trim for PhDs to be dark blue if desired. 'In the case of the Doctor of Philosophy degree', the ACE said,

> the dark blue color is used to represent the mastery of the discipline of learning and scholarship in any field that is attested to by the awarding of this degree and is not intended to represent the field of philosophy.[24]

But again the ACE fumbled the ball. By explaining the dark blue colour assignment as a way of indicating 'mastery of the discipline of learning and scholarship' the Council obfuscated a very simple fact: since 1895 American degree colours have been used to indicate the wording of the degree as it appears on one's diploma, and the wording of one's degree is very important because it indicates the substantive differences between a research degree and a vocational degree in the same subject.

Strickland and Fluitt's research demonstrated that most American colleges and universities understood this better than the ACE and therefore in the mid-1980s these institutions were still following the degree colour regulations of the 1895 Intercollegiate Code of Academic Costume. Fewer were following the subject colour regulations of the 1960 Academic Costume Code. This division of practice has continued to the present, which means that today there is no longer a single standard for determining the colour of the hood edging used by all American colleges and universities, or by American academic costume manufacturers.[25] Sadly, the goal of having a standardized, shared, and uniform system of American academic costume envisioned by the 1895 Intercollegiate Commission on Academic Costume was achieved, but has not endured.

---

23 This is one of the reasons US First Lady Jill Biden's insistence on being called Doctor Jill Biden rubbed many people the wrong way in December 2020. Biden is a Doctor of Education, which is not as academically (or culturally) prestigious as a Doctor of Philosophy or a Doctor of Medicine.

24 'An Academic Costume Code and an Academic Ceremony Guide', *American Universities and Colleges*, 13th edn (New York: Walter de Gruyter, 1987), p. 1918.

25 See, for example, the brochure illustrated in Figure 7 from Jostens, a company still using the degree colour system of the 1895 Code. But then there is the University of the State of New York, the governing body responsible for accrediting all of the educational institutions incorporated in the state of New York, which uses what appears to be the standards of the 1935 Academic Costume Code, whereby the degree title still determines the colour used for the velvet edging of the hood, but the subject of a tagged degree is given preference over the faculty in the degree title. Notice, for example, that on p. 3 of *Academic Heraldry* (Albany, N.Y.: The University of the State of New York, 2000), the 'bachelor of science in engineering degree' should have orange trimming for engineering, rather than the golden yellow of science. The doctor of philosophy degree requires dark blue because the degree designation does not necessarily identify the major field of study.'

Colours for academic legitimacy

The American Council on Education and the Intercollegiate Bureau of Academic Costume may have been reluctant to add new subject or degree colours to their official palettes after maroon for Home Economics was approved in 1961, but this has not prevented academic costume manufacturers, colleges and universities, and academic professional organizations from authorizing new hood edging colours to meet a specific purpose: academic legitimacy for new, narrowly defined, and specialized professional degree programmes. And in the higher education marketplace, one way to symbolize the pedagogical legitimacy of a new vocational programme is to stake a claim on a new subject or degree colour for that profession.

Chiropractic: silver
Design: yellow
Human Environmental Sciences:[26] *maroon*
Industrial Arts: burnt orange
Technology: red

Many of the official degree and subject colours in the 1895 and 1960 Codes began as unauthorized hood edging colours that had been adopted by a particular college or university to represent a new pedagogical faculty at their institution. Sometimes the Intercollegiate Bureau of Academic Costume would officially approve one of these local colour choices for national use: Dentistry (lilac), Humanics (crimson), Nursing (apricot), Optometry (seafoam green), Physical Education (sage green), and Veterinary Science (grey) all began this way. But sometimes the Bureau would decide not to authorize a local colour for national use. In the 1940s, for example, degree colours for Statistics (light rose) and Textiles (rose) were used at North Carolina State College, but these colours were never officially approved by the IBAC.[27]

To complicate matters even further, the American Council on Education never approved the Intercollegiate Bureau's official colours for Optometry (seafoam green), Podiatry (Nile green), and Social Science (cream). Regarding the colour for Optometry, the Bureau had officially authorized seafoam green in 1949, but ten years later the Council refused to add it to the 1960 Code.[28] Efforts by the American Academy of Optometry to obtain ACE approval of seafoam continued in 1975[29] and 1988[30] but were unsuccessful. Situations like this led to slightly different lists of 'official' degree and subject colours in the United States by the Intercollegiate Bureau of Academic Costume and the American

---

26 Human Environmental Sciences is different from Home Economics. At the universities I reviwed, the degree seems (to me) to be a hodgepodge of barely related subjects: fashion merchandising, nutrition, child education, hospitality management, health sciences, etc.

27 See Suit, 'Conforming to the Established Standards', pp. 39–75.

28 Compare Raymond F. Howes, 'Memorandum to Members of the Committee on Academic Costume and Ceremonies' (23 June 1959) with 'A Code for Academic Costumes and Ceremonies: Second Version' (7 July 1959), both in the Hoover ACE Box 468, Folder 9.

29 Henry W. Hofstetter, 'The Mysteries of Optometry's Green', *Optometry and Vision Science* [The Journal of the American Academy of Optometry], 67.2 (February 1990), p. 72.

30 'Council Activities: Miscellaneous Activities,' *Journal of Optometric Education*, 14.1 (Fall 1988), p. 27.

Figure 5. A Doctor of Chiropractic hood from Sherman College of Chiropractic in Spartanburg, South Carolina, manufactured in 2011 by the Herff Jones Company. The hood is edged with 'silver' (light grey) velvet and lined with satin in an approximation of the school colours of the college in 2006 when the student graduated: an unusual medium reddish-brown colour (PMS 478—a colour similar to the colour of dyed leather) and white. Other manufacturers of hoods for this college have used a very dark brown shade of satin, also with a white chevron. Many American college and universities are strangely inconsistent in the shades they allow hood manufacturers to use to depict their school colours.

In the US, holders of doctoral degrees are permitted to wear a cap with a gold tassel, as here. For doctoral degrees that are assigned light degree colours like silver, the velvet trim on the gown is usually black (as here), but velvet matching the colour of the edging of the hood is permitted. Doctor of Chiropractic hood, gown, and cap courtesy Dr Ashley Stiltner.

Council on Education, not including various 'unofficial' lists of degree and subject colours published by American academic costume manufacturers today, and published lists of sometimes unique degree or subject colours used at individual colleges and universities.

The short list of new degree or subject colours on the previous page has been gleaned from the lists of various academic costume manufacturers and from the commencement programmes of various colleges and universities. This list is by no means exhaustive; rather, it is intended to illustrate a few of the unofficial degree or subject colours one may see at a commencement ceremony today. Because the IBAC and the ACE have already officially assigned some of these colours to other subjects, or the colours are so similar to the existing official colours of other disciplines, sartorial confusion is the inevitable result, leaving these degree and subject colour choices with little to recommend them.

For example, the silver hood edging some chiropractic colleges are using for their doctoral hoods is indistinguishable from the silver grey colour the IBAC and ACE officially assigned to Speech (which itself is sometimes redefined at some schools as being the colour for Communication and/or Mass Media).[31] So from a pragmatic perspective, silver should not be used for degrees in chiropractic medicine. Instead, cerise would be a better option for the Doctor of Chiropractic hood. It was the colour historically assigned to Naprapathy, a medical practice related to Chiropractic.[32]

---

31 Still other schools use journalism's crimson as the colour for communication and/or mass media. Further complicating matters is the light shade of grey some academic costume manufacturers use for Veterinary Medicine hoods.

32 For more about this historical precedent, see Suit, 'Conforming to the Established Standards', pp. 46–47.

Harvard University uses hoods edged with yellow velvet for degrees in design,[33] which is easily confused with the official lemon yellow colour of Library Science or even the golden yellow colour of Science. At the University of Missouri, degrees in Human Environmental Sciences use maroon trim for their hoods,[34] the colour the IBAC and ACE already assigned to Home Economics in 1961. Until 2007, an academic costume company named Academic Apparel sold hoods edged with burnt orange velvet for graduates in the Industrial Arts, a color intentially similar to the official orange of Engineering.[35] And degrees conferred by the Polytechnic Institute at Purdue University, like the Doctor of Technology degree, use hoods edged with red velvet,[36] making them indistinguishable from hoods for theological degrees (scarlet).

Human Resources: dusk
Physician Assistant: jade green
Gerontology: gold
Dance: amethyst

Occasionally a school will select a unique or distinctive degree or subject colour for a new degree, discipline, or major. Rutgers University and the University of New Hampshire both use 'dusk'[37] as the hood edging for degrees in Human Resources. The University of Southern California trims the hoods for its Physician Assistant degrees with jade green velvet, which is intentionally within the green colour family the Intercollegiate Bureau traditionally assigned to medical degrees. But the University of Southern California also uses gold for Gerontology (easily confused with the golden yellow of Science) and amethyst for Dance (easily confused with the purple of Law).[38]

Architecture: blue-violet
Commerce, Accountancy, and Business: sapphire blue

Sometimes an existing official IBAC or ACE degree or subject colour has been reassigned an alternative colour for academic or aesthetic reasons. For example, in the early 1900s

---

33 See Cynthia W. Rossano, 'Reading the Regalia: A Guide to Deciphering the Academic Dress Code', *Harvard Magazine*, May 1999, as well as Nicholas A. Hoffmann, 'Crow's Feet and Crimson: Academic Dress at Harvard', *TBS*, 9 (2009), p. 52, https://doi.org/10.4148/2475-7799.1071.

34 At <https://www.themizzoustore.com/p-191297-masters-maroon-human-environmental-sciences-hood.aspx> [accessed 25 May 2021].

35 See <www.capsngowns4less.com>, then Faculty & Judicial, and download the Word document University Colors [retrieved 25 May 2021]. Academic Apparel (also known as Academic Cap & Gown) is one of the subsidiaries of the Academic Church and Choir Gown Manufacturing Company, Inc., established in 1946. The company no longer offers burnt orange for degrees in the Industrial Arts, having reassigned this discipline 'science gold' (golden yellow). See: <www.academicapparel.com/caps/regalia_colors.html> [retrieved 25 May 2021].

36 At <https://www.purdueglobal.edu/student-experience/graduation/cap-gowns/> [retrieved 25 May 2021].

37 Rutger's 2018 commencement programme included the description. For the New Hampshire, see <http://www.unh.edu/unhtoday/2013/05/colors-commencement> [accessed 25 May 2021]. Dusk is typically a greyish light blue or greyish light violet colour, like the colour of the sky immediately after sunset, as twilight begins.

38 'Official Colors for Degrees', University of Southern California, at <https://commencement.usc.edu/history/official-colors-for-degrees/> [retrieved 25 May 2021].

Harvard preferred to use 'golden brown' instead of maize for its degrees in Agriculture, a minor variation of hue.[39] Other colour substitutions have been more extreme.

The Bureau considered architecture to be one of the fine arts, so Bachelor and Master of Architecture degrees were assigned the brown degree colour of Fine Arts.[40] But many art historians consider architecture to be a field of design or applied art, separate from the fine arts, and it is a fact that many universities have created Schools or Colleges of Architecture outside their Schools or Colleges of Fine Arts.[41] In these cases, blue-violet has been used as a degree or subject colour for architecture at places like Yale University, Virginia Tech, the University of Notre Dame, and the University of Southern California.[42]

The colour drab used for Business degrees has been singularly unpopular ever since the Intercollegiate Bureau of Academic Costume officially adopted that unattractive shade of greyish khaki around 1903. By the 1970s, so many prominent east coast schools had substituted sapphire blue for drab that the American Council on Education felt obligated to address the problem.[43]

In the 11th edition (1973) of *American Universities and Colleges*, the ACE began to officially permit the use of sapphire blue instead of drab for Commerce, Accountancy, and Business. However, the ACE also stated in a footnote that sapphire blue was 'not recommended because of the likely confusion with blues previously assigned to other subjects'.[44] This alternative colour (and the ACE's opprobrium) was included until the 13th edition (1987) of *American Universities and Colleges* when it disappears, leaving drab as the only *official* colour for Business degrees today.

The sapphire blue alternative colour for degrees in Business was never officially authorized by the Intercollegiate Bureau of Academic Costume. But because the official degree colour of drab has remained unpopular, today many colleges and universities ignore both the ACE and the IBAC and continue to use sapphire blue instead of drab as the colour for Commerce, Accounting, and Business degrees, including Yale University, the University of Pennsylvania, and others.[45] Even so, the ACE was correct: sapphire blue is easily mistaken for the dark blue of Philosophy, the royal blue of Psychology (see below), or even the peacock blue of Public Administration.

---

39 G. P. Baker, 'The Spring Term', *The Harvard Graduates' Magazine*, 11.44 (June 1903), p. 542. See also 'Academic Costume', *The Harvard Graduates' Magazine*, 18.70 (December 1909), p. 293. Harvard no longer offers degrees in Agriculture.

40 See Hoppner, *Academic Costume in America*, p. 14.

41 Historically, music is another example of this institutional division of the creative arts into separate schools or colleges: most large universities have a School or College of Music and a School or College of Fine Arts. Accordingly, the IBAC assigned separate colours to Music (pink) and Fine Arts (brown).

42 The Academic Cap & Gown company is one of several firms creating hoods for Architecture degrees using blue-violet edging: <www.academicapparel.com/caps/regalia_colors.html> [retrieved 25 May 2021]. Confusingly, some manufacturers will use a violet colour for Architecture (similar if not identical to Dentistry's lilac) instead of blue-violet. See Fig. 7 for an example from Jostens.

43 For more information about the drab and sapphire blue degree colours for Commerce, Accounting, and Business, see Suit, 'The Iridescent Web', pp. 57–58.

44 Furniss, 'An Academic Costume Code', p. 1756. Also American Council on Education, 'An Academic Costume Code and an Academic Ceremony Guide', *American Universities and Colleges*, 12th edn (New York: Walter de Gruyter, 1983), p. 2069.

45 Harvard uses medium grey, the colour the Intercollegiate Bureau assigned to Veterinary Science.

Occupational Therapy: slate blue
Physical Therapy: teal
Audiology: spruce green
Criminal Justice: midnight blue
Psychology: royal blue
Interior Design: bilberry

On rare occasions, professional organizations were able to convince the Intercollegiate Bureau of Academic Costume to authorize an academic colour for degrees in their occupation. For example, the Society for the Promotion of Engineering Education selected orange as the degree colour for Engineering in 1905, a decision that was officially approved by the IBAC a year later.[46] Forty years later, the Association of Schools and Colleges of Optometry played a significant role in securing Bureau approval of seafoam green as the official degree colour for Optometry,[47] and in 1961 the American Home Economics Association requested a subject colour for degrees in Home Economics; the Intercollegiate Bureau and the American Council on Education assigned it maroon.[48]

As the late twentieth century moved on the Intercollegiate Bureau of Academic Costume fell on hard times. Cotrell & Leonard, the 'depository' for the Bureau, had seen its share of the academic costume manufacturing market collapse in the 1960s. As their business waned, so did their influence on academic costume policy, and by 1970 the American Council on Education no longer included a representative from the IBAC on its Committee on Academic Costumes.[49] Labour problems at Cotrell & Leonard were followed by student boycotts of the firm at various east coast universities, which led to Cotrell & Leonard's bankruptcy in 1980 and purchase by the rival E. R. Moore company that same year.

By 1987 the ACE had omitted reference to the Intercollegiate Bureau of Academic Costume from the historical prologue to the Academic Costume Code.[50] But the Bureau appears to have survived, at least in rump form, until 2011 at least, when it approved slate blue as an 'alternate' colour for degrees in Occupational Therapy.

In 1995, the American Occupational Therapy Association Commission on Education had declared slate blue as the official colour for the Master of Occupational Therapy (MOT) and Doctor of Occupational Therapy (OTD) degrees.[51] The Association then petitioned the Intercollegiate Bureau of Academic Costume to approve this colour as the official faculty colour for occupational therapy, which it did—sixteen years later!—as an 'alternate' colour for occupational therapy (see Fig. 6). The Bureau approved slate blue as

---

46 Society for the Promotion of Engineering Education, Proceedings of the Thirteenth Annual Meeting [28 and 29 June 1905], 13 (1906), p. 5. Also Suit, 'The Iridescent Web', p. 61.

47 Hofstetter, 'The Mysteries of Optometry's Green,' p. 72. Also Suit, *loc. cit.*

48 See the letter from Raymond F. Howes to O. J. Hoppner (7 April 1961) and the letter from Raymond F. Howes to A. June Bricker (20 April 1961), both in Hoover ACE. Also Suit, *loc. cit.*

49 'Committee on Academic Costumes' (July 1970), Hoover, ACE, Box 602, Folder 8.

50 The last time the American Council on Education mentions the Bureau's existence is in *American Universities and Colleges*, 12th edn (New York: Walter de Gruyter, 1983), p. 2069.

51 This topic had been discussed on the OT Connections forum, which was taken down on 29 June 2018 and replaced by a new forum called CommunOT. The content of the old OT Connections forum was deleted.

Intercollegiate Bureau of
Academic Costume
156 COLONIAL AVENUE   ALBANY, NY 12208
TEL. 518-489-8170   FAX 518-43-9251
capandgown@me.com

September 26, 2011
Dr. Florence Clark, PhD, OTR/L.
Assoc. Dean & Chair of the Division of Occupational Science and Occupational Therapy
President of the American Occupational Therapy Association
1540 Alcazar Street, CHP-133
Los Angeles, CA 90089-9003

Dear Dr. Clark,

Thank you very much for contacting the IBAC in hopes of registering slate blue as the official color for Occupational Therapy. Let me first lay out the process and the determinations based upon our research.

The general framework for the designation of academic colors originated in the 19th century in hopes of setting a standard that would be used and recognized throughout the United States.

This framework of academic colors was adopted by colleges and universities in the United States and continues to be followed by nearly all institutions of higher learning.

This voluntary standard only applies to the academic disciplines and the colors used in such standard are only broad classifications.

Since the 19th century, the number and variety of degrees has expanded greatly. In the 1960's, the IBAC determined that a moratorium would be placed on the adoption of new colors.

Instead, the general classification would continue to serve a model and would offer sufficient variety to cover specialized degrees.

As professional associations began to grow in prominence and as degrees began to become more specialized, various groups have requested an exemption from this moratorium.

When sufficient reason exists, an "alternate" color has been established. However, in doing so the following applies:

• The exemption is for an alternate color and does not replace another color that may already be in use at a higher institution

• Institutions voluntarily comply with the academic code. Institutions of higher learning are not "wrong" to use another color within their schema of hood colors.

• Colors that are being used to designate Occupational Therapy such a green (health related area) or gold (science) are valid options if an institution decides to use these colors.

With the above stipulations in place, we have registered slate blue as an alternate color for Occupational Therapy.

Sincerely yours,

John P. Harden, Esq.

President

Intercollegiate Bureau of Academic Costume

cc: Dr. Samia Rafeedie

Fig. 6. A 2011 letter from the Intercollegiate Bureau of Academic Costume regarding a suitable hood edging colour for degrees in Occupational Therapy. Courtesy Neil Harvison.

an 'alternate' option to, for instance, green (Medicine) or golden yellow (Science) that are 'official' colours in the Code.[52]

Why slate blue? According to Neil Harvison, Chief Academic and Scientific Affairs Officer at the American Occupational Therapy Association:

Histories of occupational therapy credit the work of the reconstruction aides of World War One with providing impetus for the development of the profession. The reconstruction aides were civilian women appointed to provide therapy for World War One casualties in military hospitals. They were hired by the War Department but had no military standing. They did, however, have the opportunity to apply credit for service time in gaining civil service appointments after the war. In 1917, immediately after the war, the Society for Promotion of Occupational Therapy and the profession were formerly established. The Aides uniform was made of 'blue-grey' colored cloth. Slate blue was selected as it is 'blue-grey.'[53]

Not wanting to be left behind and not wanting to use the same colour as Occupational Therapy, in 1997 the American Physical Therapy Association selected teal as its degree colour. A year before, the first students earning the newly created Doctor of Physical Therapy

52 Letter from John Hardin, Intercollegiate Bureau of Academic Costume, to Dr Florence Clark, President of the American Occupational Therapy Association, 26 September 2011.

53 Email from Neil Harvison, Chief Academic and Scientific Affairs Officer at the American Occupational Therapy Association, 18 April 2014.

(DPT) degree had graduated from Creighton University wearing hoods edged with velvet in this blue-green colour. Faculty at Creighton and the University of Southern California (two of only a handful of DPT programmes at the time, including New York University and Slippery Rock University of Pennsylvania) had earlier begun a conversation with the Intercollegiate Bureau of Academic Costume regarding an appropriate colour for this degree, and teal was proposed as it fell within the green colour family of other medical and allied health subjects in the Code.[54] Teal was then selected as the official degree colour for Physical Therapy in November 1997 at the Board of Director's meeting of the American Physical Therapy Association.[55] Official recognition of this selection from the Intercollegiate Bureau does not seem to have been given.

In 2001, University of Louisville members of the National Association of Future Doctors of Audiology needed to order academic regalia for their upcoming Doctor of Audiology hooding ceremony.[56] This group of students then contacted one of the manufacturers of the apparel to determine options. No colours had been 'assigned' to audiology so the students undertook to petition for a colour unique to audiology. This was a student-driven effort, without the involvement of any professional association or group. The students did, however, coordinate with the students at the other universities that were offering the degree.

The students chose spruce green as the velvet edging colour of these hoods because it was a unique shade that harmonized with the other green colours of medical and allied health subjects in the 1960 Code.[57] It was first used at commencement ceremonies in the spring of 2001 at the University of Louisville and the Pennsylvania School of Optometry College of Audiology.[58]

The Academy of Criminal Justice Sciences 'is an international association established in 1963 to foster professional and scholarly activities in the field of criminal justice. ACJS promotes criminal justice education, research, and policy analysis within the discipline of criminal justice for both educators and practitioners'.[59] The Academy authorized midnight blue as its academic hood edging colour on 4 March 2002 because it 'symbolizes the following characteristics thought to represent the best in the field of criminal justice and criminology: trustworthiness, truthfulness, professionalism, intelligence, respectability,

---

54 From email correspondence with Deborah Givens, PT, PhD, DPT, Chair of the Department of Physical Therapy, Creighton University, 24 April 2014.

55 From email correspondence with Gini Blodgett Birchett, Lead Information Resources Specialist and Librarian, American Physical Therapy Association, 22 April 2014.

56 From email correspondence with Ian Windmill, PhD, University of Mississippi Medical Center, 28 June 2010. The National Association of Future Doctors of Audiology became the Student Academy of Audiology in 2009.

57 See these notes from a 2003 lecture by Dr George S. Osborne, Dean of the School of Audiology at the Pennsylvania College of Optometry: <www.audiologyonline.com/articles/pf_article _detail.asp?article_id=505> [retrieved 25 May 2021]. See also Veronica Heide, 'Mission Accomplished!' *Audiology Practices*, 2:2 (June 2010), p. 35.

58 See <http://web.archive.org/web/20190502120518/http://www.audible-difference.com /Articles/veronica_h_aud_degree.htm> [retrieved 25 May 2021] and point 5 at <www.audiology online.com/news/news_detail.asp?news_id=213> [retrieved 25 May 2021].

59 'About ACJS,' at <www.acjs.org/page/AboutACJS> [retrieved 25 May 2021].

Courtesy Jostens

Fig. 7. A page from a 2017 brochure from Jostens, one of the major manufacturers of academic costume in the US today. Surprisingly, the chart on the right is a listing of 'degree colors' (1895 Code) and not 'subject colors' (1960 Code). The chart also exhibits some oddities and several new colours (some of which have been discussed in this article): Architecture and Landscape Architecture are listed separately with different colours; Journalism and Home Economics are listed together with the same colour; Chiropractic is listed here with Veterinary Science grey, not Oratory/Speech silver or something new; and separate colours are cited for Occupational Therapy, 'PhD Philosophy', Physical Therapy, as well as something called 'Liberal Science' (!), which seems to use the cream colour of Social Science. The chart concludes with a cautionary disclaimer: 'Color shades may vary from finished product.' For the complete brochure, see www.jostens.com/apps/shop/images/pdf/FineQualityRegalia_TrifoldBrochure.pdf.

security, and dignity'.[60] It is probably not coincidental that police uniforms in the United States are traditionally dark blue.

In 2007 the National Council of Schools and Programs of Professional Psychology adopted royal blue as the official colour for the Doctor of Psychology degree. Goldenrod and rose had also been proposed but were not chosen.[61] Historically, royal blue was a dark blue with a purple tint, but today royal blue is typically defined as a mid-range blue with a purple tint. To avoid confusion with the dark blue velvet trim of the PhD hood, the PsyD hood is sometimes edged with royal blue velvet of this lighter (or modern) variation.

In 2009 the Fellows of the Interior Design Educators Council selected bilberry (a 'deep eggplant purple') as the hood edging colour for degrees in Interior Design, to be 'separate and distinct from architecture and the other design professions.'[62] This colour was chosen with the help of Academic Cap and Gown, a judicial and academic regalia company founded in 1946 in Chatsworth, California.[63]

These six new degree and subject colours have been selected or approved by professional and academic organizations to be used by graduates of college and university programmes accredited by those organizations. Thus these academic colours have a serious claim to legitimacy, even though most of the colours have not been officially authorized by the Intercollegiate Bureau of Academic Costume or the American Council on Education. Having said that, there are several arguments that can be mustered against the use of these colours. First of all, most of these new degree or subject colours are too similar in shade to authorized colours already in the official IBAC and ACE lists, which makes these new colours difficult to distinguish from other degree or subject colours at a commencement. Further, the separate colours for Occupational Therapy, Physical Therapy, and Audiology illustrate the unfortunate tendency—a tendency that is now more than a century old in American academia—for similar vocational degrees to create separate professional doctoral degree titles and then demand separate degree colours. The precedent of the 1895 Code would be to combine these narrowly defined vocational degrees under a single faculty colour assigned to Therapeutic Medicine, Allied Health Professions, or something of that sort.

Epilogue: Heirloom seeds for a healthy crop

It is long past time for a reform of the American faculty colour system. For the past sixty years the American Council on Education has shown little interest in maintaining the integrity of the subject colour regulations it published in the 1960 Academic Costume Code—

---

60 From email correspondence with Cathy Barth, Manager, Academy of Criminal Justice Science, 21 May 2014.

61 From a 2007 news bulletin that was once archived online but no longer exists. Perhaps unaware of this decision by the NCSPPP, today a few colleges and universities use gold as the subject colour for Psychology, which obviously leads to confusion with the golden yellow of Science. The University of Minnesota Duluth is one example, and the Academic Cap & Gown company tailors psychology hoods with gold-coloured velvet edging: <www.academicapparel.com/caps/regalia_colors .html> [retrieved 25 May 2021].

62 From a 2010 news bulletin that was once online but the page no longer exists.

63 The report was once online but the page no longer exists. Academic Cap and Gown is online at <www.academicapparel.com/> [retrieved 25 May 2021].

regulations it would permanently cement before the end of that decade in its moratorium on new colours. The Intercollegiate Bureau of Academic Costume, having abandoned the degree colour framework of its 1895 Intercollegiate Code of Academic Costume, published nothing after the mid-1960s as its representatives became increasingly adverse to correspondence. Even today, letters can be sent and phone calls can be made to the Bureau, but they are rarely answered,[64] and its former website is a dead link (see Fig. 6). Apparently, as of 2021 the IBAC no longer exists.

Since the support of the ACE or IBAC cannot be counted upon, perhaps the best strategy to combat the entropy of American faculty colours today is to educate consumers, who are the ones ultimately holding the most power in this situation. A purchaser of academic regalia who has been well educated in these matters is a purchaser who can demand a better product from academic costume manufacturers. Likewise, faculty who have been well educated in the history of academic dress can make sure the proper hood edging colours are being purchased by their school for their graduates.

But with two competing and incompatible faculty colour systems being used today—the 'degree color' approach of the 1895 Intercollegiate Code and the 'subject color' approach of the 1960 Academic Costume Code—which is the best? Or is there another system that is better?

From time to time, academic costume historians have proposed reforms to the current systems. In his seminal 1962 book *Academic Heraldry in America*, Kevin Sheard recommended an expansion of the heraldic patterns used in the linings of American hoods; George Schweitzer devoted one of the appendices in *The Doctorate* (1965) to 'Degree, Subject Color, and Academic Regalia Reform'; in 1985 Mark Strickland and John Fluitt proposed stricter adherence to the 1960 Academic Costume Code and an increase in the number of subject colours to avoid 'Academic Confusion'; David Boven suggested that American academic costume needed more variety in his 2009 examination of 'American Universities' Departure from the Academic Costume Code'; and in 2011 Stephen L. Wolgast presented a 'Manifesto for Change' in an article on American subject colours.[65] Sadly, none of these reform proposals have borne fruit.

But it's hard to resist the fatalistic temptation to toss another reform proposal into the abyss. So as a way to popularize the research I've done for the three articles I've now written on American academic colours for the *Transactions of the Burgon Society*, as a way to better educate academic costume consumers about the history of academic regalia

---

64 This is from personal experience; however, the Bureau's poor communication skills are legendary: see, for example, comments by S. Mark Strickland and John L. Fluitt, 'Academic Colors … Academic Confusion', *College and University: The Journal of the American Association of Collegiate Registrars*, 61.1 (1985), p. 30; Hofstetter, 'The Mysteries of Optometry's Green,' p. 72; and Robert Armagost, 'University Uniforms: The Standardization of Academic Dress in the United States', *TBS*, 9 (2009), p. 145, https://doi.org/10.4148/2475-7799.1074. The last known documented action by the Bureau was in 2011, when an 'alternate' colour for occupational therapy was approved (see Fig. 6).

65 See Sheard, pp. 1–6; Schweitzer, pp. 100–03; Strickland and Fluitt, pp. 30–31; David T. Boven, 'American Universities' Departure from the Academic Costume Code', *TBS*, 9 (2009), pp. 169–71, https://doi.org/10.4148/2475-7799.1075; and Wolgast, 'The Demise of "Faculty" Meanings in U.S. Hoods and a Manifesto for Change', *TBS*, 11 (2011), pp. 76–90, https://doi.org/10.4148/2475-7799.1093.

in the US and to be more responsive to their questions and needs, and as a way to create a new organization designed to promote the standardized use of academic costume in the US, in 2018 I created the Intercollegiate Registry of Academic Costume as an homage to the apparently defunct Intercollegiate Bureau of Academic Costume. I also began to create a website that summarizes the published work others have done on the history of American academic costume and the research I've done on the history of the degree and subject colours used on the velvet trim on American academic hoods and gowns as well as the unpublished research I've done on the collegiate colours and heraldic patterns used in the silk or satin linings of American academic hoods. My hope is that the Intercollegiate Registry website can be an up-to-date and easily accessed location where people curious about American academic costume can go for useful information about this topic.[66]

So in this epilogue to my final article on American subject and degree colours, I would like to suggest what I think is a good way to correct the confused state of our academic colour systems in the US.

It seems to me that any reform of the American subject and degree colour systems must first address these two basic problems:

> 1. It is impossible to assign a distinctive colour to every academic subject or major. There are too many academic subjects or majors today.
>
> 2. It is impossible to assign a distinctive colour to every academic degree title. There are too many academic degree titles today.

The obvious solution to these problems is that some manner of 'clustering' must be used, regardless of whether one uses a subject colour approach or a degree colour approach. We cannot have individual subject colours for the broad categories of science like biology, physics, chemistry, mathematics, and so on, much less a collection of individual subject colours for specializations of those subdivisions of science like molecular biology, zoology, biotechnology, anatomy, botany, and so on. Either way, we would run out of distinguishable hood edging colours long before we even came close to finishing the natural sciences and moved to the social sciences, the liberal arts, the creative arts, or any of the professions. We need a subject or degree colour for the broadly defined category of 'Science' that would include all of these sub-disciplines.

But which sub-disciplines should be included in Science and which should not? How should we delineate the edges of other subject or degree colour clusters? Where should we draw the circles? Which stars should be in our constellations?

Here I think we should look at the academic structures of our universities and recognize that the administrators of our institutions of higher education have already done this clustering work for us, which means that we need to once again think in terms of *faculty* colours.

American universities are divided into colleges, schools, and departments. Pedagogically, these departments are further subdivided into the major subjects that are taught. Clearly we cannot assign colours to each of the major subjects in an academic department (*contra* the 1960 Code) because there are too many of these major subjects. But because these academic departments have been grouped into a limited number of larger colleges and schools, we can certainly assign distinct colours to most of these 'faculties' (colleges and schools), which can then be used to corral similar degree titles (as in the 1895 Code).

---

66 At <http://intercollegiate-registry.org/>.

Most American degree titles are based upon the names of the colleges and schools that confer them. Look, for instance, at the eight degree colours initially authorized by the 1895 Code. All of these colours represented a degree title conferred by a college or school that usually had a similar name:

White, which represented a Bachelor, Master, or Doctor of **Arts** or Letters from a College of **Arts** and Sciences.

Scarlet, which represented a Bachelor, Master, or Doctor of Divinity or **Theology** from a College or School of **Theology**, from a Divinity School, or from a Seminary.

Dark brown, which represented a Bachelor or Master of **Fine Arts** from a College or School of **Fine Arts**.

Purple, which represented a Bachelor, Master, or Doctor of **Law** from a College or School of **Law**.

Green, which represented a Doctor of **Medicine** from a College or School of **Medicine**.

Pink, which represented a Bachelor, Master, or Doctor of **Music** from a College or School of **Music**.

Golden yellow, which represented a Bachelor, Master, or Doctor of **Science** from a College of Arts and **Sciences**.

Dark blue, which represented a Bachelor, Master, or Doctor of **Philosophy** degree from a College of Arts (historically: **Philosophy**) and Sciences (historically: Natural **Philosophy**).

Today's universities are hardly different. If one looks at the academic colleges and schools of the major American institutions of higher education, one sees that there is a remarkable consistency in the way these various institutions are logistically subdividing themselves into constellations of related pedagogical subjects and majors. The names of these colleges and schools may vary a little—'College of Agricultural and Environmental Sciences' or 'College of Agriculture, Food, and Natural Resources' or 'School of Forestry and Environmental Studies'—but the cluster of subjects they encompass in what we might call 'Natural Resources and Environmental Sciences' is very similar. I believe these clusters of academic faculties (colleges and schools) should guide us in a revision of the degree colour system of the 1895 Intercollegiate Code.

A compilation of the academic units of the Association of American Universities is a good place to start. Founded in 1900, the AAU is a consortium of sixty-two of the most influential research universities in the United States and Canada.[67] When lists of the colleges and schools within each of these institutions are compiled, a surprisingly manageable number of shared pedagogical divisions appears:

Arts and Sciences, Liberal Arts, Humanities, or Science	62 universities
Business, Business Administration, Management, Accounting, Business and Economics, or Commerce	61 universities
Engineering, Engineering and Applied Science, Engineering and Computer Science, or Technology	53 universities
Law	47 universities
Medicine	47 universities
Education	42 universities
Nursing	35 universities
Public Health	25 universities
Social Work, Social Welfare, or Social Service	22 universities

67 At <www.aau.edu/> [retrieved 25 May 2021].

All of these large college or school divisions already have degree colours the Intercollegiate Bureau of Academic Costume created a century ago.

Other large pedagogical clusters of related subjects also exist, but have not yet collectively agreed upon a shared umbrella term for their disciplines. For example, twenty-five AAU members have a large pedagogical division devoted to the study of government and the political sciences, but these colleges and schools are identified by a variety of names: Government, Public Affairs, Public Policy, Public Service, International Affairs, International Studies, Leadership, Social Policy, and so on. Perhaps this cluster of related governmental academic subjects will eventually develop a singular term to describe itself, but in the meantime, we may propose a descriptive term for it (I chose 'Government and Political Sciences') and assign it a faculty colour based upon traditional American degree colours authorized by the Intercollegiate Bureau of Academic Costume or other organizations (I chose royal blue). Other AAU colleges and schools without a shared disciplinary vocabulary or degree colour could be treated in a similar way.

As a specific example, we can compare and contrast the large academic units of two universities randomly selected from the list of AAU members: Boston University (a private, historically Methodist university) and the University of North Carolina at Chapel Hill (a public, state-funded university).

Boston University	University of North Carolina at Chapel Hill
College of Arts and Sciences	College of Arts and Sciences
School of Business	School of Business
College of Communication	School of Journalism and Media
School of Dental Medicine	School of Dentistry
College of Education	School of Education
College of Engineering	
College of Fine Arts	
School of Global Studies	School of Government
College of Health and Rehabilitation Sciences	
School of Hospitality Administration	
	School of Information and Library Science
School of Law	School of Law
School of Medicine	School of Medicine
	School of Nursing
	School of Pharmacy
School of Public Health	School of Global Public Health
School of Social Work	School of Social Work
School of Theology	

These are two universities with different histories, geographic locations, emphases, and missions, but nonetheless they share many of the same academic divisions. That said, even the differences in their academic divisions are instructive. UNC Chapel Hill has a School of Nursing, but Boston University does not. Boston *used* to have a School of Nursing, however. It opened in 1946 and closed in 1988 due to declining enrolment and competition from subsidized nursing programmes at state universities. So even though Boston no longer has

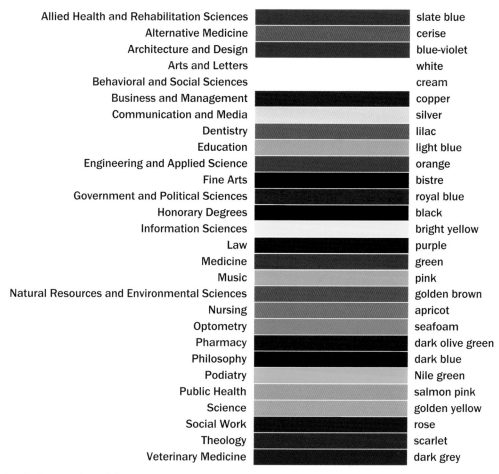

Allied Health and Rehabilitation Sciences	slate blue
Alternative Medicine	cerise
Architecture and Design	blue-violet
Arts and Letters	white
Behavioral and Social Sciences	cream
Business and Management	copper
Communication and Media	silver
Dentistry	lilac
Education	light blue
Engineering and Applied Science	orange
Fine Arts	bistre
Government and Political Sciences	royal blue
Honorary Degrees	black
Information Sciences	bright yellow
Law	purple
Medicine	green
Music	pink
Natural Resources and Environmental Sciences	golden brown
Nursing	apricot
Optometry	seafoam
Pharmacy	dark olive green
Philosophy	dark blue
Podiatry	Nile green
Public Health	salmon pink
Science	golden yellow
Social Work	rose
Theology	scarlet
Veterinary Medicine	dark grey

Fig. 8. Categories of the most common academic colleges and schools among members of the Association of American Universities with degree colours derived from the Intercollegiate Bureau of Academic Costume and other traditional sources.

a nursing school, there is no shortage of Colleges or Schools of Nursing among other AAU members.

Likewise, Boston has a College of Engineering but UNC Chapel Hill does not. This is because UNC Chapel Hill was founded as a state liberal arts university in 1789. But in 1887, North Carolina created North Carolina State University as a land-grant college emphasizing technical and industrial education, including engineering. So there has been no need for UNC Chapel Hill to create another state engineering programme, and there is no shortage of Colleges or Schools of Engineering among other AAU members.

Looking at both columns, we can see that *most* of Boston and UNC's colleges and schools already have colours historically authorized by the Intercollegiate Bureau of Academic Costume. So if we make sure we do not lose sight of the forest because of the large number of trees, the astonishing thing to notice is that, taken as a whole, the sixty-two members of the Association of American Universities share a huge number of the same college and school divisions—Engineering, Business, Law, Science, Fine Arts, Nursing, Education, Social Work, Music, Theology, Medicine, and so on—divisions that already have Intercollegiate Bureau degree colours assigned to them.

The colours assigned to these groups of colleges and schools could be used for the degree titles associated with those faculties, which would help us avoid colours for the narrowly defined and/or uncommon degrees that have consistently hamstrung the two American academic colour systems, like bachelor, master, or doctoral degrees in humanics, physical education, home economics, physical therapy, occupational therapy, audiology, and so on.[68]

Traditionally, the colours assigned to the large pedagogical divisions I am describing would be considered *faculty* colours. But employing the *degree* colour approach of the 1895 Intercollegiate Code of Academic Costume has one very attractive benefit. As I mentioned earlier, the American academic system distinguishes between liberal arts (or research) degrees and professional (or technical) degrees, and typically only a handful of degree titles are used for the former. The Master of Arts, Master of Science, and Doctor of Philosophy degrees are most often used to designate a liberal arts or research degree. Professional degrees typically use the name of the subject as part of the degree: Master of Agriculture, Doctor of Medicine, Doctor of Occupational Therapy, etc.[69]

Among terminal research degrees, the PhD is dominant. And professors are very conscious of the honour attached to this degree. The degree colour system of the 1895 Code preserves this dichotomy between (and hierarchy of) liberal arts/research degrees and professional/technical degrees in a way the subject colour system of the 1960 Code and the traditional faculty colour system cannot.

So in my opinion, the degree colour system of the 1895 Intercollegiate Code of Academic Costume—*as originally applied to clusters of degrees*—is the best solution to the problems we see in American academic hood edging today. Because this system would

---

68 In situations like these, it would not be a doctoral degree in Audiology I object to. Rather, it would be a 'Doctor of Audiology' degree I object to, when a shared doctoral degree title like 'Doctor of Allied Health Sciences' or 'Doctor of Rehabilitation Sciences' could instead be used to describe a cluster of related doctoral programmes. One could then receive a Doctor of Allied Health Sciences degree with a concentration in audiology, or physical therapy, or occupational therapy in the same way one receives a Doctor of Philosophy degree with a concentration in biology, or chemistry, or physics. My complaint here is primarily one of pedagogical terminology, not of academic costume, although they are related. The use of standardized degree titles has been debated for over a century in the US; for a specific example, see an interesting discussion in 1903 by the American Society of Naturalists about appropriate degree titles for coursework in the sciences, recorded in *Science*, 19.491 (27 May 1904), pp. 809–21.

69 Here I must admit that on rare occasions this rule of thumb is not always so neat: a student interested in practising law would earn a Juris Doctor (or Doctor of Jurisprudence) (JD), but a student interested in the history of law can earn *either* a Doctor of Philosophy (PhD) in law or a Doctor of Juridical Science degree (SJD). The PhD and SJD are terminal degrees; the JD is not. The nomenclature of law degrees is atypical for historical reasons I will not go into here, but it is worth emphasizing that most professions have but one terminal research degree: the PhD.

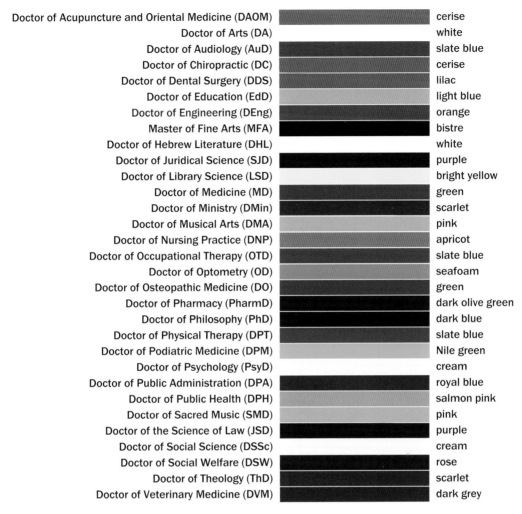

Doctor of Acupuncture and Oriental Medicine (DAOM)		cerise
Doctor of Arts (DA)		white
Doctor of Audiology (AuD)		slate blue
Doctor of Chiropractic (DC)		cerise
Doctor of Dental Surgery (DDS)		lilac
Doctor of Education (EdD)		light blue
Doctor of Engineering (DEng)		orange
Master of Fine Arts (MFA)		bistre
Doctor of Hebrew Literature (DHL)		white
Doctor of Juridical Science (SJD)		purple
Doctor of Library Science (LSD)		bright yellow
Doctor of Medicine (MD)		green
Doctor of Ministry (DMin)		scarlet
Doctor of Musical Arts (DMA)		pink
Doctor of Nursing Practice (DNP)		apricot
Doctor of Occupational Therapy (OTD)		slate blue
Doctor of Optometry (OD)		seafoam
Doctor of Osteopathic Medicine (DO)		green
Doctor of Pharmacy (PharmD)		dark olive green
Doctor of Philosophy (PhD)		dark blue
Doctor of Physical Therapy (DPT)		slate blue
Doctor of Podiatric Medicine (DPM)		Nile green
Doctor of Psychology (PsyD)		cream
Doctor of Public Administration (DPA)		royal blue
Doctor of Public Health (DPH)		salmon pink
Doctor of Sacred Music (SMD)		pink
Doctor of the Science of Law (JSD)		purple
Doctor of Social Science (DSSc)		cream
Doctor of Social Welfare (DSW)		rose
Doctor of Theology (ThD)		scarlet
Doctor of Veterinary Medicine (DVM)		dark grey

Fig. 9. A list of currently conferred terminal degree titles and abbreviations authorized by the Regents of the University of the State of New York married to the degree colours proposed in this epilogue. This list includes research and professional degrees. Note that the Regents have not authorized Doctor of Architecture and Doctor of Business Administration degrees for New York institutions of higher education, but these terminal professional degrees are conferred by other universities in the United States. The colours for the DArch and DBA would be blue-violet and copper, respectively.

assign a single colour to a constellation of related academic faculties using contemporary college and school divisions as a guide, you may call this a 'faculty color' system if you wish, but it is still essentially a 'degree color' system that *suggests* (but not necessarily *indicates*) the *title* of the wearer's degree, with similar degree titles clustered into faculty colour categories assigned to the academic fields of the most common colleges or schools in American universities. Tagged degree titles would follow the customary Intercollegiate Bureau system whereby the degree colour is determined by the faculty in the title, not the subject or major tagged to the faculty, so all Master of Arts degrees regardless of tag would use white and all Master of Science degrees regardless of tag would use golden yellow. This proposal is an heirloom of the 1895 Intercollegiate Code, preserving what I think are the best qualities of that system, gently limited and restrained by the natural pedagogical divisions of contemporary academia.

As you may recall, in 1903 the Regents of the University of the State of New York charged the Intercollegiate Bureau of Academic Costume with the responsibility to assign new degree colours to degrees authorized by that state, which explains why the Bureau approved certain degree colours at certain times during its history. Today, the Regents of the University of the State New York continue to limit the number of degree titles and degree abbreviations colleges and universities may confer in that state.[70] To illustrate how my proposed reform of American degree colours would work, in Figure 9 I have applied the twenty-eight degree colours shown in Figure 8 to current terminal research and professional degrees approved by the Regents and conferred by New York institutions of higher education. Keep in mind that some of these degrees are extremely obscure, only offered at perhaps one university in the state. Not shown are honorary degrees; according to my proposed system all hoods for honorary degrees would be edged with black velvet.

This proposed revision of the degree colour system of the 1895 Intercollegiate Code is conservative, not radical. It improves the system already being used by most colleges and universities in the US, and it possesses at least five advantages over the 1960 Academic Costume Code used by the rest. First, this revised degree colour system preserves the distinction between research and professional degrees. Second, there are fewer degree colours to memorize. Third, fewer of these colours are so similar in hue as to be easily confused. Fourth, a greater percentage of these colours have symbolic associations with the disciplines they represent. And fifth, a broader spectrum of academic disciplines can claim a representative colour of their own. Taken as a whole, then, these advantages permit one to 'read' a hood with a greater amount of specificity than the 1960 Academic Costume Code while avoiding the confusing excess of degree colours in the 1895 Intercollegiate Code of Academic Costume.

ERRATUM:

An error on page 58 of Kenneth L. Suit, 'The Iridescent Web: American Degree Colours (1895–1935),' *Transactions of the Burgon Society*, 15 (2015), resulted in the deletion

---

70 The current list of registered degrees for New York colleges and universities (Section 3.50) can be accessed from a link on this page: <www.nysed.gov/college-university-evaluation /education-law-rules-and-regulations> [retrieved 25 May 2021].

of information about Forestry, here in italics: 'But catalogues from Cotrell & Leonard (the depository of the records of the Intercollegiate Bureau) and other contemporary sources indicate that Dentistry was added between 1898 and 1901 *and Forestry was added in 1900 or 1901 ... .*' The source for Forestry is the same as that cited in Vol. 15 for Dentistry: 'School Equipment: Graduation Gowns', *The School Journal*, 62.22 (1 June 1901), p. 603.

Appendix A

Approximate "Degree Color" Adoption Dates By The Intercollegiate Bureau Of Academic Costume (1970 – Present)

Whenever possible, the colour shades in this chart have been closely matched to the velvet edgings of vintage Cotrell & Leonard hoods, although there are often slight differences in the same hue due to dye variations and age fading of the fabric. Not shown are five degree colours either officially authorized or considered for official authorization that were deleted during the tumultuous 1959-1960 period: Humanics (crimson), Naprapathy (cerise), Philanthropy (rose), Political Science (royal blue), and Retailing (turquoise). For more on this subject see Suit, 'Conforming to the Established Standards'.

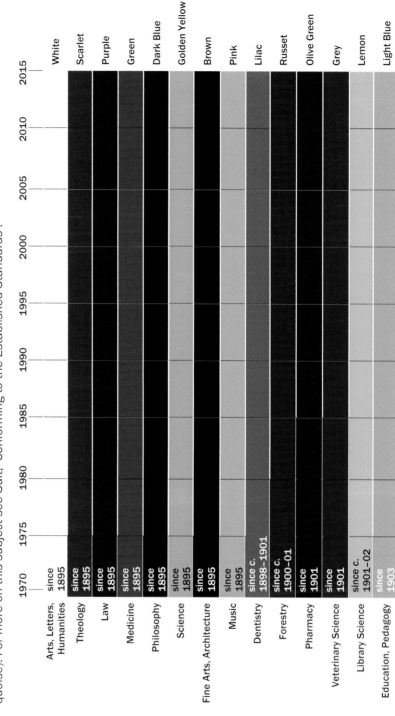

Discipline	Since	Color
Commerce, Accountancy, Bus.	since c. 1903–05	Drab
Engineering	since c. 1906–09	Orange
Oratory (Speech)	since c. 1906–09	Silver Grey
Agriculture	since c. 1909–15	Maize
Physical Education	since c. 1912–15	Sage Green
Economics	since c. 1912–15	Copper
Public Health	since c. 1915–18	Salmon Pink
Podiatry-Chiropody	since c. 1936	Nile Green
Nursing	since c. 1936–37	Apricot
Social Work	since c. 1936–37	Citron
Optometry	since c. 1949	Sea Foam
Public Administration, Foreign Service	since 1959	Peacock Blue
Journalism	since 1959	Crimson
Social Science	since c. 1959–60	Cream
Home Economics	since 1961	Maroon
Occupational Therapy	[1]	Slate Blue
Physical Therapy	[2]	Teal ?
Audiology	[3]	Spruce Green ?
Criminal Justice	[4]	Midnight Blue ?
Psychology	[5]	Royal Blue[6] ?
Interior Design	[7]	Bilberry ?

139

1 In 1995 the American Occupational Therapy Association selected 'slate blue' as the degree colour for Occupational Therapy. This was approved as an 'alternate' colour for Occupational Therapy by the Intercollegiate Bureau in 2011.

2 In 1997 the American Physical Therapy Association selected 'teal' as the degree colour for Physical Therapy. It is not known whether this colour was approved by the Intercollegiate Bureau.

3 In 2001 the National Association of Future Doctors of Audiology selected 'spruce green' as the degree colour for Audiology. It is not known whether this colour was approved by the Intercollegiate Bureau.

4 In 2002 the Academy of Criminal Justice Sciences autho-rized 'midnight blue' as the degree colour for Criminal Justice. It is not known whether this colour was approved by the Intercollegiate Bureau.

5 In 2007 the National Council of Schools and Programs of Professional Psychology selected 'royal blue' as the degree colour for Psychology. It is not known whether this colour was approved by the Intercollegiate Bureau.

6 Sometimes a lighter shade of royal blue is used to avoid confusion with the dark blue of Philosophy.

7 In 2009 the Fellows of the Interior Design Educators Council selected 'bilberry' as the degree colour for Interior Design. It is not known whether this colour was approved by the Intercollegiate Bureau.

Appendix B

'Subject Color' Adoption Dates by the American Council on Education (1970–Present)

To illustrate the difference between the darker degree color shades the IBAC and Cotrell & Leonard used (see Appendix A) and the brighter degree color shades typically used by academic costume manufacturers today, in this chart I have used the 'faculty color' hues shown in Wikipedia, at <en.wikipedia.org/wiki/Academic_regalia_in_the_United_States> [retrieved 12 July 2021]. Some variation within a given degree color may be expected, even on vintage hoods. But generally speaking, academic costume manufacturers today use degree colors that are much brighter and more vivid than the colors Cotrell & Leonard used a century ago, which makes it easier to distinguish among most of the degree colors but gives a more aesthetically lurid appearance to the garments.

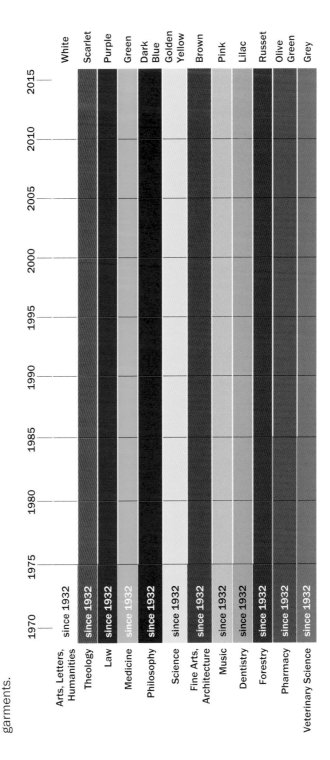

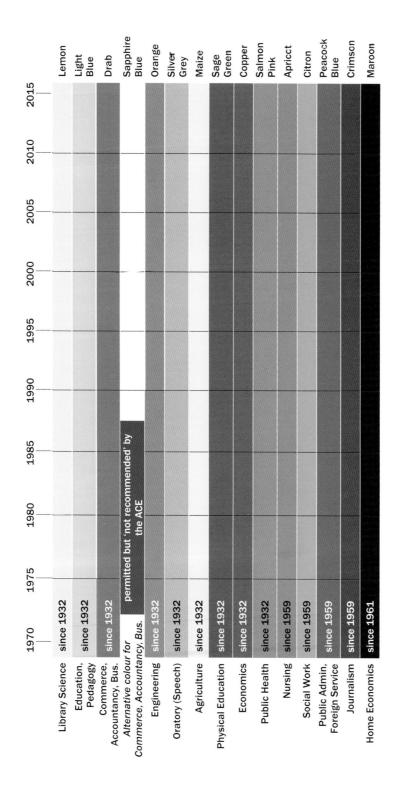

Transactions of the Burgon Society, 20 (2020), pages 143–149

The Hoods of the Three Senior Doctorates at Edinburgh

Nicholas Groves

A post on the Facebook Academical Dress group showed the Edinburgh DD hood of James Martineau, currently held by the Library at Harris Manchester College, Oxford.[1] It is of the standard Edinburgh simple shape [s4], but does not have the 'appended cape' we associate with the DD, LLD, and MD hoods, which gives the Edinburgh full shape, [f8]. Some correspondence on this followed, and it prompted me to examine some early sources about these three hoods, which I recalled did not mention the cape. The following table (next page) is the result. Shapes are noted if given.

Allowing for the sources to lag behind actual practice, it would seem that the cape was first added to the MD hood around 1890, being first mentioned in *Whitaker's Almanac* for that year—and we note that the 'appended cape' is mentioned for the MD and not the DD or LLD. It is an odd addition. The simple hood (of which the Edinburgh version [s4] is a variant) is worn back-to-front, so what has happened is that the cape has been attached to the wrong side—it is attached to the cowl edge. There is a parallel: the American ICC doctors' hood [f14] does this, also, although that is cut as a single piece. Scottish-American links were strong. Scottish universities awarded the MD as the first degree in medicine until the Medical Registration Act of 1858, when they were forced to institute the MB in line with nationally reorganized practice, and it is known that it was Scottish medics who played the major part in setting up the new transatlantic medical schools:[2] hence it is still the case that the MD is the first degree in medicine in the USA. Whether this can be translated to the academic dress is another matter.[3]

The other oddity of this style of hood is that the cape is attached back-to-front—i.e., so that the crimson lining is on show; the side that lies against the back is black.

Quite why the cape was added is unclear. We do know that medics attended conferences in their robes (this was a leading factor in the Scottish universities re-adopting robes

I am grateful to Dr Jonathan Cooper and Professor Bruce Christianson for reading initial drafts of this article, and for their comments.

1 Post by R. A. Hanford, 18.15, 20 January 2020. James Martineau, 1805–1900), Unitarian minister and theologian. He was principal of the College when it was in Manchester. He was awarded the Edinburgh DD in 1884; he was also STD (Leiden), 1874; DCL (Oxford), 1888; and DLitt (Dublin), 1891.

2 See, for example, Klieforth and Munro, p. 238: '… and Scots founded four of the first six major American universities, as well as the first three medical schools in America.' In addition, the authors note that Edinburgh attracted more colonial students than any other British university—particularly for its medical school. See also Bonner, p. 43: 'When the first medical schools were created in the United States and Canada, it was the Edinburgh graduates who planned and taught in them.'

3 Harvard graduates appear to wear the original (non-caped) MD hood, but in fact they are wearing the Oxford MA hood as it was when academic dress was adopted there. The [s4] shape was in use at Oxford at the time, and the 'flat' crimson lining is still an option at Oxford as opposed to the (now more usual) crimson shot orange.

Source & date	DD	LLD	MD
1843 Senatus minutes[A]	*no hood*	*no hood*	black lined scarlet [exact shape unknown]
1860 Installation Report[B]	black silk lined purple silk	black silk lined blue silk	black silk lined crimson silk
Edinburgh University Calendar 1865–66, p. 145[C]	black cloth lined purple silk	black cloth lined blue silk	black cloth lined crimson silk
Edinburgh University Calendar 1871/72, p. 163[D]	black cloth lined purple silk	black cloth lined blue silk	black cloth lined crimson silk
T. W. Wood, *Ecclesiastical and Academical Colours*, 1875, p. 50	black cloth lined purple	black cloth lined blue	black cloth lined crimson
Girls' Own Paper, Vol I, no. 35, 28 August 1880, pp. 564–56	black cloth lined purple silk	black cloth lined blue silk	black cloth lined crimson silk
DD hood of James Martineau, 1884 (held at Harris Manchester College)	black cloth lined purple silk, [s4] shape—no cape.	*n/a*	*n/a*
Whitaker's Almanac, 1885, p. 425[E]	black cloth lined purple silk	black cloth lined blue silk	black cloth lined crimson silk
T. W. Wood, *Degrees, Gowns, and Hoods …*, 1889, p. 21	black cloth lined purple	black cloth lined blue	black cloth lined crimson
Whitaker's Almanac, 1890, pp. 641–43	black cloth lined purple silk	black cloth lined blue silk	black cloth lined crimson silk with appended cape faced and lined with crimson silk
Notes & Queries, 7th series, 12 (26 September 1891), p. 241	black silk lined purple silk	black silk lined blue silk	black silk lined crimson silk
Whitaker's Almanac 1893, pp. 643–46	black cloth lined purple silk	black cloth lined blue silk	black cloth lined crimson silk with appended cape faced and lined with crimson silk

A   Cooper, p 124. This hood was for use outside the University only.
B   Quoted in Cooper, p 139.
C   Quoted in Cooper, p 125.
D   Accessed via Google Books.
E   The Whitakers are from a series of scans of those in the Bodleian Library provided for me by Dr Alex Kerr. They list the hoods by degree and not by university.

Source & date	DD	LLD	MD
Whitaker's Almanac 1896, pp. 681–82	black cloth lined purple silk	black cloth lined blue silk	black cloth lined crimson silk with appended cape faced and lined with crimson silk
Whitaker's Almanac, 1898, pp. 702–03	black cloth lined purple silk	black cloth lined blue silk	black cloth lined crimson silk with appended cape faced and lined with crimson silk
Whitaker's Almanac, 1900, pp. 690–91	black cloth lined purple silk	black cloth lined blue silk	black cloth lined crimson silk with appended cape faced and lined with crimson silk
Boys' Own Paper, coloured chart, 1903	[schematic only: black and purple]	black lined blue [s4] shape.	[schematic only: black and crimson]
Encyclopædia Britannica, 11th edn, 1910, p. 779	black cloth lined purple	black cloth lined blue	black cloth 'with cape attached, lined and faced crimson silk'.
British Medical Journal, 'Academic Costumes', 23 July 1910, pp. 202–04	*not listed* (it lists medical hoods only)		'Foundation': black Lining: crimson
Edinburgh University Calendar 1919/20, p. 39[F]	'black cloth lined with purple silk'	'black cloth with appended cape, lined with blue silk'[G]	'black cloth with appended cape, lined and faced with crimson silk'
Athena: A Yearbook of the Learned World, C. A. Ealand (ed.), 1920, p. 91[H]	black cloth lined with purple silk	black cloth with appended cape, lined with blue silk	black cloth with appended cape, lined and faced with crimson silk
F. W. Haycraft, *Degrees and Hoods of the World's Universities and Colleges*[I] 1923, p. 15; 1924, p. 14; 1927, p. 14	black cloth lined purple	black cloth lined blue	black cloth with an appended cape lined and faced with crimson silk.

F   Accessed via Internet Archive.

G   Does this imply that the LL.D cape was not faced with blue, and so showed black? See the MD entry.

H   Most likely copied direct from the Calendar.

I   All three editions have identical entries.

Source & date	DD	LLD	MD
Wills' cigarette cards (text by C. A. H. Frank-lyn), 1926	_not illustrated_ (the only Edinburgh hood shown is the MD.)		'all the hoods ... are of the simple shape, but the MD has in addition a crimson cape ...'
T. Baty, _Academic Colours_, 1934, p. 23	black cloth lined purple	black cloth lined blue	black cloth lined crim-son
Everybody's En-quire Within, ('What colours are university hoods?') C. Ray (ed.), 1937, p. 1513	black cloth lined and faced purple	black cloth lined and faced blue [this hood is illus-trated in three-quar-ter view, and seems to have no cape, but 'and faced' may mean that it has]	black cloth with a cape faced and lined crimson silk
F.W. Haycraft, _De-grees and Hoods of the World's Univer-sities and Colleges_, 1948, p. 25	black cloth lined purple silk and an appended tippet faced with purple.	black cloth lined blue silk and an ap-pended tippet faced with blue.	black cloth lined crim-son silk and an append-ed tippet faced with crimson.
G.W. Shaw, _Academ-ical Dress of British Universities_, 1966, pp. 56–57, 'all of ... special sim-ple shape'	black cloth lined purple silk	black cloth lined blue silk	black silk lined crimson silk
H. H. Smith, _Academic Dress and Insignia of the World_, 1970 (Vol. I), p. 770 [J]	black cloth with an appended cape lined and faced with purple silk.	black cloth with an appended cape lined and faced with blue silk.	black silk with an ap-pended cape lined and faced with crimson silk.

[J]   The simple [s4] and full [f8] hood shapes are illustrated at plates 203 and 204.

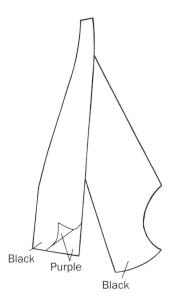

Fig. 1. [f8] shape laid flat; the cape is folded back on itself.

Fig. 2. The [f8] DD hood as worn.

Fig. 3. Robin Hanford wearing James Martineau's DD hood.

in the 1860s),[4] and the black and crimson was possibly a little too un-doctoral. Edinburgh doctors had had scarlet gowns since just before 1874,[5] but maybe the conference use was to wear the hood with the black gown.[6] Cambridge had given its MB its own hood in 1889— of black lined crimson (and its own gown—the doctoral robe in black stuff, but with no coloured facings or sleeve linings), and maybe the two outfits were felt to be too similar. (Though in that case, why Edinburgh did not follow Glasgow (1891) and Aberdeen (1895)

---

4   Indeed, this seems to be behind the 1843 MD hood, which was for use outside the University. St Andrews also had hoods for the MB and MD in use from 1862 until the full scheme was adopted in 1868.

5   They are listed in the Calendar for 1874 (p. 181), where they are specified as scarlet cloth, with facings and sleeve linings of degree colour. Interestingly, they are mandated for LL.D, MD, and DSc—but not DD: was this Presbyterian disapproval manifesting itself? (The DLitt, presumably, had not been instituted at that date.)

6   See Murray, p. 120. When J. A. H. Murray was awarded an honorary LL.D by Edinburgh in 1874 he 'wrote to the gown makers. He chose, without hesitation, the full-dress gown of extra Saxony light scarlet cloth, faced with rich blue silk … These had recently been introduced in place of the "undress robes" of black silk'. The University Calendar for 1871/72 says that all gowns are 'black, with long sleeves'—i.e., the MA gown—and does not mention the scarlet ones, so they must have been a very recent introduction. (It is known from photographs that the doctors in fact wore the MA gown with black velvet facings.) Alas, Murray says nothing of the hood. Edinburgh doctors' gowns (with the noted exception of the PhD) are now faced and lined with scarlet silk, regardless of the faculty: it is unclear when the change took place.

in 'upgrading' their doctors to scarlet hoods remains a mystery, also.[7] Both universities allowed them scarlet robes on those dates, so Edinburgh was ahead of the game in that respect.)

As to the other degrees, Wills's card of 1926 can be taken as definitive;[8] Baty less so, as he was working with information gained at a distance, both in time and physically; *Everybody's Enquire Within* is ambiguous; but Haycraft 1947 can (usually) be relied on. It is strange that George Shaw took no notice of it in his 1966 book, implying these three hoods are the same shape as the rest.[9]

So it seems that the LL.D had been given the 'appended cape' by 1920, and the DD possibly by 1937,[10] and definitely by 1947.[11] Was this to show that these are the senior—indeed, original—doctorates? It has never been granted to the later additions, DLitt, DSc, DMus,[12] DDS, DVM&S, or PhD, nor to the very late addition, Doctor *honoris causa* (Dr.h.c.)—the equivalent of the DUniv elsewhere.

As a footnote, the [f8] shape remained peculiar to Edinburgh, until 2014, when Queen Mary, University of London, adopted it for its doctors.

References

'Academic Costumes', *British Medical Journal*, Vol. ɪɪ (1910), pp. 202–05 (23 July).

Baty, T., *Academic Colours* (Tokyo: Kenkyusha Press, 1934).

Bonner, T. N., *Becoming a Physician: Medical Education in Britain, France, Germany, and the United States, 1750–1945* (Baltimore: Johns Hopkins University Press, 1995).

Cooper, J., 'Reforms to Scottish Academical Dress During the 1860s', *TBS*, 19 (2019), pp. 122–51. Available at <newprairiepress.org/burgonsociety> https://doi.org/10.4148/2475-7799.1168.

Ealand, C. A. (ed.), *Athena: A Year-book of the Learned World—the English-Speaking Nations* (London: A. & C. Black, 1920) , vol. ɪ (no more published).

Edinburgh University Calendar 1865/66, 1871/72, 1919/20.

Encyclopædia Britannica, 11th edn, 1910, p. 779.

Franklyn, C. A. H., *University Hoods and Gowns* [illustrated by Bt-Major A. V. Wheeler Holohan], a set of twenty-five large cigarette cards (Bristol: W. D. & H. O. Wills, 1926).

Groves, N., 'Popularizing University Hoods and Gowns: Wills's Cigarette Cards, 1926', *TBS*, 7 (2007), pp. 48–74. Available at <newprairiepress.org/burgonsociety> https://doi.org/10.4148/2475-7799.1056.

Haycraft, F. W., *The Degrees and Hoods of the World's Universities and Colleges*, 1st edn (Ware, Herts.: privately printed by Jennings & Bewley, 1923), 2nd edn (London and Cheshunt: privately printed by Cheshunt Press, 1924), 3rd edn (London and Cheshunt: privately printed by Cheshunt

---

7 It seems that the scarlet gown was originally worn without the hood (pers. comm. Jonathan Cooper). The gowns were originally faced with faculty colour silk. When the facings were changed to scarlet silk for all, possibly the use of the hood with the gown was seen as necessary to indicate the faculty.

8 See my 'Popularizing University hoods … ', p. 74.

9 It was corrected in the 1992 edition.

10 If we take 'lined and faced purple' of *Everybody's Enquire Within* to mean the cape.

11 Dr Cooper informs me that he has seen in a note dated 1951–53 that the changes took place 'about twenty years ago'.

12 Although at least one example of the DMus with cape (scarlet with white facing) is known to exist, it is assumed that this is an error or misinterpretation of the regulations.

Press, 1927), 4th edn, revised and enlarged by E. W. Scobie Stringer (Cheshunt: privately printed by Cheshunt Press, 1948).

Klieforth, A. L. and Munro, R. J., *The Scottish Invention of America, Democracy and Human Rights: A History of Liberty and Freedom from the Ancient Celts to the New Millennium* (Dallas: University Press of America, 2004)

Murray, K. M. Elisabeth, *Caught in the Web of Words: James A. H. Murray and the Oxford English Dictionary* (New Haven and London: Yale University Press, 1977).

Notes & Queries, 7th series, 12 (26 September 1891), p. 241.

Ray, C. (ed.), *Everybody's Enquire Within* (London: Amalgamated Press, 1937), p. 1513.

Shaw, G. W., *Academical Dress of British Universities* (Cambridge: Heffer, 1966).

Smith, H., assisted by Sheard, K., *Academic Dress and Insignia of the World*, 2 vols (Cape Town: A. A. Balkema, 1970), vol. I.

'University Hoods', *Boy's Own Paper*, 26, No. 25 (19 March 1904), pp. 413, 414. Fold-out colour plate entitled 'Hoods of the Academical Degrees of the Universities of Great Britain & Ireland', collected in the *Boy's Own Annual* for 1903/04.

'University Hoods and How to Make Them', *Girl's Own Paper*, 1, No. 35 (25 August 1880), pp. 564–66.

Whitaker's Almanac, 1890, 1893, 1896, 1898, 1900.

Wood, T. W., *Ecclesiastical and Academical Colours* (London and Derby: Bemrose & Sons [1875]).

—— T*he Degrees, Gowns and Hoods of the British, Colonial, Indian and American Universities and Colleges* (London: Thomas Pratt & Co. [1882 or 1883]; reissued [c. 1889]).

Transactions of the Burgon Society, 20 (2020), pages 150–161

Reflections on Designing the Academic Dress of the University of Hertfordshire

By Bruce Christianson and Philip Waters

Thirty years ago the authors were involved in the design of the academic dress for the new University of Hertfordshire. Here we reflect upon the process, and try to remember what we thought we were doing. We stress that our recollections are unreliable, our opinions are our own, and what we say may not represent the official view of the University of Hertfordshire or, for that matter, anybody else.

The University of Hertfordshire began life as Hatfield Technical College in 1952, and our degree candidates were presented as external students of the University of London.[1] In 1969 we became a polytechnic. Following this, the vast majority of our students were registered for qualifications awarded either by the CNAA, the Council for National Academic Awards, or by BTEC, the Business and Technology Education Council.[2] A small minority of our students continued to study for awards made by other bodies, including some certificates and diplomas awarded by the Polytechnic itself.[3]

Awards ceremonies were held each year, but these were not conferment ceremonies, even in the case of the institution's own awards. Instead, the ceremonies were presentation ceremonies, where the new graduates and diplomates were presented to the Academic Board of the Polytechnic, wearing the academic dress prescribed by the awarding institution for their award, and which they were by then already entitled to wear.[4]

The CNAA academic dress incorporated a grade-hood system, based on a variant of the Aberdeen shape.[5] All the hoods were made of a distinctive gold-yellow panama, with

We would like to thank Roxanne Garara (née Measey), Assistant Registrar (Exams & Awards) at the University of Hertfordshire, for sourcing the photographs; and her predecessor Anne Austin (née Walmsley) for incisive comments on an early draft of the paper.

1   The College also had students studying for a wide variety of other qualifications. For a potted history of the institution visit <www.herts.ac.uk/about-us/the-history-of-our-university> [retrieved 28 March 2021].

2   All degrees and postgraduate qualifications, including doctorates, were awarded by the CNAA; both bodies awarded sub-degree certificates and diplomas.

3   The Polytechnic Diploma, for example, was an award accredited as equivalent to a bachelor's degree without honours.

4   The awards had been conferred by an administrative action, well prior to the ceremonies. This practice differs from that of the ancient universities in the British Isles, where conferment of the award takes place during the ceremony. However ceremonies held by the University of London have always been of the type described here.

5   The CNAA shape is [a1] in the Groves classification system. The [a1] was probably the 'altered' pattern adopted by the University of Aberdeen in 1861, and was certainly being used there by 1891: see Cooper p. 127 n 23; and p. 128, Fig 3 & n 29. The [a7] pattern currently used at Aberdeen (and depicted in Shaw) is a later variation. The [a1] shape was also in use at the University of York prior to its adoption by the CNAA.

a silk lining denoting the level of the award: turquoise for bachelors' degrees, white for masters', turquoise with a white facing[6] for four-year first degrees such as the MEng, and maroon for the PhD. The hood for higher doctors was lined and bound with cream damask in the St Aidan pattern.

The bachelors' gown was a Cambridge BA pattern, but without the strings or the slit in the arm seam:[7] at the front, the sleeve of the CNAA bachelors' gown reached only to the elbow. The masters' gown was of the standard Oxbridge pattern, but had no cut-out in the boot of the sleeve. The doctors' gowns were made in the masters' pattern: a black gown with maroon silk yoke and facings in the case of the PhD, and a gold-yellow gown with cream brocade facings in the case of a higher doctorate. Unusually, the CNAA academic dress regulations precisely specified the length of the gowns: bachelors' gowns were to be worn twelve inches off the ground, and all other gowns eight inches off the ground.

Higher doctors wore a velvet Tudor bonnet with a gold cord, PhDs wore a cloth bonnet with a maroon cord, and everyone else wore the traditional black trencher and tassel.[8]

Those holding diplomas wore the CNAA bachelors' gown, usually without a hood, although by 1990 BTEC had prescribed a hood for the holders of its Higher National Diplomas and Certificates (HND and HNC). The BTEC hood was also in the CNAA Aberdeen shape, with a scarlet body and a deep blue lining, and so bore a superficial but startling resemblance to the hood for the Oxford DPhil.

A series of awards ceremonies was held over the period of a week in November, allowing those who had to re-sit examinations in the autumn[9] to be presented along with the rest of their cohort. This delay meant that the ceremonies had more of the flavour of a reunion than of a passing-out parade.

The government had signalled that The Hatfield Polytechnic (as the institution was then known) was to receive University Status in 1992 under the Further and Higher Education Reform Bill, thus allowing us for the first time to award our own degrees.

Relatively late in 1991 it became clear that the government proposed to abolish the CNAA at the same time as the new universities came into being.[10]

This meant that the cohort graduating in the summer of 1992 would not be able to complete their degrees under the regulations upon which they had embarked, but would need to receive degrees from the (very) new University of Hertfordshire. Our new academic dress would therefore need to be in place in time for the November 1992 ceremonies, less than a year away.

A working group was established by the Academic Board to develop the academic regulatory framework for the new university. Another ad-hoc group was set up by Marketing and External Relations to address the corporate image implications of the transition to university status. These included (amongst many other more conventional branding is-

---

6 We follow Smith's terminology, so a facing is a narrow band placed on the lining, running along the inside edge of the cowl.

7 The Cambridge bachelors' gown sleeve had been steadily creeping up the forearm for a hundred years or so, and by the 1960s the slit was no longer essential for eating or writing on a chalkboard. The CNAA bachelors' and masters' gowns are [b1] and [m10] respectively in the Groves system.

8 [h2], [h2], and [h1] respectively in the Groves system.

9 Seasons mentioned are relative to the northern hemisphere.

10 On the 6th of May 1992, see <www.legislation.gov.uk/uksi/1992/831/made> [retrieved 28 March 2021].

sues) the petition for a Grant of Arms, the design and tendering process for a university mace, and the development and procurement of a system of academic dress for the University. The authors found themselves co-opted onto both the regulatory framework and the corporate image groups.

Academic dress occupied a curious niche. While most public events were the responsibility of Marketing, the awards ceremonies were firmly in the hands of Registry. And while the design of the academic dress was regarded primarily as an issue of corporate image, particularly with regard to colour, the academic dress regulations were the responsibility of the Academic Board working group. This could easily have led to tension, and the fact that it did not was largely a result of the willingness of all those involved to respect one another's expertise.

At the time, J. Wippell & Co of Exeter had the contract for providing robes to the Polytechnic, and they were regularly consulted during the design process regarding the feasibility of the different options being considered. The initial proposals set out to the ad-hoc group in the brief prepared by Marketing included the option of having no academic dress at all.[11] This possibility was firmly laid to rest by Professor Neil K. Buxton, at that time the Director the Polytechnic and subsequently the first Vice-Chancellor of the University. 'The parents will expect to see gowns and hoods,' he insisted, perfectly correctly as it turned out.[12]

At this point, it is probably worth stepping back and considering what we believed we were trying to achieve, and the constraints we were under. Our objectives were that our robes should be consistent with our corporate image, be distinctive to the University of Hertfordshire, have a clear internal logic, provide an attractive spectacle, and look modern—but be compatible with tradition.

We were under considerable time pressure, and our immediate concern was to have something that would create a favourable impression at our own awards ceremonies. However, we were also mindful that our doctoral graduates might go on to become academics, and so it was important that our robes look good at the ceremonies of other universities as well as our own.

At the time, the planned corporate colours for the new university were black, white, and grey.[13] Interestingly, it was our consideration of the spectacle of the awards ceremonies that helped to persuade the corporate image team to replace black as a corporate colour with a distinctive shade of mauve purple.[14]

Many of the decisions turned out to be quite straightforward. We wanted our hoods to be lightweight so that they would sit well on the shoulders without strangling the wearer[15] or requiring constant adjustment, and we wanted them to flourish well so as to display

---

11 There is almost a tradition of 'new' universities going through a phase of wondering whether they really need to adopt faux-medieval attire for festive occasions: both the University of London (from 1836 until 1843) and the Open University (from 1969 until 1972) at first attempted to dispense altogether with academic dress, but their students were having none of it: see the respective accounts by Goff.

12 In the case of mature students, of which we had a surprising number, their children also proved reassuringly keen on academic dress. It is a curious fact that, as at the University of London, our graduates and diplomates have never been required to wear academic dress when being presented to the Academic Board, although very few of them elect not to. On the other hand, staff who wish to take part in the academic procession are required to robe.

13 Pantone 6C.

14 Pantone 2597C.

15 Particularly when the wearer was attired in a light blouse, rather than a stiff-collared shirt

Fig. 1. Postgraduate masters queueing.

the lining. We considered alternative full shapes, but we already had considerable experience of the CNAA variant of the Aberdeen shape, and it seemed to meet our requirements.

The cloth outer of all CNAA hoods was a distinctive shade of CNAA yellow, and we decided that we would follow this approach, with the outer for all our hoods being made of cloth in the corporate shade of cool grey.

We were also enthusiastic to retain the grade-hood nature of the CNAA system. Part of the Polytechnic's mission was to bridge the two cultures[16] and to promote inter-disciplinary academic programmes, so we actively did not wish to distinguish among awards in different disciplines but only among awards made at different levels. We decided that degree hoods would be lined with watered silk:[17] white for Bachelors' hoods, and purple for Masters'. Extended first degrees, such as the MEng, had the white lining but with a purple facing.

BTEC had allowed hoods to the holders of their diplomas, for which many of our students were still enrolled[18] so, in the interest of parity, we had to allow hoods to those who were awarded University Diplomas. Diploma hoods were lined in plain (unwatered) grey silk, shaded to match the outer, but with a facing of white watered silk for higher diplomas, and of purple watered silk for postgraduate diplomas.

We did not prescribe hoods for the holders of University Certificates, partly because certificate holders were not invited to attend awards ceremonies. The exception to this

and stout kipper tie.

16 Adumbrated by Snow. Indeed, C. P. Snow had been appointed the Polytechnic's first official Visitor in 1972, and regularly spoke at the awards ceremonies.

17 This wasn't due to any influence of Birmingham, we just liked the moiré effect.

18 While the CNAA was to be abolished in 1992, BTEC was not.

rule was the teaching qualification PGCE (post-graduate certificate in education), which did qualify the holder for attendance. This anomalous situation came about because of the credit rating. Most postgraduate certificates were rated at 60 CATS points[19] but the PGCE required an entire academic year of study, and was rated at 120 points at level 7, which was the same as a postgraduate diploma. We gave some thought to a special hood[20] for the PGCE but in the end decided to stand firm by the grade-hood principle: the PGCE was credit rated the same as a postgraduate diploma, and so it should have the same hood regardless of nomenclature.[21] We left doctoral hoods to one side while we made some decisions about gowns.

While we were very concerned to ensure that, as far as possible, none of our hoods was likely to be mistaken for that of any other institution, this was not felt to be imperative for our gowns. The option of having gowns distinctive to the University was considered, but rejected for all but the doctoral robes. Apart from considerations of cost and lead-time (the first ceremonies were by now fast approaching), our feeling was that it was relatively uncommon now for gowns to be worn without hoods on any occasion when knowledge of the wearer's university was of the essence. We also noted that the black gowns of many eminent institutions, at one time distinctive to them, were now so widely worn by other universities throughout the Commonwealth as to be generally available for adoption.[22]

We therefore decided to choose our gowns so that they told a story. The gown for bachelors' degrees was to be the same gown worn by bachelors at the University of London, which had awarded degrees to our students when we were a technical college. Our masters' gowns would be the gowns prescribed for masters by the CNAA, which had awarded degrees to our students while we were a polytechnic. Our doctoral robes would be distinctive to the University of Hertfordshire, and a reminder of our responsibility as a university for awarding our own degrees.

After looking through copies of Smith and the first edition of Shaw[23] we decided to adopt an older variation of the Oxford doctors' pattern robe, with the sleeve trim forming a cuff of the same width as the facings at the front rather than reaching up to the bicep.[24]

---

19 CATS is the Credit Accumulation and Transfer Scheme, a UK framework for quantifying the size and level of a university qualification: <en.wikipedia.org/wiki/Credit_Accumulation_and _Transfer_Scheme> [retrieved 28 March 2021].
Points quoted here refer, anachronistically, to the 2020 version of CATS. In broad terms, four CATS points are equivalent to two ECTS points, or to one US credit hour.
20 We even got as far as having a prototype made: it was grey, lined plain black, with a watered purple facing, and looked really good over a black gown.
21 Later the same principle led us to prescribe the higher diploma hood for all foundation degrees.
22 In England, these patterns include at least the gowns of Oxford, Cambridge, London, and the CNAA. For a clear summary of which former polytechnics adopted which patterns in 1992 see Appendix 9.3 of Hynes, pp. 114–21, particularly the summary table on p. 120. For full details, refer to Groves.
23 Thoughtfully brought to the meeting by Robin Richardson of Wippells.
24 The sequence of gowns is thus [b4], [m10], [d2] in the Groves system. We also stipulated, *contra* the CNAA regulations, that all gowns were to be worn eight inches off the ground: although lengthening the gown for those below the grade of Master, this stopped a few inches short of the medieval stipulation that academic gowns should reach the ankles (*toga talaris*), apart from those wearing high heels.

For the PhD we followed the University of London[25] in specifying dark red cloth[26] for the body of the robe, rather than scarlet, with watered purple silk for the facings and cuffs. The hood was lined with dark red watered silk, and faced with purple watered silk to match the gown. The research-based professional doctorates were given the same dress as the PhD, on the grade-hood principle of parity of esteem.

For the higher doctorates, we chose purple[27] cloth, trimmed with white brocade in a St Aidan pattern.[28] The hood was initially completely lined with the same white brocade used to trim the gown, although this was later modified (see below).

For doctors in undress we prescribed the same gown as for masters' degrees. We did consider the addition of a row of lace above the armhole[29] but in the end decided that black gowns were more likely to be worn if they were readily obtainable and did not require special adaptation.

Fig. 2. Bachelors celebrating.

Those awarded diplomas, whether from the CNAA, BTEC, or the Polytechnic itself, had traditionally worn the CNAA bachelors' gown. We decided to continue this custom of parity, and give our diplomates the same London pattern gown as our bachelors.

Holders of certificates did not attend awards ceremonies, or wear hoods, but should they be permitted a gown if they attended an occasion when academic dress was to be worn? And if so, on the principle of parsimony, should it be the same gown worn by holders of diplomas? What about those undergraduates who had completed sufficient study

25 As by then had many other institutions.

26 Murrey we should call it, if we abide by King Henry VIII's statute: see Cox. Our choice may also have been influenced by the maroon-coloured trim on the CNAA PhD gown.

27 We chose the purple because the cloth was available in our corporate colour, but noted that it was also permitted by Henry's statute. Keele had previously adopted purple doctors' robes, albeit in Cambridge pattern, and Imperial College would later follow suit.

28 This looked nice, and was a nod to the brocade trim of the CNAA higher doctorate.

29 You may like to know, the lace would have been oak-leaf lace, and silver not black. For the use of lace on undress gowns see Tsua.

Fig. 3a. Academic Dress for Dummies: PhD/Professional Doctor (left), Postgraduate Diploma, Higher Doctor.

towards their degree to obtain a certificate, were they to request one? Should their gown reflect their standing? And did it then make sense to prescribe a different gown only for first year undergraduates?

Eventually we took a deep breath and applied the same principle to undergraduates as we had for doctors in undress: gowns were more likely to be worn if they were of a pattern ready to hand, and so all undergraduates of the University were permitted the black bachelors' gown[30] without a hood.

Hats were very straightforward. The only change was to replace the coloured cords on the doctors' bonnets with grey ones.

In the meantime, the Academic Board's regulatory framework group had determined that the University of Hertfordshire would confer awards using a similar protocol[31] to the CNAA.

---

30 I.e. the [b4]. The rejected alternative we considered was to give undergraduates the [b1]: short gowns for undergraduates are a relatively recent (mid-nineteenth century) innovation, *contra* the medieval statutes that required them still to be ankle length.

31 The qualification is conferred by administrative action within the Registry, and is effective from the date on which the candidate satisfies the Board of Examiners. This was also in essence the protocol used by the University of London.

Fig. 3b. Postgraduate Master, Higher Doctor, Bachelor, PhD/Professional Doctor.

This decision meant that our awards ceremonies would continue to be presentations of graduates and diplomates to the Academic Board, rather than being the point of conferment.[32] The only exception to this is honorary awards, which are actually conferred in the course of the ceremony. This comes about because at the University of Hertfordshire honorary degrees such as the HonDSc are, for regulatory reasons, genuinely different awards from examined higher doctorates such as the DSc, and are conferred by a joint act of the Corporation of the University and the Academic Board, rather than upon the sole authority of the Academic Board. Our honorary degrees could therefore, in principle, have different academic dress to the corresponding examined degrees, a point to which we return.

That matter being settled, we could then turn to consider a deceptively profound question: who would be entitled to wear our robes?

As mentioned before, the University would for some years continue to present at our awards ceremonies students who gained their qualification from a different awarding authority, such as BTEC, as a result of study at the University. We were clear that we wanted

---

32 This protocol had the side advantage that our students obtained their qualifications immediately, and did not need to wait for the ceremony before they could describe themselves to potential employers as graduates.

everybody who was being presented to the Academic Board to be wearing our academic dress, to symbolise their new standing within the University of Hertfordshire, regardless of who the awarding authority was.

We also wished to allow our academic dress retrospectively to those who had gained a qualification as a result of study at the Polytechnic or the Technical College, and who were thereby members of the alumni association of the University. They would also be entitled to wear the academic dress of the nearest equivalent award of the University of Hertfordshire, regardless of the awarding institution for their qualification.

The final group on which we desired to confer rights to our academic dress were the University staff. Like most modern universities, the University of Hertfordshire encourages members of staff who hold their degree from elsewhere to wear the academic dress of their alma mater at the University of Hertfordshire's ceremonies. However, academic dress for institutions outside the United Kingdom can be difficult to obtain, especially at short notice, and some universities, for example on the continent, do not prescribe academic dress for their graduates.

Accordingly, we decided to permit members of our staff to wear, as an alternative, the academic dress of the University of Hertfordshire corresponding to the nearest equivalent qualification to their own.[33]

Finally, the senior officers of the University had special dress prescribed for them. Here our objective was to follow tradition, but be fairly understated about it. For the Chancellor and Pro Chancellor (the latter being ex officio the Chair of the Corporation of the University) we adopted the standard lay pattern[34] gown, made in royal blue[35] Chelmsford pattern damask trimmed with silver oak leaf[36] lace round the facings and the flap collar, the arm holes, and across the bottom of the sleeves. The Chancellor's gown has the addition of four inverted (point up) chevrons of lace on each sleeve. The Secretary and Registrar, who is Clerk to the Corporation, wears the same gown and silver trim as the Pro Chancellor, but made in plain dark blue.

The senior academic officers of the University, the Vice-Chancellor and their Deputy, wear lay gowns in the same pattern and trim as the Chancellor and Pro Chancellor respectively, but in dark blue with gold oak leaf lace. The Vice-Chancellor's robe is Tudor Rose pattern damask, and the Deputy's robe is plain. Fellows of the University wear a lay pattern gown made of grey cloth, with flap collar and facings of purple cloth, and trimmed with purple cloth on the armholes and white St Aidan damask on the outside of the facings.

---

33 The ancient universities (Oxford, Cambridge, and Trinity College Dublin) achieve this by a process called incorporation, which involves actually conferring their own degree on the relevant staff member, although see also <www.bodleian.ox.ac.uk/__data/assets/pdf_file/0008/199664 /MA-Status.pdf> [retrieved 28 March 2021]. Our procedure (more common generally in the British Commonwealth) is to treat the staff member as if they held our degree for the purpose of their standing under the University regulations. In technical terms, our practice is *ad eundem statum*, rather than *ad eundem gradum*. See Dickson for more on these issues.

34 [d4] without the wings over the sleeves.

35 The Pro Chancellor's gown remained a conventional royal blue, but in 2005 the Chancellor's gown changed to purple Chelmsford damask with silver trim. The liturgists among you will recognize the Advent array.

36 The oak leaf pattern was picked to evoke the Hatfield Oak, which also features on the University Achievement of Arms.

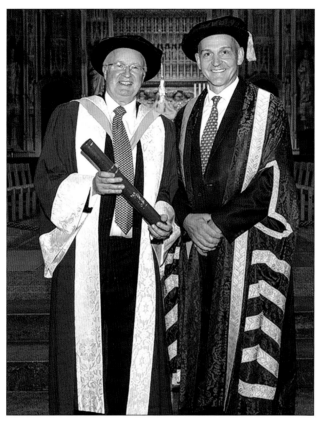

Fig. 4. Philip Waters, HonDLitt, with the Vice-Chancellor Professor Quintin McKellar.

Shortly before the first ceremonies were held, Dr George Shaw (who was in the process of preparing the second edition of his book) wrote to us expressing his dissatisfaction with a number of elements of our original scheme. He particularly disliked the fact that members of staff were allowed to wear the dress of degrees they did not hold;[37] that undergraduates appeared gowned as graduates;[38] that doctors in undress were not distinguished from masters;[39] that the higher doctorate hood had the same colours as the hood for bachelors;[40] and that the MPhil had the same hood as the PhD[41] which meant that the two degrees could not be distinguished by a hood worn over a surplice or an undress gown.

37 Although, as pointed out earlier, Oxford University also did this.

38 Although Liverpool University already followed this practice, as did scholars at Trinity College Dublin.

39 George, unaware of the detail of our deliberations, suggested a row of black Birmingham lace above the armhole. Our reply to him rather optimistically states 'we may revise this decision if there is persistent demand from our alumni'.

40 To be fair, the same is true for the PhD and MLitt hoods at Cambridge University.

41 Most masters' degrees require one year of additional study beyond that required for a bachelor; the MPhil is a research degree, like the PhD, and takes two years.

George's first three objections ran hard up against the principles underlying the decisions that we had taken, and we stood firm. Although George felt that we were departing from established practice, our intention was never so much to copy what other British universities happened to be doing at the moment. Rather, it was to rummage around in the same pool of tradition from which they had drawn their designs and practices, and to pull out something that suited our, perhaps slightly different, mission.

However, George's final two objections placed him upon very solid ground. Although it was too late to change things for the first sets of ceremonies, one of which Drs George and Mary Shaw were kind enough to attend as guests of the Academic Board, we made some adjustments later on. The colours on the MPhil hood became the purple watered silk of a masters' degree faced with the dark red watered silk of a research doctorate,[42] and the higher doctorate hood became lined with purple watered silk and faced with a wide strip of white brocade, thus bringing both doctoral hoods into line with the colour and trim of the corresponding robes.[43]

The first ceremonies were held in 1992 on the original College Lane site, in the Great Hall,[44] at that time the largest room in the University. In 1994 the ceremonies moved to the Cathedral and Abbey Church of St Alban, and since then the academic procession progresses along the longest nave in England. At the beginning of 1992 the Polytechnic had around 5,000 students; ten years later that number had increased through mergers and expansion to over 21,000. In parallel with the increase in students, the variety of degrees and diplomas offered has also greatly enlarged. Nevertheless, apart from the small changes already indicated, the University's scheme of academic dress did not require adaptation, and remained popular with all concerned for nearly thirty years.[45]

Do we have any regrets? Is there anything we wish had turned out differently? Well, it would have been pretty, and historically appropriate, for the examined higher doctorates to be trimmed with rose pink, rather than white. Pink damask was available in the appropriate shade and pattern but alas, pink was not a corporate colour. But in 2005 the University's bus company unō unveiled its new corporate livery: purple and pink.

References

Christianson, Bruce, *Academic Dress in the University of Hertfordshire*, 2nd edn (Hatfield: University of Hertfordshire, 2006). Available online at <uhra.herts.ac.uk/bitstream/handle/2299/4633/Academic%20Dress%20Lo-res.pdf?sequence=1>.

Cooper, Jonathan C., 'Reforms to Scottish Academical Dress during the 1860s', *TBS*, 19 (2019), pp. 122–51. Available online at <newprairiepress.org/burgonsociety> https://doi.org/10.4148/2475-7799.1168.

---

42 Thus placing the colours the opposite way around to the PhD hood.

43 Further information (including pictures) can be found in Christianson, where the Regulations (as they stood in 2006) are reproduced in full on p. 26.

44 Renamed the Prince Edward Hall in 1993.

45 In 2020 the University appointed new robemakers, and this resulted in some changes coming into effect from September of that year. The new robemaker is H. Tempest Ltd, and the University's current academic dress regulations are set out in version 4.0 of UPR AS01: <www.herts.ac.uk/__data/assets/pdf_file/0014/230540/AS01-Academic-Dress.pdf> [retrieved 28 March 2021]. You may like to see if you can spot all the changes from the scheme described here.

Cox, Noel, 'Tudor Sumptuary Laws and Academical Dress: An Act against Wearing of Costly Apparel 1509 and An Act For Reformation of Excess in Apparel 1533', *TBS*, 6 (2006), pp. 15–43. Available online at newprairiepress.org/burgonsociety> https://doi.org/10.4148/2475-7799.1047.

Dickson, Neil, 'Degrees of Degrees', *TBS*, 19 (2019), pp. 183–203. Available online at <newprairiepress .org/burgonsociety> https://doi.org/10.4148/2475-7799.1171.

Goff, Philip, *University of London Academic Dress* (London: University of London Press, 1999).

——, 'Blithering Nonsense: The Open University and its Academic Dress', *TBS*, 19 (2019), pp. 7–37. Available online at <newprairiepress.org/burgonsociety/> https://doi.org/10.4148/2475 -7799.1160.

Groves, Nicholas (ed.), *Shaw's Academical Dress of Great Britain and Ireland*, 3rd edn, Vol. i: *Universities and Other Degree-Awarding Bodies* (London: The Burgon Society, 2011), Vol. ii: Non-Degree-Awarding Bodies (London: The Burgon Society, 2014).

Hynes, Alice, 'Development of Academic Dress in Kingston University: A University for the Twenty-First Century', *TBS*, 19 (2019), pp. 7–121. Available online at <newprairiepress.org /burgonsociety/> https://doi.org/10.4148/2475-7799.1167.

Shaw, George W., *Academical Dress of British Universities* (Cambridge: Heffer, 1966).

——, *Academical Dress of British and Irish Universities*, 2nd edn (Chichester: Phillimore, 1995).

Smith, Hugh, assisted by Kevin Sheard, *Academic Dress and Insignia of the World*, 3 vols (Cape Town: A. A. Balkema, 1970).

Snow, Charles Percy, *The Two Cultures and the Scientific Revolution* (London: Cambridge University Press, 1960).

Tsua, Charles Rupert, 'A Study of the History and Use of Lace on Academical Gowns in the United Kingdom and Ireland', *TBS*, 12 (2012), pp. 103–27. Available online at <newprairiepress.org /burgonsociety>, https://doi.org/10.4148/2475-7799.1103.

Transactions of the Burgon Society, 20 (2020), pages 162–165

The Lack of a Theology Hood
at The University of the West Indies

By Mitchell A. Nicholls

The University of the West Indies (hereafter The UWI), formerly the University College of the West Indies (UCWI), was established in 1948, and gained full university status in 1962. It came after much dedication, research and funding thanks to the Commission on Higher Education in the Colonies formed by Oliver Stanley in 1943 when he was the Secretary of State for the Colonies. High Court Judge Cyril Asquith was made head of the Commission and a West Indies Committee was formed of which Sir James Irvine was made head.

This Commission made provisions particularly for key areas of study to be taught and thus catered for, within the university setting. The curriculum proposed initially for the new University was limited to the Faculties of Arts, Science and Medicine. No school or institution was set up for the teaching of agriculture or of engineering; but 'provision [was] made for education leading to graduation in these important branches of applied science', particularly for agriculture through the Imperial College of Tropical Agriculture in Trinidad which was established in St Augustine, Trinidad, on 30 August 1921 (His Majesty's Stationery Office, 1945).

No arrangements were made for the study of law, music or of theology, though these subjects would have been common to find in many other universities predating the UCWI. Though theology was not included within the proposed curriculum, there was already a college—and a considerably renowned one—which facilitated theology and pastoral studies, within the Island of Barbados.

Codrington College, completed in 1743 and opened in 1745 in St John, Barbados, was established by the will of Christopher Codrington dated 22 February 1703 and later branched into the Codrington Theological College and the Lodge School in 1830—the latter so named after the Mansion House, which later became the Principal's 'Lodge'.[1] The College was affiliated with Durham University from 1875 in which students at Codrington read theology (for either the BA or LTh) whilst others read classics. The Durham degree in classics ceased in 1955, and students studied at the UCWI as external students of London University until 1962. Codrington then became affiliated with the UCWI in 1965 where the Licentiate (LTh) started the same year and subsequently the newly Senate approved BA in Theology was introduced in 1971 (Holder, 1988).[2] As a result of the affiliation with Durham, the holders of the BA in Theology, BD (Bachelor of Divinity) or the BCL (Bachelor of Canon Law) or any other degree from Durham, would have worn Durham's academic dress for degree ceremonies at The UCWI/UWI. This was the case up until 1974 when the

---

1   Read more about the history of Codrington College in Holder.

2   The Right Revd Dr. John W. D. Holder is the former Archbishop and Primate of the Anglican Church in the Province of the West Indies and Lord Bishop of Barbados; he retired in 2018.

first holders of the BA in Theology from The UWI were graduated, by this point wearing academic dress of The UWI which was adopted in 1966. Durham's BA hood is full [f6], black, the cowl part-lined and the cape bound 1" [white] fur, Figure 1 (Groves, 2001).[3]

The BA in Theology is still offered at Codrington to this day however, as well as Durham's degrees in Theology, though since the introduction of the BA at The UWI, degrees in theology from Durham through Codrington are particularly at the postgraduate level. It is interesting that theology was not made or rather designated a 'professional' degree as is the case for degrees in education, medicine, law as well as agriculture and engineering—some of which came long after the BA in theology. The custom at The UWI was—as was the case at many other universities—that every faculty would have had its own colour and as faculties developed and new programmes were introduced, new colours were added. Due to the complexity of the academic system and the creation and development of specialist areas, faculty colours eventually became discipline colours. These discipline colours were coordinated in such a way to reflect the principal area of study—the Faculty—and were differenced with other colours to show specializations. The colours are then reflected in the lining of the academic hood indicating which degree the graduand would be receiving or rather, the degree to which they have been admitted.

These discipline colour variations could be seen at The UWI where, for example, the colour of the Faculty of Science and Technology (formerly Pure and Applied Sciences, hereafter SciTech), was once Allamanda Yellow regardless of the area of study, however today a BSc in Natural Sciences is Allamanda Yellow, whilst a BSc in Engineering is Aluminium Grey, and a BSc in Agriculture is Avocado Green.[4] (Nicholls, 2020.) These advances and distinctions never happened for the area of Theology, like as though theology as a specialization was all but forgotten.[5] Many other universities included theology amongst their primary degree areas, for example, the Regulations for the Academic Dress of London *c.* July 1952, listed their faculties and their colours: Theology—Sarum Red, Arts—Russet Brown, Law—Blue, as well as a variety of colours for varying specializations in Medicine.

Academic dress of The UWI began to be formally developed circa 1962, with the finally agreed dress being worn for the first time in 1966. The gowns feature the use of the lightweight and very breathable blue princetta fabric[6] of a modified shape—which is essentially a Cambridge BA [b2] gown with the forearm seam opened to the shoulder and the inner side of the sleeve removed. The hoods are of the old Fellow of the Royal College of Organists shape c.1930, similar to the Wales [s5], maintaining a rounded cowl, and a rounded cutout towards the liripipe, however unlike Wales, which has a pointed liripipe, the Organists' pattern is rounded downwards. The hood generally is cut at a steeper angle.

3　Nicholas Groves PhD, MA, FRHistS, FBS, is a historian who has published widely on the topics of ecclesiastical history and academic dress.

4　UWI Archives, 'Did You Know?!: The UWI Academic Dress'.

5　There is no set or particular process to denote an area as a professional degree which would grant it its own postnominals, discipline colour and recognition, other than a decision via the Senate of the university. What particularly makes these areas worthy of 'professional or specialization' status can range from the niche area of the subject—for example music (BMus)—to the focus, type or quality (credit weightings) of courses involved. A BMus more than likely contains more 'hard core' music topics than a BEd(Mus) or a BA(Mus), which would contain more education and liberal arts topics respectively. Comparatively, the same is true of the BA in Theology and the LTh at The UWI.

6　Princetta is a fabric made of wool and cotton, it is light, thus suitable for use especially in tropical climates.

As the degree, the BA in Theology is offered within the Faculty of Humanities and Education (HumEd), holders of the BA in Theology or the Licentiate (LTh), would be entitled to wear the hood lined with the faculty colour for Humanities (formerly Arts) which is a blue princetta hood, lined Plumbago Blue bound University Red. As Education has been denoted as a professional degree and is taught within its own school—The School of Education (SOE), it was assigned its own discipline colour which is White. One may posit, that because theology was not included in the main faculties of The UCWI and later The UWI, nor was it formally recognized as a special degree within HumEd, theology was never denoted a specialist or professional degree, and thus never gained its own distinct colour or post-nominals. Due to the aforementioned points, no hood was ever developed for the specific area of theology.

To 'combat' this, theology would first have to be designated as a professional or special degree, gaining it a particular post-nominal and recognizing it as the first professional degree for priests and religious scholars—where it would gain an extension of the BA, through BA(Th) or BA(Theol) as in the case of the science degrees like BSc(Eng) or BSc(Agr). It could also be denoted as a BTh or BD if given its own school faculty as per the BEd in the School of Education; for example, 'The Faculty of Theology and Religion'. It could finally be structured—as stated before—where there are different degrees for different 'classes' or qualities of course content. Perhaps the LTh and BA in Theology would remain in HumEd, whilst the BD or BTh would only be offered through the Faculty of Theology and Religion—as is the case for the geography degrees at The UWI—Mona, where there are three different geography degrees: BSc (SciTech), a BA (HumEd) and the BEd (SOE).

Secondly, a colour would be chosen usually to reflect the principles, or the nature of the degree, particularly a colour not in use for other faculties, as well as a colour with reasonable significance and meaning—for example blood red to represent the blood of Christ, or perhaps palatinate purple with a trim of white fur as tribute to Durham's BA and BD degrees. Thirdly, this colour is then reflected within the academic dress whether the hood be differenced with these colours or solely containing them, similar to The UWI's medical degree hoods—particularly those of nursing and of basic medical sciences.

In conclusion, as the university grows and develops and new areas of study are introduced, the university usually makes every effort to highlight the importance of every area. Not to say that the degree in theology would increase in rank or specialty if granted 'professional or specialty status' compared to the other degrees offered by the university, as to date, there is no set hierarchy of degrees at The UWI outside of the general ranking from Bachelor degrees to Honorary Doctorates. However, granting such status is an outward symbol that the area and discipline of theology forms one of the fundamental areas of study within academia and this is important as it is the only area that caters specifically to the spiritual needs of those who read for their degrees—particularly those preparing for the priesthood within the faculty.

And, in light of the College's much esteemed history, one spanning 275 years, as well as the nature of the degree, I am sure the designation of a discipline colour would be welcomed with open arms by all those who study in the faculty and receive their BA in Theology or LTh, thus placing it among the 'ranks and dignity' of the much esteemed and revered degrees such as the BEd, LLB, MBBS and BSc(Eng).

References

Groves, N. (2001). 'Towards A Standard Terminology for Describing Academic Dress', *Burgon Society Annual 2001*, pp. 9–12. Available at <newprairiepress.org/burgonsociety> https://doi.org/10.4148/2475-7799.1001.

Groves, N., et al. (2007). 'Popularizing University Hoods and Gowns: Wills's Cigarette Cards, 1926], *TBS*, 7 (2007), pp. 48–74, Available at <newprairiepress.org/burgonsociety> https://doi.org/10.4148/2475-7799.1056.

His Majesty's Stationery Office (1945, June). Report of the Commission on Higher Education in the Colonies, online at <obtienearchivo.bcn.cl/obtienearchivo?id=documentos/10221.1/29331/2/213787.pdf> [retrieved 12 December 2020].

Holder, J. (1988). *Codrington College: A Brief History* (Bridgetown, Barbados: Codrington College, 1988).

Nicholls, M. A. (2020). 'Tropical Raiment: The Academic Regalia of The University of the West Indies 1946–2020' (unpublished dissertation for Fellowship in the Burgon Society).

UWI Archives (31 October 2011). 'Did You Know?!: The UWI Academic Dress', online at <uwiarchives.wordpress.com/2011/10/31/did-you-know-the-uwi-academic-dress/> [retrieved 15 June 2021].

Transactions of the Burgon Society, 20 (2020), pages 166–174

'Degrees of Degrees'[1]: An Alternative Structure

By Graham Zellick

As Dr Neil Dickson wrote: '… in order to understand the customs surrounding the wearing of academic dress, it is necessary to understand the history of how and when degrees are awarded'.[2] In advancing that understanding, he identifies six types of degrees which he styles as follows: earned degrees, honorary degrees, incorporation degrees, official degrees, dignity degrees and prerogative degrees.[3] This is a welcome analysis in the course of a scholarly and stimulating exposition much of which is of historical interest. It has provoked my own thinking with a view to offering an alternative taxonomy with the emphasis on contemporary practice and designed to facilitate a better understanding of academic dress.

It affords an understanding of academic dress because academic dress varies not only with specific degrees but with the category of degree, subject to the caveat that nearly all generalizations about academic dress tend to be wrong. Gowns vary as to the category. Thus, most bachelors' gowns have an open sleeve very different from the closed sleeve found on masters' gowns. Both are typically black, but some masters' gowns have an element of colour introduced by way of facings. Doctors' gowns in their festal or ceremonial form are much more ornate and elaborate, especially in the case of the higher doctorates. The original doctoral colour was scarlet—hence the commonly seen dress-code formula: 'Academic dress: Doctors wear scarlet'—but many other colours are now employed. Headwear also differs: bachelors and masters wear the flat cap or mortar-board while doctors usually sport a Tudor bonnet.

I shall also discuss the use of the title 'Dr', since Dr Dickson raises this point in his discussion of honorary degrees. I begin with some comments on Dr Dickson's analysis of degrees.

The Dickson scheme: a critique

Earned degrees is the category covering the vast bulk of degrees awarded. They are, says Dr Dickson, degrees obtained by studying and taking examinations, which may be written or oral, including assessment of a thesis. He also includes in this category the Oxford and Cambridge MA 'because … the right to the MA stems from sitting and passing the BA examinations'.[4]

The weakness of this category is that it conceals more than it reveals and as a category embracing the whole gamut of degrees from first degrees to higher doctorates it provides no guidance on the hierarchy of degrees which is crucial to an understanding of the different styles of academic dress attached to each level.

---

1   Neil K. Dickson, *TBS*, 19 (2019), pp. 183–203, available at <newprairiepress.org /burgonsociety> https://doi.org/10.4148/2475-7799.1171.
2   Ibid., p. 183.
3   Ibid., pp. 187–99.
4   Ibid., p. 189, n. 30.

Dr Dickson writes of 'study and examination' but he should say 'study and/or examination', since there are earned degrees—notably the higher doctorates but also in some institutions the PhD—where there is no period of study preceding the scrutiny, which is not of a thesis but of a body of original published work. This is different from the 'scrutiny of a thesis' mentioned by Dr Dickson.

The inclusion of the Oxbridge MA in this category is especially problematic. I do not question it because, like many others, I find it an objectionable tradition. On the contrary, I take the view that its justification, rooted in its origins and long history, is compelling. The mystery is why later universities, aware of the use of the MA in Oxford, Cambridge, Trinity College, Dublin and the Scottish universities, chose to make the MA a postgraduate degree awarded after a prescribed course of study and examination. To envelope it within this category, however, is unhelpful. Dr Dickson rightly says that it stems from the BA which itself follows study and examinations, but the MA calls for no further study or examinations and some BAs choose not to proceed to it. It differs from the MA in all other universities throughout the world where that degree is awarded and it is controversial. In my view, it is better to recognize its distinct nature and treat it transparently rather than rely on a fiction or a contrived explanation.

Most of us would suppose that there was only one other category, namely honorary degrees, to cover the full range of degrees conferred other than after study and/or examination. Dr Dickson helpfully elucidates the different kinds of non-earned degrees but some of the distinctions are highly subtle. For a scheme seeking to capture contemporary usage, a single category, noticing minor technical distinctions, will be sufficient.

I have no comments on Dr Dickson's category **Honorary degrees** save for a statement about the use of the title 'Dr' to which I shall return at the end of this note.

Incorporation degrees, or rather degrees by incorporation, arise in the UK at present only at Oxford and Cambridge. If a Cambridge graduate accepts a post at Oxford, or an Oxford graduate at Cambridge, the new employer will 'incorporate' the individual's degrees from 'the other place', meaning they will be admitted to the equivalent degrees in their new university; so, for example, an MA, PhD, LLD from Cambridge will acquire the corresponding Oxford degrees of MA, DPhil, DCL. This curious practice flows from the fact that degrees obtained elsewhere, and their academic dress, were not formally recognized. Why only Oxford and Cambridge? Because at the time this practice originated there were no other universities in England. Dr Dickson explains all this more fully, including the wider scope of incorporation in times past.

These degrees are clearly not 'earned' in the sense discussed above, nor are they 'honorary', so their explicit recognition is necessary, but in my arrangement they are treated as a specific kind of substantive degree. Moreover, although 'incorporation' is the official term employed by the two universities for this kind of degree and it is not inapt, it is not illuminating and I have adopted an alternative which I think better conveys its nature.

Dr Dickson's remaining categories call for explanation. **Official degrees** are similar to degrees by incorporation in that they give an Oxford or Cambridge degree, as the case may be, to a new member of staff who does not already have a degree either from the newly employing university or 'the other place'. The rationale is that it is the degree (usually MA) that confers membership of the university. For my purposes, I prefer to treat it as a sub-category of substantive degrees.

Dignity degrees are similar to honorary degrees but confer full substantive rights on the holder. The only practical difference I can discern is that it would not be necessary or appropriate to add 'Hon' or *honoris causa* in brackets after the abbreviation for the degree. They were at one time not uncommon at Oxford and Cambridge, particularly in respect of any alumnus who became a diocesan bishop and who did not have an earned doctorate. It is only Oxford that now confers 'dignity degrees', limited for the most part to royalty and heads of state, where they are termed 'degrees by diploma'. Diocesan bishops without an earned doctorate no longer receive a DD either from their own university or the Archbishop of Canterbury. Even the present Archbishop himself is without a doctorate, unthinkable in times past. In my view, this attenuated category is no more than an honorary degree by another name.

Finally, there are Dr Dickson's **Prerogative degrees**, defined as 'degrees awarded by, or on the direct instructions of, a senior person with prerogative powers such as a pope, king, emperor or archbishop who is not part of a university or college'.[5] He says these *include* Lambeth degrees, which are degrees awarded by the Archbishop of Canterbury.

As the Archbishop of Canterbury is the only contemporary degree-awarding authority of this kind, the use of the word 'include' is odd, as is the use of the word 'prerogative'. The Archbishop's power derives from statute; he has no prerogative power. If there is a prerogative power in play here, it is that of the Sovereign, but every university established by royal charter has degree-awarding powers deriving from the royal prerogative. The fundamental problem with this category, however, is that it refers not to the nature and character of the degree but to the nature and character of the authority awarding the degree. It is therefore different from all Dr Dickson's other categories: it is not a type of degree at all. Lambeth degrees are of several kinds: (a) some may be earned following a course of study and examinations; (b) some may be conferred in recognition of the recipient's standing as a scholar and thus correspond to a higher doctorate; and (c) some are bestowed for service to the Church or similar distinction and correspond to an honorary degree, even if not explicitly described as such.[6] They are therefore all covered by the earlier categories. In any event, the award of Lambeth degrees other than following a course and examinations is currently in abeyance.

An alternative scheme

My schema is designed to enumerate the different kinds of earned degrees with a view to facilitating an understanding of academic dress. Explanation of the hierarchy of degrees is important because academic dress changes and becomes more elaborate as the hierarchy is ascended. It also de-emphasizes distinctions which are largely formal and technical, are almost entirely devoid of practical implications and are irrelevant to questions of academic dress. I have used only three categories, though the first has a number of classes to specify the different levels and kinds of degrees. The last two categories complete the picture, but are irrelevant to questions of academic dress, since these degrees (with only rare exceptions) take the same costume as the corresponding degree in the first category. I have also devised a different nomenclature, although any such terms can only be understood with their explanations and definitions.

---

5   Ibid., p. 196.
6   See further William Gibson (ed.), *The History of Lambeth Degrees: Sources and Studies*, Burgon Society Historical Reprints 2 (London: Burgon Society, 2019).

I. Substantive degrees awarded after formal assessment

• *First degrees* (chiefly bachelor's, some MAs (e.g., in Scotland), four-year (or longer) first degrees with a master's designation, e.g., MSci). Qualifying medical, dental and veterinary degrees (MB, ChB; BDS; and BVetMed), although around five years' duration, also fall into this group.

• *Taught masters' degrees* (e.g., MSc, LLM, the Oxford BCL).

• *Postgraduate degrees based on course work and a dissertation* (mostly master's, but including professional doctorates).

• *Research degrees* (e.g., MPhil, PhD, MD, ChM).

• *Degrees awarded on the basis of original published work* (chiefly higher doctorates, such as DLitt, DSc, LLD, MusD, and DD; but also the PhD in some universities).

II. Nominal degrees

The degrees falling within this category are actual degrees indistinguishable from those in the first category, but awarded without study, examination or assessment of any kind. The titles for each of these sub-categories are mine.

• *Maturation/complementary/choate [the opposite of 'inchoate'] degrees*. This refers specifically to Oxford and Cambridge, where the first degree in all disciplines was until recently the BA which after about three years entitles the graduate to proceed to the MA without further study or examination. It is the MA that confers full membership of the university. The BA may therefore be seen as a provisional or inchoate qualification, which matures into an MA. Hence the designation 'maturation' or 'choate'.[7] As the BA may be regarded as an incomplete qualification and status, the MA may also be said to be 'complementary'.

• *Reciprocal or derivative degrees*. These are the degrees by incorporation discussed above whereby Oxford and Cambridge will recognize the degrees awarded by the other university and will accordingly admit a new member of staff to the same or equivalent degrees. Thus, for example, an Oxford MA, DPhil employed by Cambridge will be admitted to the degrees of MA, PhD; a Cambridge MA, ScD on taking up a post in Oxford will be given the degrees of MA, DSc, and an MA, LLM will become an MA, BCL. This recognition of degrees may be described as 'reciprocal' or alternatively as 'derivative' since they derive from the degrees previously conferred by the other university.

• *Membership degrees*. This is shorthand for the conferment of a degree, typically the MA, for the singular purpose of conferring full membership of the university. It arises where a new member of staff in Oxford or Cambridge without an Oxbridge degree and therefore not eligible for incorporation may acquire full membership of the university by being given the local MA.

III. Honorary and titular degrees

Any degree conferred by a university to honour an individual for that person's achievements or in respect of his or her appointment to high office may be styled an honorary degree, or degree *honoris causa*, whatever technical label may be attached to it by a particular university's statutes or ordinances. For present purposes, and particularly in view of

---

7   The word 'choate' is not recognized in British usage, although it has currency in American English, especially in the law, but it is controversial even there and on etymological grounds is indeed questionable.

contemporary practice, no purpose is served by refining this category and distinguishing a degree conferred on, say, a head of state because, for example, it is expressed to be a 'degree by diploma', not least because this is confined to a single university, the expression has no wider connotations and in itself is a meaningless term of art. Also included in this category are the so-called dignity degrees described by Dr Dickson, now of only historic interest.

Use of the title 'Dr'

In the course of his discussion of honorary degrees, Dr Dickson writes:

> ... holders of honorary Doctor degrees are entitled to use the title Dr, as stated in Patrick Montague-Smith (ed.), *Debrett's Correct Form*, revised edn (... 1992), p. 266. The practice of universities also makes this clear. For example, T. R. Craig, who was Chancellor's Assessor (senior lay member of the University Court) at the University of Glasgow in the 1970s, and whose only degree was a Glasgow honorary LLD, was always addressed and referred to as Dr Craig within the University (personal recollection).[8]

I make four preliminary comments. First, Dr Dickson speaks of 'entitlement' without any analysis of where this is found or its logical or legal basis. Secondly, he relies on *Debrett's*, but not only is this out of line with other guides on forms of address, it dates from 1992 and no longer represents *Debrett's* current thinking.[9] Thirdly, a single example from one university some years ago affords inadequate evidence to support the assertion. Fourthly, internal practice does not support use of the title outside the institution.

The fundamental point to note is that use of the title 'Dr' is not a matter for universities at all, at least in any technical sense. Universities are empowered to confer doctoral degrees; they will prescribe the abbreviation which may then be used post-nominally; but nothing authorizes a university to pronounce on use of the title and I know of no university that purports to do so. Aside from use of the title by medical professionals and certain others, where it may be the subject of legislation or rules of a regulatory authority—often, it should be noted, where there is no doctoral degree at all[10]—the title of 'Dr' is entirely unregulated. It is purely a matter of social or professional custom and convention, as indeed is the title of 'Professor'.

This is the nub of the difficulty. There is no royal warrant to which to turn; no legal basis on which to rely; no official ruling from the Crown or those empowered to pronounce with authority. Social custom is not always easy to capture. Practice varies. Views differ. And times change. There are today far more universities, and honorary degrees have proliferated. They are being given to different kinds of people. Many recipients are celebrities—prominent figures from the worlds of entertainment and sport, for example. Any opinion about the propriety or correctness of use of the title by the holders of honorary doctorates needs to take all this into account. Indeed, that recipients may call themselves 'Dr' has been used by critics of the award of honorary degrees as one of the arguments justifying the abolition of the practice.

The near universal adoption of the title 'Dr' by dentists in the UK presents striking

---

8 Ibid., p. 190, n. 34.

9 See <www.debretts.com/expertise/.forms-of-address/.professions/>, [retrieved 4 June 2021]. 'In practice, ... the recipient [of an honorary doctorate] does not generally adopt the title of "Doctor" ...'

10 Few medical practitioners in the UK have a doctorate: the standard degrees are MB, BS/MB,ChB; most dentists also now use the title Dr: see below.

evidence. Dentists in the UK, as in many other Commonwealth countries, qualify with the degree of Bachelor of Dental Surgery. Very few go on to acquire the postgraduate research degree of Doctor of Dental Surgery. Until 1995, the dentists' statutory regulatory body, the General Dental Council (GDC), had a rule prohibiting the use of the title 'Dr' by dentists, since it was thought to imply that they were also medical practitioners, which would mislead their patients or potential patients. In 1995, the GDC rescinded the prohibition provided that there was no implication that the dentist was qualified to carry out medical procedures. The consequence of this was a rush of dentists who began to call themselves 'Dr', as if the GDC had actually licensed them to adopt the prefix.

This is bizarre. The GDC did not tell dentists they could adopt a title they had no claim to either historically or logically; and indeed would have had no power to do so. But there was a growing head of steam among dentists to have the title enjoyed by their physician colleagues. They argued that they should have full parity with physicians; that their course of study was just as long and arduous; and that dentists in the US and throughout the EU had long been called 'Dr'. With the support of their professional body, they just went ahead and did it. Their patients were left with no choice but to accept it.

There is, perhaps surprisingly, also a divergence of views about the use of the title by the holders of substantive doctorates. Some argue that the holder of a PhD or other doctorate should not use the title socially and even professionally should use it only where it relates to the occupation in question.

No better example is afforded than that of the new First Lady of the United States, Jill Biden, who has had a long career as a teacher, currently in a community college, and has over the years steadily upgraded her qualifications from bachelor's degree to master's and eventually to an EdD, since when she has styled herself 'Dr Biden' for both professional and social purposes.[11] Most people see no problem with this, but some ridicule and decline to acknowledge it, insisting on calling her Mrs Biden. They say, variously, her thesis was pedestrian; the University of Delaware which conferred the degree is of low standing; the EdD is a so-called professional doctorate that does not rank as a real doctorate; the title should be used only in connection with her teaching role and it is an affectation to use it socially; and only medical doctors are real doctors entitled to the honorific. This resistance is odd in a country which has compensated for its refreshing lack of titles of nobility and chivalry by turning many job titles into prefixes in a way unknown in Britain and most other English-speaking countries. Job titles such as Dean, Principal, President, Ambassador, Director and Chairman are all used as prefixes; and it is customary to cling tenaciously to some of these titles in retirement, such as President, Vice-President, Senator, Secretary [of State], Ambassador, Governor and Judge.

Some of the objections to Dr Biden's use of the honorific hardly require refutation. Are we to assess the merits of a particular thesis or the standing of a particular institution or degree before conceding that an individual's doctoral title should be acknowledged? The one argument that deserves any consideration is the assertion that only medical doctors should be accorded the title: in other words, that physicians are the only true doctors.

In the US, of course, all medical practitioners will have an MD and may therefore base their honorific on possession of a doctorate, but that is not the case in many English-speaking countries whose higher education systems are based on the British where

11 See, e.g., *The* [London] *Times Magazine*, 9 January 2021.

the qualifying degrees are Bachelor of Medicine and Bachelor of Surgery awarded simultaneously. They are nevertheless styled 'Dr' (as are dentists and veterinary surgeons). The simple fact is that the word 'doctor' has two distinct meanings. First, and originally, it refers to people who hold a university doctorate. Secondly, it refers to medical practitioners, but the reason this second meaning evolved is that the early physicians trained in Europe where they received MDs and thus were called 'Dr'. Hitherto, the only doctors had been those in possession of the degrees of DD and LLD/DCL from Oxford and Cambridge. The true doctors, therefore, insofar as that term has any significance—or, more accurately, the original doctors—were not medics but lawyers and clerics.

The refusal to credit Jill Biden with the title she has earned flows, it seems to me, from a blend of misogyny, ignorance, envy and arrogance and it is not attractive. Their objections are mere canards. Common sense and common courtesy demand that Dr Biden, and all those who have acquired earned doctorates, should be so styled if that is their wish. To deny them the title is an act of disrespect, bordering on insult.

For the individual holder of the degree, it is wholly a matter of personal preference. We see this clearly in public life. Many politicians with PhDs do not call themselves 'Dr', but some do. Courtesy dictates that we respect their choice. *The Times Style Guide* takes the lofty view (which I do not share) that 'there is little to be said for a German-style flourishing of doctorates in public life, and we should resist'.[12] What may be apt for a newspaper report or article, however, may be very different from a social and personal context where failure to recognize the title is likely to be taken as disrespectful. It is not only the title 'Dr' that is disliked by *The Times*. They have recently introduced a policy on their news pages to dispense with all honorifics after a person's first mention. Thereafter they are referred to by surname alone, even, for example, in the case of Cabinet ministers, judges, and the victims of crime. This is a surprising and regrettable development, but it puts their reservations about the title of 'Dr' in context.

It follows that no single university is able to shape the practice. It has no power to do so. I suppose a policy formulated on behalf of all British universities by its representative body (Universities UK) might carry some weight, but no such policy exists and is unlikely to emerge. A university may choose to use the title internally, though I am certain it is not common to do so, just as many universities will use the title 'Professor' for its visiting and honorary professors, but it is generally accepted that it does not carry beyond the campus. I have only ever come across one institution that habitually used the title 'Dr' for its honorary graduates: it was a small American liberal arts college based in London and clearly wished to humour its honorary graduates, many of whom were its trustees or benefactors.

The example of Dr Craig in Glasgow tells us very little. If Craig adopted the title himself, as was very likely the case, it would have been churlish and risk causing serious offence if the University insisted on calling him 'Mr'. I can cite similar examples. I recall a case in the University of London of the head of one of its colleges whose only earned degree was a BSc but who had several honorary DSc's, including one from the University of London itself, conferred prior to his appointment. He called himself 'Dr' as head of college until he received a knighthood some years later. Was the University to insist on addressing him as 'Mr' prior to the knighthood? Clearly that was not a feasible option, but to infer from this instance of acquiescence that the University of London approved of the use of the title

---

12 2nd edn (2017), p. 80.

by its honorary graduates, or even prescribed, permitted or encouraged it, would not be correct. There was also the case of a senior administrator in the University of London who on his retirement was awarded an honorary LLD and thereafter was styled 'Dr'. Neither the Glasgow nor the London examples lend support to the use of the title generally. If universities were canvassed on the point, I should be surprised if there was much, if any, enthusiasm for the title's use by honorary doctors.

It is true that some holders of honorary doctorates call themselves 'Dr', but that proves nothing. It is generally deplored, even derided. Clerics seem especially prone to the conceit. Their use of it does not make it correct, let alone establish an 'entitlement', but there is no power to stop it; and quite often common courtesy dictates that we acquiesce. We commonly see these breaches of etiquette in the use of other titles, even by their holders, such as life peers and the wives of knights including their first names, as in Lord John Smith and Lady Mary Jones. This misuse, widespread though it has become, does not make it correct or acceptable.

At least in these instances we can confidently state that the usage is wrong—which is not to say that it will not eventually supersede the correct forms—but it is more difficult when the usage is governed purely by custom and convention. Take the prefix 'Mrs' used by married women together with their husband's surname. We know that many women these days on marriage eschew the title 'Mrs' and retain their maiden name together with the prefix 'Ms', but a very few choose to retain their maiden name and combine it with 'Mrs' which they assume they may do because the prefix accurately denotes their marital status. Traditionalists will object that the honorific cannot be separated from the husband's surname and it is therefore incorrect, but no one can proscribe the practice and it would be difficult and churlish to refuse to follow such women's preference, even though it is confusing: if Mr Smith is accompanied by Mrs Brown, no one will suppose they are married to each other. To take an analogy, could Sir John Smith's wife, Jane Brown, call herself Lady Brown because she has retained her maiden name? The answer is surely no.

In determining whether the holder of an honorary doctorate may use the prefix 'Dr', regard must be had to usage, analogies, logic and common sense.

A particularly powerful argument relates to the inherent nature of an honorary award or appointment. Just as an honorary knighthood does not give rise to the title 'Sir' and an honorary professorship to the title 'Professor', so an honorary doctor should not be styled, or style himself, 'Dr'. Interestingly, *Who's Who* does not accord the title even to its biographees who use it socially or professionally.[13]

Custom and practice in such matters can be elusive and contradictory, and it has a tendency to change over time, but to assert unequivocally that an honorary doctorate *entitles* the holder to use the title 'Dr' is at best questionable and at worst wrong. Perhaps we might at least agree that use of the title is problematic and should be discouraged.

Conclusion

There are any number of ways of classifying degrees. For example, there is a legal classification based on the source of the degree-awarding power—whether Act of Parliament, Order-in-Council, Royal Charter or some overseas authority. Or there is the classification

---

13 I do not, however, necessarily defer to *Who's Who* in these matters. It is far from infallible. For example, it thinks the title 'Dr' can be combined with 'Sir'; that retired High Court judges are entitled to the honorific 'The Hon'; and that serving High Court judges may use that honorific in conjunction with their non-judicial title.

developed by Dr Dickson, with its predominantly historical accent. Other classifications might be based on types of course and study or on methods of assessment. All are legitimate and have their uses. It depends on the purpose which the analysis is intended to serve. None of the examples chosen, however, would shed any light on academic dress or lead to an understanding of the different kinds of dress attaching to particular categories or levels of degree.

By looking at the hierarchy of degrees, my scheme makes it easier to appreciate the different styles of academic costume typically attaching to the different levels of degree, even if that is not its only or even primary purpose. Degree structures in all universities are hierarchical and academic dress varies with that hierarchy. Thus, a clear understanding of that hierarchy is essential to an understanding of the different styles of academic dress attaching to each level, culminating in the elaborate robes worn by higher doctors.

The use of the title 'Dr', raised by Dr Dickson in the context of honorary degrees, is a discrete issue. The salient point here is that there can be no laying down of the law on the use of this honorific since there is no law to lay down. The title is a product of social and professional custom and practice, informed and shaped by history. That custom and practice, or usage, is fascinating and arcane.

There are people called 'Dr' who have no doctorate, namely, the majority of British medical, dental and veterinary practitioners. There are those who would be entitled to use the honorific but in practice do not—holders of the American JD degree and UK surgeons (even if they have an MD or PhD). There are those with substantive doctorates who eschew the title in either their social or professional life or both. And there are a few people with honorary doctorates who make use of the title. In the absence of law, we fall back on social custom and usage, or occasionally professional edict. Custom is often varied and may be uncertain or divided. What can be said with certainty, however, is that it is not for universities to prescribe use of the honorific. They have no power to do so, except perhaps within their own institutions.

The two prominent areas of controversy are the use of the title by the holders of honorary degrees and its use by those with substantive doctorates in their lives beyond any relevant occupation or profession to which the degree relates. My own view is that it is wholly inappropriate for the former to call themselves 'Dr'; and in the case of the latter it is entirely a matter for them, and their choice should be respected in all contexts.

Transactions of the Burgon Society, 20 (2020), pages 175–176

Response to Professor Zellick's Article

By Neil K. Dickson

I am very grateful to the Editor for deciding to let me see Professor Zellick's article[1] prior to publication and for offering me the opportunity to publish this response alongside it.

Professor Zellick and I share the view that an understanding of how and when degrees are awarded will aid the understanding of the customs surrounding academic dress. My analysis of the types of degrees was based on the historical context. Professor Zellick takes an alternative approach based on contemporary practice to which he adds a discussion on the hierarchy of degrees, and thus provides important additional insight. I find myself in agreement with much of what he says. Readers will however identify that there are some issues where we differ.

One of these is the arcane area of the Archbishop of Canterbury's degree awarding powers. The archbishop's powers derive from the Ecclesiastical Licences Act 1533. The wording of that Act makes it clear that the king is delegating his prerogative powers to the archbishop and not giving the archbishop absolute powers. It also put in place arrangements involving the Clerk of the Crown in Chancery and the requirement for certain degrees to be confirmed under the Great Seal that enabled the king to monitor the exercise of these powers.[2] This contrasts with the wording of the papal bulls, royal charters and acts of parliament under which universities were granted absolute and unmonitored powers. Therefore in my historical analysis I treated the archbishop differently from universities. On the other hand, the practice of the current archbishop to award degrees only on the basis of study and examination, and not on his own initiative or the recommendations of others, means that in an analysis of contemporary practice like Professor Zellick's it is perhaps more appropriate to treat the archbishop as a 'one-man university'.[3]

The principal area of difference between Professor Zellick and me would appear to be the question as to whether honorary doctorates 'entitle' the holder to the use of the title 'Dr'. The word 'entitle' was perhaps an infelicitous choice when I wrote my article. As Professor Zellick correctly points out, there are no statutes governing the use of that title. Rather, what Professor Zellick, the successive editors of *Debrett's* and I are trying to capture is custom and practice, and what is acceptable to public opinion. These are shifting sands that subtly change from time to time and even from place to place. I think that changes are currently taking place that can perhaps explain why Professor Zellick, based in London, with his extensive experience in England and overseas, can appear to interpret the current position differently from me with my particular knowledge of Scottish universities. For example, Professor Zellick cites the 'near universal adoption of the title 'Dr' by dentists': that may be the case in England but it is currently not common practice in Scotland.

---

1 Graham Zellick, 'Degrees of Degrees: An Alternative Structure', *TBS*, 20 (2020), pp. 166–74.

2 <https://www.legislation.gov.uk/aep/Hen8/25/21/contents> [retrieved 14 June 2021].

3 Neil K. Dickson, 'Degrees of Degrees', *TBS*, 19 (2019), p. 199, at <newprairiepress.org /burgonsociety> https://doi.org/10.4148/2475-7799.1171.

Professor Zellick rightly draws attention to the large increase in the number of universities, particularly in England, the proliferation of honorary degrees, and the increasing number of such degrees conferred on what he describes as 'celebrities'. I agree that this is shifting public opinion as to when it is acceptable to use the title 'Dr'.

Nevertheless, if we leave to one side the 'celebrities', it is my view that it has been accepted custom and practice, certainly in Scotland, for holders of honorary doctorates to use the title 'Dr'. I cited as an example Dr T. R. Craig of the University of Glasgow. I chose him because it was the University that decided to confer the honorary doctorate on him and, while he may well have enjoyed being called 'Dr', I formed the impression from personal observation that it was the University that had initiated the use of the title in relation to him and then used it with great consistency in a wide range of official documents. In any case, he is simply an example of what I saw as common practice. Another more widespread example concerns Church of Scotland ministers. A Church of Scotland minister Hamish McBlogs is generally referred to in writing as Rev. H. McBlogs (note not the Revd, which is an English custom) and when spoken to is called Mr McBlogs. If however he has received an honorary DD, these references change to Rev. Dr H. McBlogs and Dr McBlogs, respectively. This is not, in my view, a 'conceit' of the clergy (to quote Professor Zellick). Rather, it represents the long-accepted custom and practice of the Scottish universities, the Church, newspapers, publishers and the general public.

I think that, despite the differences between the views of Professor Zellick and myself, we might agree that we embarked on a hazardous task when we tried to record custom and practice, a fickle thing that resists being pinned down even by time or place. I suggest that a comment that Professor Zellick makes about academic dress applies equally to custom and practice regarding titles: 'nearly all generalisations … tend to be wrong'.

With the Editor's indulgence, I also take the opportunity to report the result of further personal communications with Dr Nicholas Groves and Dr W. B. Stewart following the publication of my article. I am advised by them that persons holding MA status at the University of Oxford in the late twentieth century adopted the practice of wearing MA gown and hood on formal occasions, which caused the 'unseemly row' to which I referred because the academic dress regulations did not cover MA status.[4] The Vice-Chancellor could have resolved the situation by a pronouncement, but apparently never did.

---

4 Ibid, pp. 201–02, n. 80.

Authors

Bruce Christianson, MSc (Victoria, NZ), DPhil (Oxon), FNZMS, FBS, joined The Hatfield Polytechnic in 1987, and has been Emeritus Professor of Informatics at the University of Hertfordshire since his retirement in 2018. His previous article, with Joan Kendall in Volume 15, investigated a portrait of James Cecil, Fifth Earl of Salisbury. He is a Foundation Fellow of the Society and was Dean of Studies from 2003 until 2016.

Neil K. Dickson, BSc (St And), MSc, DPhil (Oxon), ACIE, FICB, FBS, lectured in Mathematics at the University of Glasgow for thirty-five years, was a member of the University's Academic Dress Committee for nineteen years, and is the author of articles on the University's academic dress in Volumes 12 and 14. His previous article, in Volume 19, reviewed the various degrees awarded by universities.

Philip Goff, BD (London), AKC, FSA, FBS, is a founder and was the first Chairman of the Burgon Society. He has been associated with academical and ecclesiastical robe-making since he was a teenager and was Academic Consultant to Ede & Ravenscroft Ltd for ten years. More recently he was Area Dean of West Haringey and Vicar of St Augustine's Church, Highgate, London until retirement in 2015 and previously Senior Practice Counsellor at Clapham Family Practice. His previous article, in Volume 18, reviewed the academic and official dress of the University of the Arts London.

Nicholas Groves, MA, BMus, PhD (Wales), MA (EAng), BA (Lond), PGDip (York), FRHistS, FBS, is Director of the Centre for Parish Church Studies in Norwich and a freelance lecturer and writer. He was previously an Associate Tutor in Continuing Education at UEA. His previous article, in Volume 17, was on the hood of a Determining BA at Oxford. A Foundation Fellow of the Society and Dean of Studies 2000–03, he is the editor of *Shaw's Academical Dress*, and the author of a forthcoming study of Charles Franklyn.

Martin J. Hardcastle, BA (Open), MA, PhD, ScD (Cantab), FInstP, FRAS, FIMA, FHEA, FBS, is Professor of Astrophysics at the University of Hertfordshire and currently the Head of the Department of Physics, Astronomy and Mathematics.

Alex Kerr, MA (Oxon), MA, PhD (Reading), FBS, was a lecturer in medieval studies and is now Director of a training consultancy specializing in technical writing. His previous article, in Volume 18, examined academic dress on picture postcards in Oxford in the early twentieth century. He was the Society's Publications Editor from 2003 to 2011 and its Secretary from 2011 to 2020.

Brian M. Newman, MA (Cantab), MBA (Penn State), CEng, FIMechE, FIET, FRSA, FIoD, FBS, is retired after a career as CEO of a number of global engineering businesses. Non-executive Director experience includes manufacturing, an NHS hospital, The Woodard Corporation (education), and charities. In 2022/23 he will be Master of the Shrewsbury Drapers' Company. A now all-but-retired semi-professional singer, he sings in the choir of, and is occasionally organist at, Shrewsbury Abbey, where the wearing of hoods by choir members has been actively encouraged!

Mitchell A. Nicholls, FBS, is reading for a BEd in geography at the University of the West Indies, Mona, Jamaica, with a particular interest in socio-cultural history. He designed the insignia of the Order of Freedom of Barbados (constituted in 2019) and was elected to the fellowship for his submission on the academical dress of UWI in 2020.

Kenneth L. Suit, Jr., BA (Baylor), MFA (Ohio), FBS, is Professor of Cinema in the School of Arts and Humanities at Milligan University, Tennessee. He previously wrote about the historical sources for US degree colours in Volumes 15 and 17.

Scott Pilkington, BA (Hons), MA (Auck), DipILS (OPNZ), GradDipTheol, PGDipArts, PGCertEd (Auck), PGCertArts (AUT), PGCertSciComm (Otago), FBS, is an Honorary Research Fellow in Museums & Cultural Heritage at The University of Auckland and works in higher research degree management of Auckland University of Technology in Aotearoa New Zealand. His fellowship submission in 2020 examined the development of university doctoral academic dress in Aotearoa.

Philip Waters, BSc (So'ton), HonDLitt (Herts), FRSA, FIOD, became Deputy Secretary and Registrar of The Hatfield Polytechnic in 1989. He was Secretary and Registrar of the University of Hertfordshire from 2001 until his retirement in 2013, and was also the founding Director of the University's bus company unō. He is a member of the Society, and presented a paper on 'Overseas ceremonies organised by the University of Hertfordshire' to the 2016 Spring Conference.

Graham Zellick, CBE, QC, MA, PhD (Cantab), LHD (NYU), LLD (Birm & Richmond), DLit (Lond), FAcSS, Hon FRAM, FBS, is President of the Society and a judge of the UK Investigatory Powers Tribunal. He is Emeritus Professor of Law in the University of London, Honorary Fellow of Gonville & Caius College, Cambridge, and Barrister, Senior Master of Bench and former Reader of the Middle Temple. He was formerly Principal of Queen Mary & Westfield College, University of London, Vice-Chancellor and President of the University of London, Chairman of the Criminal Cases Review Commission and President of the Valuation Tribunal for England. His previous article, in Volume 7, used his correspondence with Lambeth Palace to demonstrate the intricacies of Lambeth academic dress.

A Special Issue of:
Transactions of the Burgon Society,
Volume 20:

Hoods by the Armful: Academic Dress and the Founding of the Burgon Society

By Philip Goff

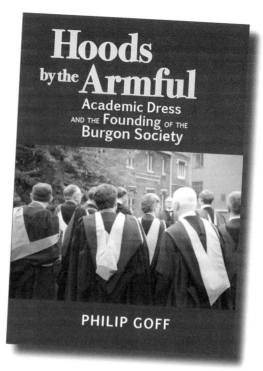

From online chat groups and a meeting at the Wheatsheaf pub in London, enthusiasts of academic dress came together to form a group for researchers who examine the history of academic robes around the world. In *Hoods by the Armful*, the Revd Philip Goff, one of the Burgon Society's founders and the Society's first Chairman, assembles recollections of the people who were there at the beginning. Includes photos from the first Congregation, at Charterhouse in London.

Burgon Society Shop

For deliveries within the UK, send your order with your remittance to: *Ian Johnson, Treasurer, The Burgon Society, 9 Pymore Road, Bridport, Dorset, DT6 3XE, UK.*

For deliveries to the US and Canada, you may order in two ways. You may receive an invoice through PayPal (in US Dollars) by writing to slw53@columbia.edu; or you may send your order with a cheque payable to The Burgon Society to: *Stephen Wolgast; 1435 Jayhawk Boulevard; Lawrence, Kansas 66045-7594; USA.*

All prices include postage and packing to the UK, US, and Canada.

If you are making a payment to the Society from outside the UK, US, or Canada, you may either: transfer your payment by PayPal to the Society at this email address: sales@burgon.org.uk; or you may pay by banker's draft in UK pounds drawn on a corresponding UK bank.

Books

Hoods by the Armful: Academic Dress and the Founding of the Burgon Society

By Philip Goff
Published in 2021 by the Burgon Society as a history of its formation and early days. Soft cover. 113 pages. A5, perfect binding, with colour photographs.

Recollections of the people who were there at the beginning. Includes photos from the first Congregation, at Charterhouse in London in 2000.
Members £8/$10; Non-members £10/$12.50

The History of Lambeth Degrees: Sources and Studies

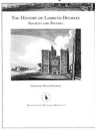

Edited by William Gibson
Published in 2019 by the Burgon Society as the second in a series of important texts on the history of academic dress and related topics. Hardback. 200 pages.

The book brings together ten important sources and articles on the nature of Lambeth degrees and their academical dress. It includes the complete text of Bishop Francis Gastrell's legal claim in 1717 that Lambeth degrees were not equivalent to university degrees; a complete list of Lambeth degree recipients 1539–1995; an examination of Charles Franklyn's claim that the degrees are really 'state' or royal degrees; reprints of articles by Noel Cox, FBS, and by Graham Zellick, FBS, on the robes for the degrees.
Members £24.99/$21.25; Non-members £33/$41.

Ackermann's Costumes of the Universities of Oxford and Cambridge

Edited by Nicholas Jackson
Published in 2016 by the Burgon Society as the first in its historical reprint series on academic dress and related topics. Hardback. 84 pages. Includes 37 plates (34 colour, 3 B&W).

Here are reprinted all the plates of academic dress that appeared in Rudolph Ackermann's two-volume histories of the Universities of Oxford and Cambridge published in 1814 and 1815, giving a valuable snapshot of the academic and official dress in use at these Universities at the beginning of the nineteenth century.
Members £18.50/$22; Non-members £24.99/$29.99

Shaw's Academical Dress of Great Britain and Ireland, *3rd edition, Volume I*

Edited by Nicholas Groves
Published in 2011 by the Burgon Society. Crown Quarto, bound, soft cover. 450 pages.
Members £20/$25
(Non-members can buy direct from the printers at www.lulu.com at £27.50 or $49)

Shaw's Academical Dress of Great Britain and Ireland, *3rd edition, Volume II: Non-Degree-Awarding Bodies*

Edited by Nicholas Groves
Published in 2014 by the Burgon Society. Crown Quarto, bound, soft cover. 236 pages.
Members £14.50/$17.50
(Non-members can buy direct from the printers at www.lulu.com at £18.50 or $31.50)

Burgon Society On-line Bibliography

The aim is to build up a comprehensive resource for those researching the design, history and practice of academical dress.

The Introduction is a brief survey of the key materials on academical dress that are either in print or available in the larger public and university libraries.

The Alphabetical list that follows is intended to cover what has been published on the subject since the beginning of the nineteenth century; earlier items are listed if they include engravings that provide important evidence of robes of the period.

The bilbliography grows every year. Suggestions for additions (or corrections) are welcome. Please send e-mails to: webmaster@burgon.org.uk.

Find a list of books and articles to help your research at www.burgon.org.uk/society /library/biblio.html.

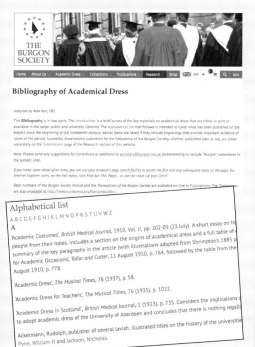

The Vice-Chancellor's Committee: The University of West Bromwich Considers the Place of Academic Dress in a Contemporary University, *A dramatic discussion with three papers as appendices*
By Les Robarts
Published in 2012 by the Burgon Society. Soft cover. 76 pages. A5, perfect binding.
No longer in print.

Key to the Identification of Academic Hoods of the British Isles, *4th edition*
By Nicholas Groves
Published in 2010 by the Burgon Society. A5, comb bound. 65 pages.
Members £8.00; Non-members £12.00

Malachite and Silver: Academic Dress of the University of Stirling
By Colin Fleming
Published in 2009 by the Burgon Society. A5, stapled.
Members £7.50; Non-members £10.00

University of London Academic Dress
By Philip Goff
Published in 1999 by The University of London Press. A5, bound, soft cover. 56 pages.
Members £6.50; Non-members £8.75

Journal

From the *Transactions*' first volume in 2001 until its fourth volume in 2004, it was called *The Burgon Society Annual*. Since 2005 it has held its present title.

Transactions of the Burgon Society   *Crown Quarto format*
Volume 20 (2020)   Further copies of this volume are available.
Members £12.50/$15.50 per copy; Non-members £15/$19 per copy

Transactions of the Burgon Society   *Crown Quarto format*
Volume 19 (2019)   *206 pages. The academic dress of The Open University; of the University of Exeter; of the University of Hong Kong, 1911–1941; of Kingston University; reforms in Scottish academical dress in the 1860s; academic dress in the Middle East and the Maghreb; faculty attitudes regarding academic dress at a second Land-Grant university in the US; the degrees of degrees.*
No longer available in print.

Transactions of the Burgon Society   *Crown Quarto format*
Volume 18 (2018)   *126 pages. Academic and official dress for the University of the Arts London; faculty attitudes regarding academic dress at a Land-Grant university in the US; academic dress at Nashotah House Theological Seminary; academic dress on picture postcards in Oxford; academic dress at Eton College.*
Members £12.50/$15.50 per copy; Non-members £15/$19 per copy

Transactions of the Burgon Society   *Crown Quarto format*
Volume 17 (2017)   *126 pages. Harvard returns honorary doctors' third crow's foot; academic dress of the University of Essex; American degree colours, 1936–61; the hood of the Determining BA at Oxford; the MA full-dress gown and its use by the proctors and assessor of Oxford; an argument for wider adoption of academic dress in the Roman Catholic Church.*
Members £12.50/$15.50 per copy; Non-members £15/$19 per copy

Transactions of the Burgon Society *Crown Quarto format*

Volume 16 (2016) *96 pages. The source and artists of Oxford academic dress engravings identified; academic dress of the University of Bradford; academic dress in British Columbia, 1866–1966; Tailors' labels; academic dress in China, 1994–2011.*
Members £12.50/$15.50 per copy; Non-members £15/$19 per copy

Transactions of the Burgon Society *Crown Quarto format*

Volume 15 (2015) *96 pages. French influence on the dress of Scottish Doctors of Medicine; how academic dress is mobilized in degree ceremonies; a portrait of an early 18th Century nobleman; American degree colours; and the tradition of academic costume at Acadia University.*
Members £12.50/$15.50 per copy; Non-members £15/$19 per copy

Transactions of the Burgon Society *Crown Quarto format*

Volume 14 (2014) *112 pages. Articles cover the discovery of an image of a Glasgow Court member's gown; an account of receiving a Lambeth degree; the influence of the Church on the development of the trencher; academic dress at the Ionian Academy; the history of academic dress in Japan; the introduction of academic dress in China; guidelines for academic dress and colours in Spain; creating officers' robes for the University of Divinity, Melbourne; and students' writing on academic dress at Columbia University.*
No longer available in print.

Transactions Online Resource for Researchers

While the Burgon Society shares articles published in the *Transactions* on its web site, researchers unfamiliar with the journal can find its topics through targeted searches in scholarly databases.

Open access publishing makes the *Transactions*' articles available through New Prairie Press at no cost and with few restrictions. Digital object identifiers make authors' work easily discoverable in academic searches, with the result of researchers (and the curious) making more than 1,300 article downloads per month, on average, in the first seven months of 2021.

Our home page on the site features a map which shows where articles have been downloaded over the previous week and which articles they were. The site is also the online home to our house style sheet. It appears on the 'information for authors' page under 'Formatting Guidelines'.

New Prairie Press, hosted by Kansas State University, offers a home for the *Trans-*

Articles from the *Transactions* are published online at http://newprairiepress.org /burgonsociety/.

actions and other scholarly publications edited or written by scholars committed to the principles of open access publishing. The Press focuses on journals, monographs, and conference proceedings in the humanities, social sciences, and the arts.

The *Transactions* has been on the New Prairie Press site since October 2016.

The Burgon Society Member's Tie
Available only from the Burgon Society.

Pure silk, produced by James Morton Ties, showing small crimson Burgon shaped hoods between narrow triple stripes of silver, crimson and silver on a dark blue background.

Members £25/$40

Transactions of the Burgon Society   *Crown Quarto format*
Volume 13 (2013)   *144 pages. Academic dress at Kenyatta University, Kenya; academic dress in Sweden; a sumptuary law of Mary I in 1554–5; Scottish ecclesiastical dress from the Reformation to the present day; academic robes of graduates of Cambridge from the end of the eighteenth century to the present day; the development of academic dress of Oxford from 1920 to 2012.*
Members £12.50/$15.50 per copy; Non-members £15/$19 per copy

Transactions of the Burgon Society   *Crown Quarto format*
Volume 12 (2012)   *128 pages. The issue includes a memoriam of Dr John Birch, who served as President of the Burgon Society from the Society's foundation in 2001 until October 2011. It also reports on academic dress of the University of Glasgow; the conservation of a nineteenth-century student gown of the University of Glasgow by the Hunterian; the dress of rectors at Scottish universities; Queen's College Oxford and purple as the blood of the Lord; gowns worn by MAs in early-seventeenth-century England and Thomas Thornton's curious sleeves; a survey of variation in US academic dress and a system of categories for departures; and a study on the history and use of lace in academic gowns in the UK and Ireland.*
Members £12.50/$15.50 per copy; Non-members £15/$19 per copy

Transactions of the Burgon Society   *Crown Quarto format*
Volume 11 (2011) *112 pages. Academic dress in Canterbury; academic dress of the University of Hull; academic dress of the University of Leicester; the demise of 'faculty' meanings in US hoods; revisions to the academic dress of the University of Malta.*
No longer available in print.

Transactions of the Burgon Society   *Crown Quarto format*

Volume 10 (2010)   *128 pages.   This issue includes articles on the history of the Scottish undergraduate scarlet gown; Walter Pope's successful fight against the abolition of academical dress at Oxford in 1658; the robes for new doctorates at Oxford, 1895-1920; the debate on proposed academical dress for the Royal Institute of British Architects. 1923–24; and an investigation into the perceived decline of academical dress—and how this trend might be reversed or abated—by tracing the social and cultural forces that have acted upon the tradition in the last hundred years.*
Members £10.00/$12.50 per copy; Non-members £13.00/$16.50 per copy

Transactions of the Burgon Society   *Crown Quarto format*

Volume 9 (2009) — Special North American Issue   *224 pages.   Three studies on the Inter-collegiate Code of Academic Costume, its development and departures from it; three covering the history and use of robes at Harvard, Princeton, and Columbia Universities; two on Canadian universities in Nova Scotia; an article with detailed illustrations on the making of an American doctoral gown; and a timeline of key events in the history of academic dress in North America.*
Members £15.00/$19 per copy; Non-members £20.00/$25 per copy

Transactions of the Burgon Society   *Crown Quarto format*

Volume 8 (2008)   *160 pages.   The academical dress of the University of Warwick; trends in the manufacture of gowns and hoods (with detailed descriptions and illustrations); the robes for the Master of Midwifery of the Worshipful Society of Apothecaries of London; the origins of the University of Wales robes; the use of the academic hood in quire; notes and corrections to Hargreaves-Mawdsley's* History of Academical Dress; *and the personal reminiscences of a life-long student of academical dress.*
No longer available in print.

Transactions of the Burgon Society   *Crown Quarto format*

Volume 7 (2007)   *144 pages.   Academical dress at the University of Toronto; the question of Lambeth degree holders and the University of London; Wills's cigarette cards of university hoods and gowns; the robes of the medical Royal Colleges; and academic attire as a component of the livery of the Chapel Royal.*
Members £9.00/$11.50 per copy; Non-members £12.50/$16 per copy

Transactions of the Burgon Society   *Crown Quarto format*

Volume 6 (2006)   *128 pages.   Tudor sumptuary laws; green as the colour for doctor's robes; Masters of Grammar; the academical dress of the University of Stirling; and academic dress and nursing.*
Members £7.50/$9.50 per copy; Non-members £10.00/$12.50 per copy

Transactions of the Burgon Society   *Crown Quarto format*

Volume 5 (2005)   *128 pages. This issue, which continues the series of Burgon Society Annuals under a new name, includes articles on the history of robes in Germany and France; the evolution of English academical dress from the Middle Ages to modern times; Lambeth academical dress; the original London University scheme; gold as the colour of science; and the use of the British Colour Council numbering system by British and Commonwealth universities.*
Members £7.50/$9.50 per copy; Non-members £10.00/$12.50 per copy

Copies of some older volumes are available online at **www.burgon.org.uk/society/shop.**